STUCK? Dealing with organizat

STUCK? Dealing with organizational trauma

Philippe Bailleur

Translation by: James Campbell – `thelastword.eu`

Originally published under title: Trauma in organisaties – Herkennen, aanpakken, voorkomen (completely revised)

© 2018, Systemic Books Publishing

ISBN 978-9492331533 (NUR 801)

# Contents

# List of illustrations

# Foreword by Catherine Carton

A severe traumatic event stops you in your tracks; suddenly your world is stilled and silent; overwhelmed and powerless, you can only sit and stare. It really hurts. No one wishes for such an experience, yet few are spared. Every significant overwhelming event leaves its traces.

In August 2013, as a result of a medical error, we lost our son Gustav. Later, we would receive honest answers from the hospital to all our questions. I'm still grateful to the hospital for this. It was crucial to our process of coming to terms with the tragedy.

It goes without saying that medical staff always do everything in their power to save lives. But when it goes wrong, they have to continue living and working with the reality of their part in that. Taking the time to talk about this together, hearing how everybody has been affected, and standing by each other, is crucial to the healing of everyone involved.

I was able to put my questions to the management, the doctors and the departmental heads as we sat around the table. They had the courage to listen and reflect on the 'pain' points in their organization. We then collectively agreed to recognize this trauma, to examine it in detail and to move ahead constructively. Everything possible was done to ensure this could never happen again. This way, lessons were learned from our 'wound' and suddenly our story could have a positive outcome. From a perspective of collective responsibility, we looked at a number of patterns within the hospital and at the structures and relationships between employees, teams and disciplines. Everything was taken on by this 'team'.

Two years later I received an invitation from the hospital. What I saw and experienced was beautiful; it exceeded all my expectations. The people, the team and the organization seemed to have become stronger through the process.

It is partly because of my personal story, but also my business experience, that I am aware of trauma in organizations. This book – which I read while it was being written – has given me much insight. Philippe has managed to give words to my experience. I hope it will inspire you as much as it has me.

Finally, I am convinced that, as a society, we have to find a way to face the traumas around us and take whatever steps are necessary to deal with them. That takes courage. But huge strength to face trauma is at our disposal even if we are not aware of it. It is up to us to take action. Facing a trauma in the present, heals the past and offers new perspectives for the future.

Happy reading!

Catherine Carton
Organizational Coach

# Foreword by Jan Jacob Stam

You're holding a remarkable book in your hands on a delicate subject. Trauma in Organizations. I only can recommend to read it… from your common sense, from your heart, from your soul and for the love of the organization you are contributing to.

In the country where I come from, the Netherlands, personal trauma is a common and accessible subject. But organizational trauma? Completely the opposite! It's not only often a no-go zone, full with shame, blaming, denial and not knowing how to…, it's also very often not recognized for those who are working in or leading the organization. Nevertheless, in my work, which is supporting companies in their development by applying the systemic phenomenological approach and organizational constellations, in two out of ten cases we stumble into trauma. Not individual trauma, but organizational trauma that even effects employees and leaders who never themselves were present during the event or era that was experienced as traumatic. And in many of the over thirty countries I've been working, it was not so different…

The bad news is: trauma needs to be addressed in order to create the framework for a change or transformative process. The good news is: I'm pretty optimistic about what we can do in order to heal trauma, to grow beyond it ánd to prevent trauma reactions after an incisive event. There is a fast growing body of knowledge and experience how to detect trauma reactions and what interventions we can do.

Philippe's book makes the understanding of, the detection of, the interventions for and the preventions from trauma reactions very accessible without taking anything away from its seriousness and relevance for organizations and society. And Philippe is a man with a big heart for organizational development. In this book you do not only meet and drink his knowledge about the subject, but you also will be submerged in his attitude to face trauma. And it's the attitude that does the work. The techniques described by Philippe are of great help.

We do hope this book helps to open up this field, beyond shame, beyond feeling guilty… and awaken the love and potential, embedded in the fields of trauma.

Jan Jacob Stam
Bert Hellinger Institute the Netherlands.

# Preface by Erik de Soir

## From Traumatized Individuals to Organizational Trauma

Recent years have seen an increase in applied scientific research on organizational robustness and organizational resilience in times of crisis. It appears that the knowledge on psychological trauma in individuals is useful to analyze the impact that threatening and unpredictable events may have on organizations and their members. The effects of trauma influence an organization's identity, the well-being of its constitutional parts and its worldview in the same way that an individual is influenced by his/her trauma experience. This book is not just another theoretical framework to analyze organizational culture. It offers a truly inspired vision of a former operational Airforce Officer who graduated from our proud Royal Military Academy and whose experiences are crucial for a better understanding of the challenges that organizations and systems may have to confront in the face of adversity.

Armed forces and crisis response organizations in general are prone to become traumatized due to their mission but in times of economical and geopolitical instability also other organizations may experience different types of trauma; e.g. direct and indirect, sudden and cumulative trauma. The recent wave of terrorism has clearly shown that the organizations of different types of first responders had to increase their resilience and their level of preparedness in order to face a new prominent threat: the presence of 'enemies' of our Western life-style in our society and the permanent state of readiness, on behalf of our institutions and crisis response organizations.

The aim of this book is to offer a detailed and comprehensive insight into the stepped process that organizations may have to endure on their way to organizational trauma. It also offers recommendations for assisting traumatized organizations to recover and for intervening in a preventive way with organizations at risk for becoming traumatized. This framework of organizational trauma makes it easier to identify the systemic and inherited aspects that improve organizational functioning and enhance the resilience and robustness of the organization. Ultimately understanding organizational trauma and helping traumatized systems to heal offer hope for the future.

Recent history has shown us that organizations can suffer from trauma in times of massive bankruptcy, due to the financial crisis, or after confrontation with direct threat. Often trauma is indirect, the result of an organization's continual exposure to trauma through the very nature of its work i.e. armed forces or non-governmental organizations working in conflict areas.

At specific risk for organizational trauma are the highly mission-driven organizations. A highly mission-driven organization is one whose mission is compelling and pervasive; the mission and values define not only the nature of the work but also the approach to the work and the nature of the relationships between the members of these organizations.

In the early 1980's researchers and practitioners began writing about the experiences of those exposed to (others') trauma. Earliest publications focused on families and friends using concepts such as secondary traumatic stress, vicarious traumatization and compassion fatigue (*"Compassion fatigue as secondary traumatic stress disorder: An overview"* (Figley, 1995, [11]) ). Researchers and practitioners expanded their thinking to include first responders and helping professionals. This expanded work offered both explanations and solutions for the posttraumatic stress-like symptoms shown by first responders and other helping professionals. *"Regardless of their theoretical frameworks, all constructs refer to the negative emotional and cognitive reactions of helping professionals, specific to their work with trauma survivors or the reactions of the survivors themselves"*.

These frameworks offer ways to understand (post)trauma symptoms and suggest how to address them. Strategies include individual self-care, team-based approaches and institutional responses.

The author of this book explains how it is plausible to accept that the effects of trauma influence an organization's identity and worldview in the same way that an individual is influenced in his/her trauma experience by the organization. That impact embeds itself in the organizational culture and the basic assumptions of the members of the organization.

Organizational culture makes sense of its members' experience, provides answers and protects against collective and individual anxiety. Those answers influence the ways in which group members perceive, think and feel about the world and the organization's place in it.

In response to external and internal forces of trauma, organizations may become redemptive organizations and/or develop reparative cultures. Redemptive organizations seek to change the wrongs of society through socially useful actions; reparative organizational cultures seek to integrate contradictory organizational elements to serve valued purposes. The need to make sense of and affirm organizational work and its place in a society not always supportive, as well as account for needs of its members, makes organizations vulnerable to traumatization.

Organizations and structured systems may become traumatized through natural disasters or human behaviors, through single events or over time. Lots of attention were given, by the media and the research community, to disastrous events such as the World Trade Center attacks (2001 Sep 11th), the Columbine school massacre (1999 Apr 20th), the Oklahoma City bombing (1995 Apr 19th) and the attacks on the Norwegian Utøya Island (2011 July 2nd). These impacts are comparable to those of the terrorist attacks in Paris: The *Charlie Hebdo* attack (2015 Jan 7th), *Le Bataclan* & *Stade de France* attacks (2015 November 13th), the attack of the Brussels Airport and the Maelbeek Metro (2016 March 22nd). But also less mediatized types of collective trauma, such as the permanent transformation and downsizing of the Belgian Armed Forces over the last two decades, may have a devastating impact on organizations.

In times of trauma, the protective emotional membrane of the organization is penetrated, violated and sometimes even destroyed beyond repair. At any level, trauma is an experience for which a person-family-group is emotionally (not only cognitively) unprepared, an experience that overwhelms ones' defensive (self-protective) structure and leaves one feeling totally vulnerable and at least temporarily helpless.

For the Belgium Army, the assassination of ten Belgian paracommandos in Rwanda (1994, April 7th) has provoked an irreparable trauma. For other societies, such as the post-9/11 US society, the wars on terror,

launched on Iraq and Afghanistan, created a whole new generation of traumatized families. In our collective memories, financial traumas, such as
the collapse of the Belgian Fortis Group (2008) or major health crises, such
as the outbreak of the influenza pandemic in Mexico (2009). It may even
come from the deleterious effects of dysfunctional internal dynamics that
develop over time, such as the poisoning of the population in the Man-
zanillo region in the state of Colima in Mexico (2009) through the construc-
tion of dangerous industry plants.

Some organizations even have traumatic beginnings. The experiences
of individuals associated with an organization's founding may influence
the initial thinking about the problem, societal response, desired changes
and the need for collective action. The Dutroux pedofile case in Belgium
(1996) has been the beginning of several societal and community-based
actions. It directly leaded to the creation of a European centre for abused
and missing children (i.e. Child Focus, 1998). It also initiated the massive
reform of the Belgian police apparatus that still generates internal dynamics up till today.

Organizational values and strategies may run counter to societal
norms: society denies the problem, marginalizes those served and deni-
grates the work. Justification of the need and effort and rationale for a pre-
ferred approach come from these individual and collective experiences. In
their struggle to survive, organizations create an affirming emotional and
cognitive worldview that frequently contains an 'against all odds' feeling.
The developing culture often includes a powerful perception (or real experience) of the external environment as unsupportive, uncaring and sometimes dangerous. These early characteristics become part of the organization's culture and continue to influence the organization's identity.

The author of this books clearly illustrates the main characteristics of
a traumatized system. To the extent that an organization experiences or
perceives its environment to be unsupportive and hostile, it will protect itself. The external environment (they) is vilified while the organization (we)
is idealized. Boundaries become less permeable and less information and
energy enters: the organizational system closes down. Closed systems
tend towards sameness, defensiveness and resistance to change. As the
system's boundaries close, the organization becomes isolated form the
external environment and incapable of correctly assessing external real-

ity. Its self-image becomes distorted. Curative interventions to cope with the trauma may then be difficult to realize.

A clear example in the Belgian Armed Forces is to find in its reaction to the beginning of the Rwandan genocide in which ten Belgian paracommandos of the 2nd Commando Battalion were massacred, as cited above. The trauma resulted in some kind of conspiracy of silence which disabled all possible long term psychological support. No one, even till today, is supposed to speak overtly about what really happened in the hours and days before and after this massacre. Sadly enough, this attitude has ever been an obstacle for psychological support for the military personnel involved and till today, wounds are still open and left untreated.

Emotional contagion, stress contagion or trauma contagion may occur as organizational members are swept up in co-workers' feelings, anxieties, and stresses. Reliance on internal relationships couples with a dependence on empathy to accomplish the work, overload the stress-absorption capacity of the organization, and the organization, as an entity, never calms down. The internal atmosphere remains stressful, and stress becomes an organizing framework, a lens through which the work is experienced. The interplay of atmosphere and organizing framework results in a culture partially defined by stress and uncertainty.

Traumatized organizations are also characterized by a loss of hope (for rescue or healing). Fueled by lack of organizational efficacy and a view of the world as unchanging, the organization may begin to doubt itself. The result may then be an organizational culture hypersensitive to the same dynamics it is trying to change, dynamics such as power, authority, oppression and exclusion. As it cannot succeed in changing the external world, it also cannot succeed in changing itself. Ultimately, the organization is damaged spiritually, losing its ability to make meaning of its work and to connect itself to wider purposes and movements.

The characteristics above, each described separately, are to be seen as interconnected and mutually reinforcing. Closed boundaries offer little new energy or perspective to organizational processes. Continuing to view the surrounding world as uncaring and unchanging reinforces protective boundaries. Both promote involvement in internal dysfunction and distract the organizational from its purpose. This in turn exacerbates the feelings of hopelessness about making any real impact on the external world. In extreme cases the organization dies. Philippe Bailleur has done an impressive work in order to cope with these organizational challenges.

The value of this book is on both the preventive and curative level. The author shows us how organizations can avoid trauma by a timely intervention in their structure. Although, intervening in an organization suffering from trauma, or having a history of trauma, urges for a practice which shows real concern, respect and care which is not always easy in uniformed masculine organizations.

Containing the anxiety and despair felt by the organization is the first step in the intervention procedure. It requires perseveration and courage. The ability of the 'trauma coach' to act as a non-anxious container is critical. But this 'coach' has to be accepted by the top-level management of the organization. A trauma coach, such as the author of this book, can offer his expertise and guidelines for protecting and stabilizing the organization. These might include calling a truce on harmful patterns and (re)structuring organization-wide conversation. Conceptualizing and the naming of the traumatic situation come next.

This book offers an insight into the concepts of organizational trauma and offers a way to talk about them. Using them also helps to normalize the reactions and patterns and to allow individual and collective recognition that they are not alone, not lost and not crazy. These concepts and discussions provide a non-personalized and non-politicized way to describe the experiences and systemic anxiety. Ultimately, the author of this book offers ideas for collective meaning making and healing.

Trauma coaches, such as Philippe Bailleur, need to be sensitive to the readiness of the organization to think in these ways. This book is critical in order to help organizational leaders and colleagues to use the right trauma concepts because these concepts help them to make sense of their experiences and view them as legitimate and normal reactions to imminent threat and danger of annihilation. Discussions about the organization's enduring and changing patterns expand the ways organizational members understand and respond to their experiences. Understanding the sources of trauma helps organizational members collectively make sense of organizational history and assess the organization's risk for (re)traumatization.

Since traumatized systems also focus inward, developing internal systems and structures that deal with tension, conflict, pressure and stress, builds capacity for resilience. They are particularly helpful to reduce stress contagion, the vehicle through which traumatic stress spreads and persists.

In any intervention leaders need support to acknowledge their role in influencing the organization and to understand how their own histories and experiences of trauma influence their work and the organization's culture. In fact, all organizational members need the opportunity to reflect about the connection of their individual history to organizational culture and work.

Finally, I think that also the spiritual dimension of organizational life is often ignored or discounted. Attending to the organization's spirit helps kindle hope. Organizations; like individuals, need ways to replenish and sustain themselves and to make meaning of their work and experiences. The organizational capacity to accept the existence of trauma and act anyway allows it to succeed. The numerous metaphors used by Philippe Bailleur in his book may help to promote and symbolize posttraumatic spiritual growth.

'Stuck. Dealing with organizational trauma' explores the various aspects of organizational trauma; ways an organization may become traumatized, characteristics of organizational trauma and ways to intervene in traumatized systems or event preventing systems to get stuck in trauma. In a short time, Philippe Bailleur has become a leading expert in organizational trauma and an ambassador of the theories of systemic healing. His book offers hope for the future but the real defeat will be to get his messages accepted by the top level management of large organizations (uniformed organizations in particular).

I truly wish that this book will find its way to the right clients in order to help organizations develop adequate survival strategies and make systems bounce back from adversity.

Erik de Soir, PhD
Military Associate Professor in Crisis Psychology
Royal Military Academy
Department of Behavioral Sciences

# Introduction

This book is about trauma, specifically about trauma in organizations. For people who really want a deep understanding of organizational trauma, I want to share, in my own way, how trauma came onto my path. I need to go back a long way; since an early age I was confronted by trauma, although I only realized this many years later. And it was my own experience that motivated me to look for ways to heal trauma. One of my main insights is the fact that trauma does not heal when we ignore it or push it away; quite the contrary. I have learned, over the years, that deep healing only happens when something is allowed out into the light. This is precisely why I believe it is important, and useful, to give you a look at the 'nest' into which I was born.

My story starts with my father. His father lost his left hand, as a result of an industrial accident from which he later died – a few years before the start of the Second World War. At the time of his death, he and his wife were expecting their fifth child, the youngest brother of my father – who was then ten years old. My grandmother raised her five children alone, in West Flanders (Belgium), during the war. As a result of losing the breadwinner, the family grew up in and out of poverty.

When my father was 28 – my parents were already married but had no children – he was blown off a roof by a gust of wind. He had been employed to fix a number of panels to the roof before the storm became too strong. Luckily he landed in newly-poured concrete, but his left arm was badly damaged. Due to a medical error – which, in those days, wasn't acknowledged – his arm eventually had to be amputated. This would colour his entire life…

A few years later my brother, Vincent, was born. Three days after the birth, he suffered a brain hemorrhage from which he sustained a very serious disability, becoming badly twisted and paralyzed for the rest of his life. My brother was put into a home for the disabled because my parents

13

could not provide the carehe needed. Now the picture widens to include my mother and brother. My mother was born, in the middle of the Second World War also in West Flanders where her family of origin also lived on the edge of poverty.

The family into which I was born, a few years later, had already experienced a great deal of suffering. The choice both my parents made, time and time again, despite all the misery, was to choose for life. They continue to enjoy each day of their lives and are surrounded by many friends from whom they get tremendous support. Yet, in a way, they are wounded. They belong to a generation which had no chance of help, therapy or healing. The message from society was, to just get on with it, day after day without complaining. I look at my parents with great respect and, at the same time, I wish them healing.

I was born into a family that was full of grief and trauma, concepts that will be worked out in more detail later in this book. Being constantly in such an environment takes its toll. The literature calls this 'vicarious' trauma, or trauma that, drop by drop, through your pores, your senses, your empathic ability or your mirror neurons slips unnoticed into your nervous system. It becomes a part of you. Since then, and throughout my life, I have been, and remain, constantly reminded of this complex and painful reality.

- I had a brother but also I didn't have a brother, because he was rarely at home. I couldn't play or talk with him and at school I didn't always know the best way to talk *about* him. Sometimes it was just easier to say that I was an only child. That made it much easier to avoid being bullied.

- From when I was a small child, I could feel my mother's deep sorrow, but I didn't know what to do with it, let alone help her with it. And I could also feel my father's helplessness, frustration and anger around his physical disability. And here too, there was little I could do.

- When I was thirteen, my brother died very unexpectedly. He was only sixteen years old. I still can see us all, sitting in the living room on the night of his death and I can still feel these painful moments. Despite all that he was in one way absent even when he was alive, in another way, he remains very present in my life.

- When our own children were little, I often thought of the fact that my father could never pick up his sons with both his hands; now I get great joy from a big family hug.

That was the way I first learned about trauma, as a witness. Later it became clear, albeit gradually, that I was more than just a witness, and so my interest and my antennas for trauma grew together. Because I work mainly with organizations, I became increasingly clear to me that this might be a very relevant theme for organizations too. As Catherine's preface testimony already shows, there is – more often than we think – a personal and an organizational side to trauma. And that is precisely why I have written this book for people that are confronted with trauma in organizations and willing to deal with it. You can be a manager, an executive, a board member, a director, a consultant or an (organizational)coach. Once you start working with organizational trauma, you become a facilitator, the overarching word that will be used throughout this book.

To make the book as accessible and useful as possible, it is positioned at the cutting edge between research and practical application. Readers wanting to dive even deeper into these matters will find much of value in the Sources section at the end of the book, or via my website.

'STUCK? Dealing with organizational trauma' has three parts:

- In Part I, I discuss the relevance of trauma to organizations. Most of us encounter trauma at the individual level, but it also manifests in families, groups and even at large-society levels. When we take a broad perspective to the theme, a number of recurring patterns become visible that are relevant to working with trauma in organizations.

- In Part II, I show how trauma can arise in organizations and show you how to identify trauma and how to track it down. Often we have no idea at all that trauma is the root of a recurring problem.

- In Part III, I offer a range of approaches and insights to start dealing with trauma in organizations.

It is important to be aware that the terrain of organizational trauma remains, to a great extent, unexplored. Now I want to make an important distinction: there are healthy organizations where individuals suffer from trauma, and there are traumatized organizations. It is only in the latter case that we speak about organizational trauma – but more on that later. Given the broad perspective of this book, however, a number of issues are always present:

- Trauma gets in your clothes; in the warp and the weft of the fabric, stubbornly remaining no matter how many times you try to wash it out. Even though someone might do his utmost to ignore old pain, he'll be pulled back to it by his body. And the same applies to groups and organizations.

- Although socially (and certainly within the context of organizations) we are not so good at dealing with negative or difficult emotions, we are definitely able to work with organizational trauma and do not have to make do with repression or denial.

- Everyday, research provides more insight into organizational trauma. This book is a stepping stone to where more stones can be laid. Growing our understanding will help us to navigate this less-obvious domain. And, whatever the situation, a certain level of insight or knowledge of organizational trauma is essential to getting started.

- Working with trauma asks a lot of those entering this field. Knowledge is necessary, but not sufficient. Facilitators need to develop profound, empathetic abilities. The importance of deep, simple presence – as a key ingredient to recognizing and working with trauma – is becoming increasingly evident. It is not a trick or a smart technique but an attitude, a way of being. Any attempt at guidance without this ingredient will be counterproductive.

- Some people seem naturally to be very sensitive to trauma. They quickly recognize the signs of pain, emotions and trauma, and many can also do so in organizations. They seem to have a nose for it. But the ability to do the work only manifests when a person has confronted their own traumas, acknowledged them in the light of compassion. This is the only way that a person can grow beyond tricks and techniques.

Feel free to contact me if you have any questions, want to further explore trauma in organizations or are looking for general or specific guidance. Finally, for now, I want to thank you for being open to the concept of trauma in organizations.

Philippe Bailleur

Experienced Guide for Organizational Renewal
www.traumainorganizations.com
philippe@livingsystemscoaching.be

# PART I

## TRAUMA, A FRINGE PHENOMENON?

# Why focus on trauma in organizations?

**1**

This chapter is intended to help you understand the why of this book. Few of us immediately associate trauma with organizations. Yet they too can be hit by events that transcend their ability to cope. This damages the relational fabric of an organization to varying degrees, negatively impacting the healthy functioning of the organization, often for several years or longer. An important distinction to keep in mind, however, is between the potentially-traumatic event itself, and how that event can continue to haunt an organization in the form of a set of symptoms that interfere with its healthy functioning. Leaders of organizations should certainly be interested in learning to recognize potentially-traumatic events, but also in being able to distinguish the symptoms of organizational trauma from those of 'everyday' organizational challenges. Whether or not a leadership is in conscious denial of this phenomenon, the consequences for the functioning of the organization are serious. For the people who work there, but also for the organization's customers, clients and target groups, especially, for example, if these include healthcare institutions.

But be warned: no matter how hard we try to avoid such drastic events, even by implementing 'zero tolerance' security and prevention measures, we will never eliminate them from our society and our organizations. Therefore, the emphasis in this book is on how we can support and guide people and organizations in the aftermath of such events. This book invites the corporate world to open its eyes to the fact that organizational trauma is a real problem.

## 1.1 Trauma requires a customized approach

Millions of people long for happiness, yet it seems the harder they strive to achieve it, the further away it gets. The global percentage of people with mental health problems is strikingly large. Data from the World Health Organization might be confronting, but it does not lie. Either there is work to be done or we are putting the bar too high for ourselves and for each other. Maybe chasing happiness is like trying to grasp the wind: the harder you grip, the less you hold. Perhaps we should reconcile with the fact that certain things are probably not possible. Or definitely not in Seven Steps, a Three-Week Course or a series of morning meetings with your Personal Coach. The more experience you build up, as an organizational coach, the more humble you become about what you can or cannot mean to an organization. This is especially true when you're faced with organizational trauma: none of the old, trusted interventions work, nothing you know appears to have any lasting effect.

People suffering from trauma need very specific help. The same applies to organizations. Most help or interventions seem to have no effect because they are not focused on healing the trauma. What you see, is that people with trauma become increasingly despondent despite the help provided, and that those trying to help become exhausted, disappointed or angry because their efforts deplete their energies while having little effect. Sometimes the lack of success gives rise to a negative judgement, a perception that the traumatized person doesn't want to heal. However, it is only after you begin to understand a little about how trauma works, that what you begin to see is a person overwhelmed by something over which he or she has little control. Like an aircraft, with an expert crew, that gets hijacked by terrorists. Brain research tells us that trauma makes changes in the functioning of our nervous system, changes that remain for as long as there is no help or support; the victim becomes trapped in a kind of vicious circle.

As a facilitator, trauma asks for something different from you, something you might not (yet) be aware of. Your capacity as a facilitator is directly proportional to what you have worked through personally and professionally. You will not be able to work with the difficult emotions of others, if you haven't worked through those same emotions yourself. This can be pretty confronting or challenging. For example: Can you allow emotional pain just to be there? Neither ignoring it or wanting it gone? Can you stay present and open when emotional pain arises in yourself or others? No matter how paradoxical this may sound, the key to healing, both individually and at the organizational level, is in this quality of being present to everything, without judgment or urge to fix it.

It's like when you have lost a loved one, and people come to your door with well-meaning, but unhelpful, intentions. While what you need is a person or place where you can share your pain without having to fix it right away. Our habit of starting immediately to work on the most difficult issues, does not work with trauma. It just makes things worse. For organizations – hell-bent on fixing problems quickly – because they must always be moving forwards, this is a significant challenge.

*A small and innovative family company was taken over by a multinational. The founder, and original owner, never managed to settle into the new company, which, after much struggle, let him go. Due mainly to the anger and the frustration the founder felt around the leaving process, it did not go well. A result was that many of the people who had worked with him believed that he had been unfairly treated.*

*Once the founder had left, the new organization underwent one change process after another:  first they called it integration, then streamlining, then process optimization… Bit by bit, everything that the family business had stood for was suppressed, while there were still many people in the 'new' company who had been there from the start.  For them, each change was like an arrow through their organizational heart.  Their loyalty to the founder who, according to them, had been unfairly pushed out, made this feeling even stronger.*

*Another important fact is, that after the founder left, the organization never experienced stable leadership.  Every so often, headquarters sent a new director, but none of these (temporary) directors was aware of the history.  None of them understood they had to address the old pain that needed healing. Each one came to the same point: looking forward to the end of their contract.  The reputation of the business steadily deteriorated until, one day, HQ announced that a thorough reorganization would take place, to get the business back on track.*

*News of the reorganization was delivered by one of the corporate directors, flown in especially to show the staff that the company cared and to get them motivated. But his speech was counterproductive: it forced the accumulated pain even deeper in the organization. Why? He did not acknowledge the organization's past, its history.  What he did was choose words that totally ignored the issue:* "We're going to move on from all the hassle of the past." "Whatever it was, it's no longer relevant.", "Turn over a new leaf". *His visit could have done a lot of good.*

*Sadly, he did not use his visit well and, in the end, he made the organizational trauma and its symptoms even worse.*

In this example, the organizational trauma became stronger and more deeply embedded in the relational fabric of the organization. Because the employees did not feel heard and their loyalty was still with the founder, they became and remained stuck. Stuck in old pain and old patterns. Recognition of their pain by the corporate director could have been the tipping point that kicked-off a healing process but, through ignorance of the systemic forces at play, he wasted the chance.

## 1.2 Healthy organizations can make the difference

Over the past few years, many books have appeared full of insights obtained by, studying how particular organizations thrive in a rapidly-changing, complex world. The effectiveness of a particular organizational design, however, is not absolute, but should be viewed in the context in which it operates. In a fairly stable world, an organization can be streamlined via tight procedures and guidelines, clear role definition and centralist or top-down management. We have the industrial revolution to thank for these kinds of mechanistic organizations, where employees are seen as replaceable parts of a machine and the executive board sits pushing buttons and pulling levers. In the classic film 'Modern Times', Charlie Chaplin pokes fun at just this kind of organization.

But organizations need to become more agile. That means, among other things, noticing changes in the market and quickly translating them into new or improved products or services. From this point of view, it seems more practical for an organization to function less as a kind of machine and more as a living system, constantly in motion. A superb example from nature is the flight behavior of bird flocks. By studying organizations designed to be more like a living system, a number of principles emerged that are very different from 'machine' organizations. The following table compares a number of principles.

| Organization as machine | Organization as living system |
|---|---|
| The organization must be designed in such a way that it can be led easily and well. | The organization must be designed in such a way that employees can do their work smoothly and can make their own adjustments when needed. |
| Information is something for leaders and intended to facilitate control. | Information is intelligently shared to promote self-regulation. |
| Control generally comes from above. | Guidance can come from anywhere. Leadership is more about coordination and facilitation. |
| Direction is determined by a market/profit driven strategy translated into increasingly granular objectives. | Direction is determined by an attractive, vibrant purpose, often linked to societal needs. |
| Profit and shareholder value are the most important in the functioning of the organization. | A balanced approach is taken that accounts for the needs of all the stakeholders of the organization. |
| The strength of the organization lies in the expertise that underlies all strategic choices. | The power of a living system is in the relational fabric between people, teams, departments, etc. |
| There is little or no eye for the invisible dynamics and the culture of the organization. These are seen as manipulable dimensions. | The culture of the organization is, as it were, the personality of the organization. Organizational change is most successful when you align with that culture. |

A machine can wear out or fail. When that happens, you replace or repair parts or buy a new machine. A living system, such as our own body, sometimes needs to restore itself, and heals, usually, from the inside out. When you cut yourself, it takes a few days for the body to heal the wound completely. This gives us a clue to how we might work with organizations in a different way. Mechanistic thinking leads to interventions from the outside world (outside-in), usually by someone offering specific expertise. If you are approaching an organization as a living system, an intervention is more a series of interventions that reactivate the system's self-regulating or healing ability (inside-out). This distinction becomes very concrete when you begin working with organizational trauma. Trauma is not something you can fix from the outside. What you can do, is offer the kind of space and presence that initiate the healing process. This is further explored in Part III.

Living systems can, therefore, be sick or healthy. However, sickness and health are not static concepts, partly because the contexts in which organizations operate are constantly challenging. Living systems are moving continually between two poles, which we might call blooming and withering. Compare it to riding a bike, which is actually a constant process of falling to the left and then to the right; a delicate balance maintained by pedaling and steering. Maneuverability and resilience – properties which many organizations seek – exist in a state of dynamic tension. Life, human or organizational, is a constant balancing act.

We recognize this too in our own lives. Frantically striving for health can make us less resistant to disease. Being sick now and then, helps our body develop resistance. You can apply the analogy to living systems. In short, excellence, resilience and durability cannot emerge when fixed to one pole, but only by being able to move between the two poles. It is, therefore, interesting to understand what makes an organization healthy or sick. When you do understand this as a facilitator you can support the natural movement of an organization through the stages shown in the visual below.

*Figure 1: Organizational blooming and withering*

You cannot lead an organization to excellence by trying to keep it close to the most attractive of these poles, but by guiding the vessel, in its different phases, as it moves between both poles. People who are attracted by superficial appearances have a tendency to ignore what is not immediately obvious. You might be able to sweep it under the mat, but it hasn't gone away. When you do this in an organization, slowly but surely the organization will end up in trouble. This book takes a different approach to examining how things go wrong in organizations. There are thousands of books full of stories about successful organizations, but very few, if any, that address the reasons why a potentially-successful company is withering when it could be blooming.

When organizations are healthy, they develop tremendous added value. It is fascinating to see how organizations manage to meld the power of people together and create something special in the world. Many of the things we regard as quite normal in our daily lives we owe to the people, in small and large organizations, who have worked on them: our clothes, our food, our furniture, our cars, our computers and so on. If you ever get a chance to see how a passenger plane is built, you might find yourself staring in wonder. Only a very-well functioning organization can manage a puzzle of such a complexity. We need this kind of organizational power to provide as many people as possible – preferably every person on the planet – with the basic building blocks of a comfortable life, lived in a sustainable way.

Even more, we will need the power of organizations to deal effectively with the tough challenges that currently face society or are looming on the horizon. Here's a list of the challenges identified to guide the United Nations initiative Global Goals for Sustainable Development:

1. No poverty.

2. No hunger.

3. Good health and wellbeing.

4. Quality education.

5. Gender equality.

6. Clean water and sanitation.

7. Affordable and clean energy.

8. Decent work and economic growth.

9. Industry, innovation and infrastructure.

10. Reduced inequalities.

11. Sustainable cities and communities.

12. Responsible consumption and production.

13. Climate action.

14. Life below water.

15. Life on land.

16. Peace, justice and strong institutions.

17. Partnerships for the goals.

Local, national, even international, authorities have important roles to play here, but they cannot succeed without allying with the power of organizations. Increasingly, out of a growing sense of altruism, organizations are looking beyond short-term profits to understand and imagine their wider responsibilities. In whatever country we live, we can see how the power of organizations is increasingly being used to address the issues on that UN list of challenges. Commonly known as social innovation or social entrepreneurship, one of its pioneers is the banker Muhammad Yunus. He founded the Grameen Bank, to provide loans to people who were refused by regular banks, offering them what we now know as micro-credit. For helping so many people to escape poverty, Yunus was awarded the 2006 Nobel Peace Prize. In similar ways, more and more organizations are becoming Forces for Good.

The extent to which an organization can take on a societal role has a direct correlation with the health, awareness and maturity of that organization. A dysfunctional person might easily do harm before they get better. But it can also work the other way around. Doing good can also make you healthier: individual, group or organization. So what we're talking about here is a positive movement that is effective in both directions: healthy people equals healthy organizations equals a healthy society.

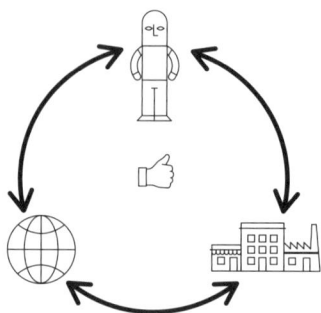

*Figure 2: Healthy individuals – Healthy organizations – Healthy Society*

An organization, like an individual, can get completely stuck trying to transform itself into a Force for Good. Someone suffering from longstanding trauma symptoms might find himself desperately longing for better times and constantly fantasizing about how he might make this happen. However, as long as the trauma is still a part of him, it will continue to have a heavy impact on his past, present and future. So, again, this is true for organizations. As an employee, manager, director, consultant or coach, finding yourself in such an organization, it is in your own interests to accept that organizational trauma exists. And if it comes across your path, you need to be able to recognize it and, more or less, know what the keys are to healing it. That's the intention behind this book: the more that organizations are also forces for good, the better for us, our planet and our children's children.

## 1.3 The special value of work

In the previous section we paid special attention to the added value of organizations in the outside world, and how organizations can have positive impacts on society. Let's now turn from the outer effects to the inner. Healthy organizations can also create added value internally, by providing meaningful work, that offers more than just a way to pay the bills, work that feeds the hands, head, heart and soul:

- Hands: a guaranteed income ensures a person can meet their basic needs and those of their family (the role of bread winner).

- Head: providing challenges that offer possibilities for professional development that result in a higher level of employability.

- Heart: the chance to be part of a community; the chance to build relationships, the opportunity to belong.

- Soul: the chance to make a positive contribution to the lives of others and/or society that, as a consequence, adds meaning in one's life.

The extent to which these needs are met allows for greater or lesser human fulfillment, passion, motivation, health, etc. 'Sick' organizations fulfill none of these needs: the increasing incidence of burnout in organizations, and people simply dropping-out completely from society, is more than just an individual issue. This phenomenon invites us to reflect on the way we view and form organizations and why we create them. Are we using the power of organizations to the advantage of a select few, or to lead the way in finding solutions for the pressing social issues of our time? After all, rotten baskets can make good apples bad too.

For many of the people working in them, organizations can provide nurturing and healing. We do not all begin our professional lives as equals; some of us take our first steps in the workplace carrying the burden of injuries suffered elsewhere, perhaps earlier, in our family of origin. Healthy organizations can provide opportunities and support to people who might be struggling, providing the kind of work that supports positive change and starts the healing process. Especially if the work is fulfilling, challenging in a way that asks for passionate engagement, motivating and healthy. Providing such work can help people reintegrate in society and, perhaps, be an attractive strategy compared to the social and financial costs of exclusion.

So we see that many people begin their careers already carrying so much baggage or trauma that they can only manage the basic minimum required. Others might enjoy a better start, but then have an accident, get on the wrong side of the justice system, or face other setbacks, ending up as long-term unemployed. Sometimes whole populations are displaced, forming long lines of desperation and hope. All these groups are at risk of exclusion. And when someone feels excluded, they are no longer inclined or able to take care of the society where they belong. The extent to which our society manages to give people a sense of inclusion and self-esteem directly determines their sense of personal wellbeing and, consequently, a healthy society.

In this context organizations, too, can make an extremely important social contribution. There are plenty of incredible initiatives, all over the world, that fit into the field of social innovation. At its core, this development contains a number of important keys; tools that can help when working with organizational trauma. Even more, these tools are crucial for organizations working with vulnerable target groups. It makes sense that an unhealthy organization can't possibly offer a safe haven – or sanctuary – to people in jeopardy. Dr. Sandra L. Bloom, who guides organizations in this field via her Sanctuary Model *Restoring Sanctuary* (Bloom and Farragher, 2013, [4]) , talks about a transformation that will take at least two generations of time.

In short, many people – whether or not they belong to a vulnerable group – owe their professional and personal development mainly to their work. Organizations also can play a particularly fine role in this area of dynamic exchange between individuals and society. Therefore it is in everyone's interest that organizations become catalysts for wellbeing in the broadest sense of the word. And, I hope, this book too will contribute.

# Trauma and organizations

**2**

The word trauma is used in many different ways and very different contexts. It is a word that comes with a lot of baggage; a word you have to be careful how and when you use it. Khaled Hosseini describes the core of individual trauma, rather beautifully, in the opening paragraph of his book *The Kite Runner* (Hosseini, 2003, [17]) :

> *I became what I am today at the age of twelve, on a frigid overcast day in the winter of 1975. I remember the precise moment, crouching behind a crumbling mud wall, peeking into the alley near the frozen creek. That was a long time ago, but it's wrong what they say about the past, I've learned, about how you can bury it. Because the past claws its way out. Looking back now, I realize I have been peeking into that deserted alley for the last twenty-six years.*

Even after years of study it remains difficult to formulate a specific definition of trauma. Although our understanding of trauma is far from complete, it is possible to offer a framework for how we might work with it in organizations. To clarify how we have learned to relate to this theme, we will look at the place trauma has in our society and how this was established, and also look at some of the different kinds of trauma. Certain patterns return again and again and it is exactly these, that we can use to create a framework for addressing organizational trauma.

## 2.1 Trauma: a concept we don't fully understand

The word trauma comes from the Greek and literally translates as: wound, hurt, defeat. Physical medicine uses the word trauma whenever there has been a serious wound, administered by an external force.

The mental health profession sees it as causing a psychic wound, an unpleasant experience which causes abnormal stress, an understanding which entered professional use around 1900. These high-impact events or chronic, overwhelming conditions can lead to lasting psychological and emotional damage. Following most stressful events, even when they are extreme, there is usually a kind of bounce back effect, for example after a rest or recovery period. Trauma, however, seems to prevent this bounce back; its lasting impact responding neither to rest or recovery. Skilled healing intervention is needed.

Trauma is as old as humanity. And because people who suffered from trauma didn't know what was happening to them, or how to deal with it, they often ended up marginalized by society. In earlier times the trauma 'workers' were healers, shamans, medicine men or priests, whose interest was in the health of the system – the group or tribe. In those histories we can see a fascinating tradition that informs how we can work with organizational trauma.

*Figure 3: Shaman*

And it is clear that, over the centuries, these healers developed a deep understanding of the invisible dynamics of trauma and how to heal them using specific rituals and ceremonies. One of the impacts of colonialization on these (mostly) indigenous tribes, was to prohibit their rituals, their natural ways of living. This contributed to the breakdown of their societies and, at the same time, made their wisdom inaccessible to the Western world. Drop by drop that wisdom is seeping back into our society via anthropologists, amongst others.

The earliest mentions of trauma in Western society are found in the context of the Greek Wars (450 BC) and, throughout the centuries, trauma has occurred most frequently and strongly in the theater of war.

Pioneers such as Sigmund Freud (individual trauma) and Wilfred Bion (group trauma), were the first to create a more-scientific framework around the phenomenon. In those days it was linked, primarily, to sexual abuse or war, but few took the impacts seriously; mostly they were laughed at or belittled. It took decades for Holocaust victims to find the courage, and be given the recognition needed, to begin talking about their experience. On the one hand was the fear of not being taken seriously but, on the other hand, an inability to truly put their experience into words.

Another example, from the First World War, describes how soldiers returning from the front were totally withdrawn, on the edge of madness. This is the origin of the term 'shell-shock'; a condition linked to the impact, for example, of a grenade.

*Figure 4: Shell shock*

Step by step it became clear that shellshock wasn't simply due to the physical impact of a grenade, but more to seeing comrades, friends and even enemies lying dead and wounded on the battlefield. Perhaps you already know that, only at the beginning of this century, some Governments rehabilitated soldiers from the first world war. Honoring and respecting those who were executed for cowardice and desertion when they were actually suffering from shell shock. Even now, war veterans get no medals for post-traumatic stress disorder while it can disrupt their lives as thoroughly as the loss of an arm or leg.

Also, victims of sexual abuse are often treated with contempt, feeling abused, ignored, excluded; sometimes even made to feel as if they are the guilty party. Although it is becoming increasingly understood that the nature of their initial reception by a professional health worker or police officer is fundamental to the process of healing and justice.

In recent years there has been tremendous progress in scientific research into trauma and, partly through advances in scanning technology, we have a growing understanding of the impact of trauma on the functioning of our brain and nervous system. This has helped widen the definition of trauma. An initial interesting distinction is that between trauma with a capital 'T' and trauma with a small 't'.

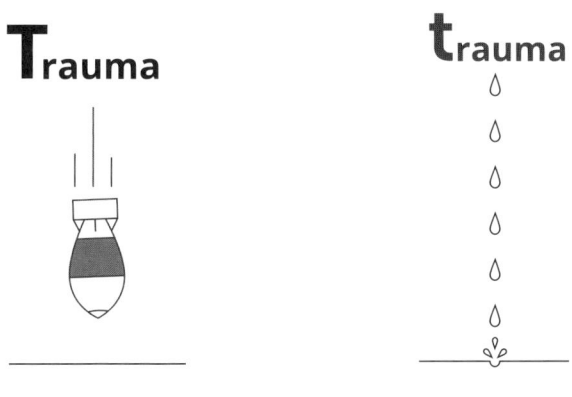

Trauma with big 'T'                           Trauma with small 't'

This does not mean there are traumatic events that are not relevant. It means that some events might, initially, not seem relevant but, eventually, go on to be traumatizing. It is not only about experiences like sexual abuse, natural disasters, wars and serious accidents, but about issues such as emotional abuse, neglect, humiliation, exclusion or bullying. These 'small t' traumas can be just as destructive, especially if they follow each other or if someone is exposed to them for a longer period.

From this we can deduce a number of important insights; in particular that an event might not necessarily be traumatizing in itself, but that it can be a function of a number of factors such as:

- the possibility to anticipate a particular (traumatic) event;
- the availability of resources (training, skills, energy, social support) to face up to and then process an overwhelming event;
- the possibility and space to give meaning to the experience.

In short, what is traumatizing for one person, might not be for someone else. And what in one situation might have been traumatizing, perhaps is not or is less so, because enough space and resources were made available to deal with it effectively. As you will see later in the book, we can translate these insights into tools for working with organizational trauma. This means that there is no list of events or circumstances that result in organizational trauma, however desirable such a list might be. It is up to everyone who works with organizations, whether coach, advisor or manager, to learn how to view an organization through the lens of trauma. The tendency to face up to organizational trauma or to ignore it will, therefore, largely depend on the willingness to do so and a measure of common sense. The following questions can elicit an initial impression of how emotions, vulnerability and feelings are given a place, within a specific context. This immediately points to whether an organization is willing to face trauma or ignore it:

- How do you personally perceive trauma and, more specifically, within organizations?
- How do those around you, in the organizations for which/where you work, perceive trauma?
- How does the organization respond to people with difficult psychological issues (depression, burn-out, mourning, etc.)?
- How does the organization work with phenomena which, according to your understanding are probably organizational trauma?

By the end of this book you should be able to verify whether an organization really is in the grip of organizational trauma or not.

## 2.2 Looking for patterns with the Trauma Cube

The emphasis in trauma seems, at first glance, to be on the individual, or perhaps this is just the view of Western society. However, in more group-oriented cultures, it is seen more as a societal trauma. In the first example, shelter and guidance occur in an individual setting, in the second in a group setting. Both approaches are relevant in the context of this book and in both we detect a number of recurring patterns. With these in mind, and with the help of the Trauma Cube, we widen our perspective.

The cube has three faces:

1. Magnitude

2. Impact and intensity

3. Nature.

**First face: Magnitude**

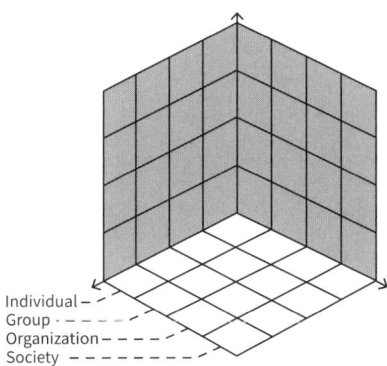

*Figure 5: Trauma Cube – Dimension of magnitude*

The first face distinguishes a range between individual and societal trauma. It begins with the individual (who endures ongoing suffering from a previous traumatic event). Then it moves on to groups, families, organizations, communities and even whole societies. When we use group, it is important to draw a clear distinction between a 'random' group and an existing group structure such as a tribe, team or family. A 'random' group could be people of the same nationality, profession, age and so on. Within an organization, random groups tend to be less visible as they are spread throughout the organization.

The following are some examples. Again, bear in mind the difference between a potentially traumatic event and how it is subsequently handled, as ultimately this largely determines the duration and impact of the consequences.

### Individual trauma

- Threatened or attacked by someone with a weapon
- A traffic or work accident where heavy injuries are sustained (possibly with lifetime disability such as loss of an arm or leg)
- A near-death experience
- Serious (sexual) abuse
- Constant bullying and teasing
- Being fired unexpectedly when you are the family breadwinner

### Group or family trauma

- Loss of a newborn child (whether or not by medical error)
- Heavy financial loss or bankruptcy
- Being forced to leave your homeland
- Victim of extortion
- Family scandal (such as abuse, murder, incest, …)

### Organizational trauma

- An acquisition where the soul or the core mission of the organization is not respected
- A key leader suddenly leaving
- Being caught committing fraud or behaving dishonestly
- Causing suffering to clients, patients or the public by, for example, pollution or the use of toxic substances
- Major environmental accidents such as factory explosions, toxic chemical release, toxic fires, ...

### Societal trauma

- When large numbers of people experience terrible events such as genocide/ethnic cleansing
- Natural disasters (hurricanes, tsunamis, forest fires, earthquakes, ...)
- Environmental disasters (Chernobyl, Fukushima, oil spills, ...)
- The flow of refugees into new countries/societies and the effects on all sides
- Wars, terrorist attacks and so on

When trauma is caused by human beings it seems to have a deeper impact than when it is a 'natural' event. Perhaps because most people experience (Mother) Nature as being impartial and impersonal. I believe the origin of a trauma does indeed impact the healing process and I will return to this issue later in the book.

It is becoming increasingly clear – within each of the categories on this face – that the effects of certain major events often continue long after the event, sometimes spanning many subsequent generations.

**Second face: Impact and Intensity**

This face of the Trauma Cube appeared earlier when we talked about trauma with a small or a big 't', and it helps us to understand the intensity or the impact of a potentially traumatic event or of certain toxic conditions. This face also determines whether, and to what extent, there is trauma. We can divide the evolution of intensity into the following categories:

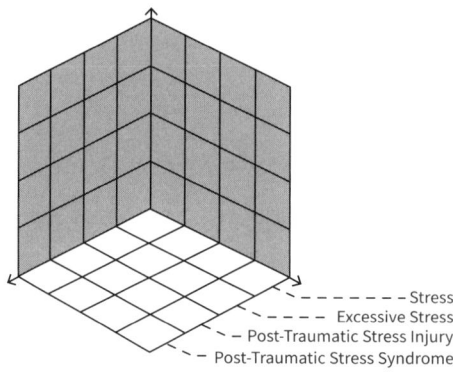

- - - - - - - Stress
- - - - - Excessive Stress
- - - Post-Traumatic Stress Injury
- - Post-Traumatic Stress Syndrome

*Figure 6: Trauma Cube – Dimension of impact*

Again here are some examples by category. This face is central to working with trauma in organizations because it makes visible to what extent a major event continues to have effects – whether it's about trauma with a small or a big 't' – and helps us identify trauma in organizations. Remember that we described this face earlier, from the individual perspective, in order to further develop the concept of organizational trauma.

***Stress***

Stress in itself is neither good nor bad. We have all experienced the kind of positive stress that keeps us sharp and well-prepared for an important event such as a major presentation, an exam or a marriage. Stress can also detract from performance, for example when there is fear of failure, or when we feel expectations of us are set too high, or when poor delegation gives an employee the feeling of being in a straitjacket. People and organizations are constantly being challenged, making stress ever-present in our society. Healthy stress makes life challenging and exciting. That is why we go to theme parks, watch horror/thriller films, bungee-jump or go parachuting. But when stress persists, individuals or groups can get stuck in a pressure-cooker environment that, ultimately, will take its toll physically, mentally and emotionally, affecting relationships at work and at home. Too little stimulation, however, can produce a sense of having not enough meaning in one's life.

*In conclusion*

Stress, on the second face of the Trauma Cube, is about the temporary tension that arises due to an imbalance between what is asked and what is possible. But this situation does not last too long. Think of recharging your proverbial 'batteries' on holiday.

- The stimulation remains manageable because there is no loss of control or no sense of disorder.
- Stress does have a biological, physiological and psychological impact, and prolonged or persistent stress can take a heavy toll. Even more, persistent stress can exhaust a person or group physically, emotionally or mentally, significantly reducing normal resilience and making them more vulnerable to further overwhelming events.

### Excessive stress

Particular events or circumstances can cause excessive stress or a stress peak. Things like unemployment, losing a loved one, learning that you are terminally ill, the breadwinner losing his or her job, a divorce, redundancies in your department, a fatal accident at work and so on. We are talking here about events that get deep inside you, that are devastating. Yet people often underestimate the impact of excessive stress, pressing on regardless. For example, because it is not the right time, or there is just no time to face up to it or because there is no possibility to be vulnerable.  Many of us know someone who lost a loved one and suddenly – sometimes after weeks or even months – they break down, only then realizing how deeply the event affected them. The distinction between stress and excessive stress is, among other things, that the latter cuts so much deeper and remains so much longer. Certainly, excessive stress can make a person or group even more vulnerable during a specific time period.  If that person or group is facing other difficult situations or contending with ever-increasing stress (whether or not work related), then something can break that opens a trapdoor into the next category.

*In conclusion*

- Here it is about a stress peak which, although very destabilizing, can be recovered from, albeit perhaps, after a longer period of time.

- Stress becomes unmanageable causing temporary loss of control in the form of panic and/or irrational behavior.

- This changes, damages or shapes those involved, but absolutely not in a lasting way.


### Post-Traumatic Stress Injury (PTSI)

Here we move from stress to trauma on this face of the Trauma Cube.  In advance I would like to explain the words I will use from now on because I made a conscious choice here to change some well-established labels. Most people will be familiar with the label Post-Traumatic Stress Disorder.  It is the official name used in the field of mental health.  The word 'disorder' is rooted in the question: "*What is wrong with that person or this group?*" More and more parties prefer using the word 'injury', rooted in the question: "*What happened to that person or these people?*" This choice fits the purpose of this book.

'Wounded' – by a major event or continuous exposure to extreme circumstances – opens a more respectful perspective than being labeled 'disturbed'. Imagine how it would be for a nurse, for example, who has worked for years in extreme emotionally or psychologically stressful circumstances, to be labeled as having a disorder, when she knows that her wounds are the result of years of commitment, dedication and exposure.

So on this face of the Trauma Cube you'll meet first Post-Traumatic Stress Injury followed by Post-Traumatic Stress Syndrome.

PTSI is defined as an event that continues to haunt someone, negatively impacting certain aspects of their daily life. There are many people who fall within this category without actually being aware of it. Babette Rothschild quotes a rather obvious example in *The Body Remembers. The Psychophysiology of Trauma and Trauma Treatment* (Rothschild, 2000, [23]) . She describes a boy who was once bitten by a dog and remained forever scared of dogs, but also could only feel safe and comfortable when he was sure no dog was in the vicinity. Due to the fact this incident was not healed, it becomes an injury the person takes with him into his future.

Usually, though, the situations that eventually lead to PTSI are far more dramatic. The resilience of the people involved, at the time the event occurs, also affects the intensity and duration of their PTSI. Therefore, it is clear that such a wide variety of potentially-traumatic events cannot be bracketed together. Here is a specific example that comes up frequently in organizations.

> *A manager dreamed of getting a particular top job in the company in which he had worked for years. He was recognized as the natural successor. However, when the time came, the organization changed its policy and chose someone else. Worse still, he was fired. Because he still had a long career ahead of him, he quickly applied for similar positions. Three times in short succession he managed to win such a job, but they were always short-lived and ended in a strange manner every time. He was too focused on avoiding another failure. Exactly that put him in a very unnatural way of working and led to what he was trying to avoid. During a coaching program, it became apparent that he was recreating these failures because he had not dealt with the pain of the first rejection. He was still being unconsciously guided by that pain.*

As you can see, PTSI is fairly easy to demarcate and only arises in certain circumstances or situations. Therefore it is possible to structure your life around this only if you can find ways to avoid or ignore the actual 'irritation'. At the same time, doing this often turns out to have a greater negative impact on the wellbeing of people than they realize. In this situation – also for groups and organizations – a part of their available potential gets stuck. If that potential becomes necessary due to some change in circumstances, first the 'irritation' must be dealt with.

In addition, it is good to be aware of the fact that events in the workplace can open old wounds. In the previous example, there was also a problem of a more-personal nature. Let's be clear that old wounds having an effect is the rule rather than the exception, but mostly we would rather not face up to this.

### Post-Traumatic Stress Syndrome (PTSS)

When a major event is extremely damaging, PTSS (commonly known as PTSD) can occur. This tends to have a severe impact on the 'victim's' day to day functioning. We're no longer talking about just irritation, but a lasting wound. Someone is stuck in their past. The person is experiencing difficulties in being in the 'now', being in touch with reality, and is regularly overcome by difficult emotions, stimuli, dreams or images that drag him back in time. Often he can't really say what exactly happened or is happening. His nervous system is disrupted and he no longer feels safe in his own body. Small, seemingly-minute triggers cause overstimulation or re-activation, bringing that person or group back into an overstimulation from their past. The effect on body and psyche is almost as destructive as the original event because people appear, as it were, to be stuck in time.

Re-activation can be linked to an event from the individual's life but can also play-out over generations. It means that, in organizations, organizational trauma can continue to cause damage even when the people involved at the time of the original incident have left the company. We have already made the distinction between an organization with traumatized individuals and a traumatized organization. How to perceive this distinction will become clear as you read on.

Using a series of diagnostic criteria in the USA's Diagnostic and Statistical Manual of Mental Disorders (DSM) it is relatively easy to identify PTSD (= the label used in the DSM). Although the DSM is controversial, it's criteria remain crucial for research, support, legislation and recognition. And its extension of the concept of trauma to include both small and large Ts, shows how the DSM's understanding and definitions have evolved over the years.

In conclusion, it is helpful in differentiating stress from trauma, to remember that trauma can continue to play-out long after the event. Time or rest are rarely enough when trauma is involved: healing interventions will be needed to restore the individual or the organization. Such healing, and subsequent recovery, ensures the person or organization does not fall back into old, familiar patterns, but will always change the person permanently. There will be a clear difference between before and after.

**Third face: Tangibility**

The third face of the Trauma Cube is the least obvious to bring into the world of organizations. In many organizations, there is little room for non-professional or personal matters. This context is littered with clichés: "*Leave your emotions at home*", "*Let's keep the conversation to facts and figures*", "*Keep work and home separate*", "*Don't let home issues affect your work*", "*Don't let them see what's going on inside you*". This means that employees, one way or another, must try to separate or hide certain parts of their humanity when in the workplace.  This of course does not work, it costs tons of energy and it creates anything but job satisfaction.

During the writing of his much talked-about book, *Reinventing Organisations* (Laloux, 2014, [18])  Fréderic Laloux found that similar issues occurred in different organizations in different countries. He was investigating the characteristics of organizations that operate in a people-friendly and sustainable way. One of these characteristics relates to this face of the cube: people were allowed to be 'complete', with their vulnerability, their beliefs and convictions, their creativity, femininity, playfulness, … what he calls their 'wholeness'. Indeed, when people can just be themselves, they do not need to invest energy in maintaining a professional persona, freeing up all their life energy for meaningful activities.

Coaches working with burn-out report something very similar. People draw on their energy and their reserves to keep on meeting – sometimes imagined – expectations. Often they would rather do something different, they would rather do the work in a different way or they would like more recognition for their contribution.  The fact that they remain trapped in that pattern ensures that their energy cannot flow in an authentic way, but must be diverted to all kinds of expectations and measures. That requires enormous amounts of energy. It is almost inevitable that someone working or living in such a situation will get burnt out. This is a part of the intangible essence of being human, and many organizations still struggle to take it seriously. This face of the Trauma Cube brings the full spectrum of being human to the table.

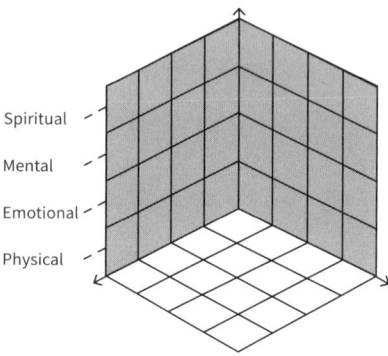

*Figure 7: Trauma Cube – Dimension of Tangibility*

### Physical

Previously I said that the term trauma is used to describe physical wounds or fractures, the kind that often need a visit to the emergency department of a hospital. Physical trauma is caused by the brute force of an external object acting on the body. This can then lead to a simple or compound fracture and eventually internal injuries almost anywhere in the body. Here, we are in the familiar reality of the visible and tangible.

### Emotional

The word trauma, in the context of this book, has a more psychological, emotional and relational meaning. This makes it less tangible despite the feeling for the people involved. In this way, someone can relive a radical event in his inner world with all the accompanying emotions and behaviors, while on the outside he appears to be perfectly safe. How people perceive this phenomenon has evolved a lot over the centuries. It is worth remembering, however, that people suffering in this way have, for centuries, been labeled as cursed, bewitched or possessed.

In most cases, it can be that the 'victim' avoids a person or place that reminds him of a fearful event or situation. If interactions between team members repeatedly cause frustration, those people start to withdraw. The proverbial relational wiring or relational fabric between the team members is gone or disturbed. Exchange within the team is no longer human, but has become 'mechanical' or 'transactional'. People now see each other as objects. In these cases, something is missing: something essential, if people are to find their work fulfilling. Every one of us is a relational being. While it might seem that nothing is wrong on the outside, each team member could be living in an internal hell.

### *Mental*

In the last decennia brain research has clearly proved that trauma actually changes the functioning of the brain – the 'hardware'. Brain scans show that, in certain situations, parts of the brain react either differently or not at all. As research makes this more visible and better understood, trauma is increasingly being taken seriously. And so we come to a persistent feature of our Western society: we really only take seriously that which we can measure or quantify. That is precisely why we need this face of the Trauma Cube.

> *Some time ago at a company site, a tanker containing chemicals exploded. There were no deaths or injuries and everyone was relieved, and rightly so, because there were no physical victims. It soon became clear, however, that there were victims; especially employees whose work required regular contact with the tankers. Some of them found it difficult to go back to work and many suffered from nightmares. For others, their workplace changed from a safe, professional environment to a place of life-threatening danger.*

Where trauma is involved, you could argue that the functioning of the brain and the structure of the nervous system could be changed. When children are raised in terrible conditions, research shows that their environment turns out to have a detrimental impact on their brain development. For a traumatized team this could mean that joint processing of emotions and/or sharing of difficult information is disrupted. In an increasingly complex world, organizations are particularly dependent on the contributions of interdisciplinary or cross-functional teams. The quality of their 'wiring', the relational fabric of the teams, is a crucial factor; one that, unfortunately, is too often ignored or undervalued.

### Spiritual

And so we come to the face of the cube, that we call the 'soul'. Ten or so years ago it was rare to use or hear this word in the context of organizations. But more and more it becomes clear that when we connect with the soul of an organization, we also connect with the inspiration that leads to quality, creativity and customer orientation. At the same time, it is clear that you cannot create or manage inspiration. You can only create a context that supports people to be in contact with their inspiration and gives them the courage to let it flow. Conversely, you can create a soulless work context that depresses people.

The eyes are the windows of the soul. Someone who has lost contact with his soul or spirit, often has dull eyes and a blank, floating look, never making eye contact. Such a person is often present only physically. The chance is high that this person's soul is somewhere else, or their inner flame has been extinguished. This can point to trauma, as a traumatized person often is no longer connected with the here-and-now.

For that reason, trauma is rather spiritual in nature, as it is about:

- The self-esteem and core values of an individual, group, organization or community.

- Loss of belief in the possibility of an ongoing fulfilling (professional) life or whatever is necessary to sustain such a life.

- The lack of a safe haven – in the mind, or in relation to the out-side world – where one can work with or share difficult emotions or events.

When in this dimension, people feel connected to each other, their country, a project or an organization. Trauma then, at its deepest level, is often spiritual in nature.

### Bringing back the soul

Shamanism, as we saw earlier, is a discipline with a centuries-old tradition in working with trauma. Shamans work in the intangible, non-material world, in particular the world of the unconscious, the soul, the invisible. Increasingly, many of their 'old' insights are being scientifically validated. Shamans view disease very differently to our Western, scientific-medical perspective. However, the openness necessary to their vision, provides us with pertinent information about the nature of trauma. Shamans approach disease holistically. For them, there is much more to us than a physical body of muscle and bone: they see us as a number of interdependent 'bodies' that mutually affect each other. Roughly speaking, the following subdivisions are often seen: a physical body (hands), an emotional body (heart), a mental body (head) and a spiritual body (soul). Contact with reality, with the ground beneath one's feet is also crucial (ground).

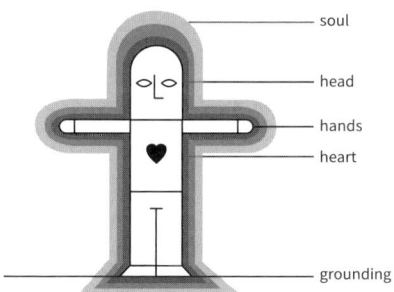

*Figure 8: Beyond the physical*

To shamans, disease occurs in much more than just the physical. Anything that makes us feel less than at ease, less than 'whole', they call disease. The roots of disease might equally well start in the soul, the mental, the emotional or the physical body. Each body can influence any other body in ways that, after time, will find their expression in the physical body, the tangible form with which we are most familiar. Our language is full of links between these different bodies. We have all said things like: "*I feel like there's a stone in my stomach*", "*I can't get it out of my head*", "*She is heartbroken*", "*She is carrying a heavy burden*".

In practice, this means that when someone comes to a shaman with a particular complaint, the shaman is first going to identify in which of the 'bodies' the problem originates. He knows that if he can 'cure' the root of the problem, then healing will take place. Sometimes it will go relatively smoothly because the complaint sits in the physical body. Sometimes the root of the illness will be deeper and purely physical work will have no effect. Examples of the latter phenomenon include problems that are growing exponentially in our modern world; conditions such as chronic fatigue syndrome (CFS), fibromyalgia, obesity, anorexia and all kinds of addictions. Over the last ten years or so, the world has begun to be more open to a holistic approach to health and disease. If you are looking for some inspiration, check out the TED-talks from Nadine Burke Harris or Gabor Maté.

So, the shaman journeys beyond the physical reality to the intangible world. If the root of the disease or disruption is on the spiritual level, for example, he will probably use a process called Soul Retrieval. Shamans have learned that we can lose parts of our souls, that souls can, in part or whole, be stolen, or even that we – albeit not voluntarily – can give them away. Shamanism sees the splitting-off of one or more parts of the soul as a result, usually, of a traumatic event. The more overwhelming the event, the greater the number of pieces, or the larger the piece of soul, that separates away or gets fragmented. So a part of the soul can still be stuck in the time and place of the causative event. Parts of one person's soul can also attach to another person who was connected to the trauma. So the souls of many traumatized war veterans are still on the battlefields where their comrades died. Even an 'ordinary' event like a car accident can leave a part of the soul stuck in that time and place. And the soul (parts) of an employee can remain, endlessly, with a previous employer or a previous project. Soul Retrieval literally means that the shaman goes in search of the lost parts of the soul. He identifies what is needed to return and integrate them and he resets the clock – that for those soul-parts was stuck in the past. This brings us to the literal meaning of the word healing: making whole again.

The concept of the soul splitting-off has been used by pioneers in the field of individual and societal trauma. People like Franz Rupert, in *Splits in the Soul* (Rupert, 2011, [24]) and Anngwyn St. Just in *A question of balance* (St. Just, 2008, [28]) point to a similar phenomenon. Their work, of guidance and reintegration, is built on a centuries-long tradition of re-embracing fragmented parts of our selves, and at the same time is supported by groundbreaking research, years of experience and their courage to travel where there are no paths or maps.

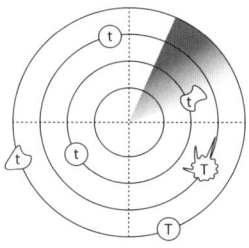

*Figure 9: Trauma Radar*

The moment you begin to approach organizations as a living system, you begin, naturally, to see them in terms of their physical, mental, emotional and spiritual 'bodies'. It follows, then, that organizations too can have a soul and can lose it, in whole or part. Can become detached from it; that it can be lost, stuck somewhere or simply just hurt. Indeed, when an organization is stuck in organizational trauma, then something is missing; lost, split off, hurt, torn, stolen, locked-away, hidden. And often that 'something' is not tangible; you can't put your finger on it. The cause can be very abrupt, such as a major industrial accident or crisis, but sometimes it can go unnoticed; quietly infiltrating the organization and doing just as much damage. In such a case, one has to look deeper than familiar and visible structures, such as business processes or organizational charts or redundancies. An organization in this kind of silent crisis needs healing of another order. When we cling to the tangible and measurable – the superficial symptoms – it usually takes far too long before we realize that the problem lies in the hidden dynamics, the not-so-visible forces running through all organizations. In the following chapters you will learn in detail how to focus your trauma-radar on those dynamics and patterns.

## 2.3 The Trauma Cube as lens

Now that we understand the three faces, we have a cube, with different areas, which we can use as a lens. It might be useful to bookmark this page so that you can easily find this picture.

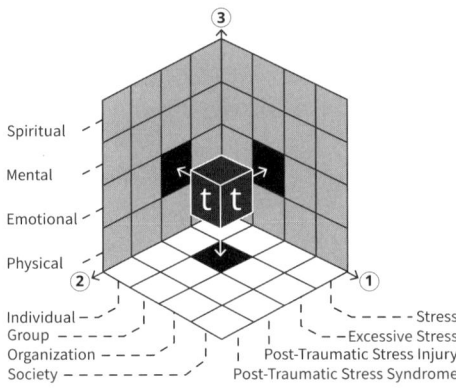

*Figure 10: Trauma Cube with three dimensions*

The Trauma Cube shows us that trauma rarely comes isolated in only one of the boxes. It can be very easy to latch onto the box where trauma first appears, only to find yourself struggling later on with the boxes that were overlooked. Problems that emerge in one part of the cube might also be an invitation to adopt a wider perspective. Just because symptoms mainly manifest in the context of an individual, don't make the mistake of assuming that's where you'll find a permanent solution. An important skill to learn – in order to work effectively with organizational trauma – is to use the entire spectrum of the cube, every face. Here are some examples:

> *John is suffering from post-traumatic stress. Every time he has to do something new, he gets cramp in his gut. Old, unhealed pain arises – from years ago at home when, time and time again, he was punished if he got something wrong. Because the risk of error is greater when attempting something new, the old pain rears its ugly head, giving him cramp every time he is asked to take on a new task or to change his way of working. Then a familiar process begins: he asks for more explanation, perhaps some extra training, more feedback and endless checklists, all costing his colleagues and supervisor loads of energy. If the team around John is resilient and willing to support him, then they can help him. However, if the team members are tired or stressed then it is more likely that there will be even more pressure on John. And this exactly reaffirms his old pattern. John's resilience will therefore be determined by his social network. Unfortunately, few organizations have any space for someone with issues like John's.*

In this example, you can see a clear link between what John experiences as the space allowed for him to work through this issue, and the dynamics of the team where he belongs. Managers, who are not aware of this phenomenon, are apt to zoom in on the employee with the problem. So they miss the fact that there might be a lot of potential resources and also potential obstacles around the employee. They do not understand how the dynamics of the team easily provide the precise stimulus needed to push John back into his old, abiding, unhealed pattern. Notwithstanding that the resources for healing exist equally in that same team. But on the employee the blame falls.

> *It could be that in some teams multiple members are suffering from post-traumatic stress. This happened in a team whose work required a high degree of accuracy. Striving for accuracy can be a strength, but it can also turn into perfectionism, where no result is ever good enough. This can be a consequence of*

*post-traumatic stress, and this was the case with a team for whom perfectionism came to be their survival strategy but also their undoing. Whenever the team received a complaint about their work, they immediately became uneasy. No one wanted to be the one blamed and a kind of barely-controlled panic would spread immediately throughout the team. The team leader was, coincidentally or not, also uncomfortable with emotions and errors and so was unable to contain the tension.*

*The team environment gradually became like a pressure cooker: people were easily triggered, there were increasingly few moments of calm, and resilience plummeted. Because it was always the 'weakest' employee who took the blame for any mistakes and the lack of cohesion, there was a severe, crippling dynamic in the team, which immediately and continuously affected new employees as they fell 'under the spell' of the existing dynamics. The team became totally exhausted and the whole situation accelerated out of control. It was very difficult to keep new employees for long; many complained that the basic new-hire training was useless. Unfortunately, no one knew how to zoom-out, to take the distance needed to see how to turn these dynamics around.*

These two examples occur at the interface between individual and team, but trauma can also manifest at the interfaces between different departments or between organization(s) and society. So an organization can do damage in or to a community: environmental pollution for example, fraud or exploitation. This can cause all kinds of emotions within those organizations, feelings of impotence, anger, disappointment, sadness and shame. Even though the symptoms are visible within the organization, the key to healing probably lies outside, in the relationship between perpetrator and victim(s) or other affected parties. As long as the key remains unnoticed, or is sought internally, and the damage is not recognized, it's likely that particular internal dynamics and emotions will continue to manifest. In a way these are recurring calls for help or resolution. In short, the solution is often to be found in more places than only where the problem appears.

A person who really understands trauma is likely to be both willing and able to work with the Trauma Cube. He already knows that what shows as a team issue might have its roots with an individual or in the dynamics of the team or how the team is embedded in its surrounding organization. When constant pressure creates an environment of continuous stress, any existing post-traumatic stress is magnified, causing an individual or team to suddenly break down, often sowing the seeds of organizational trauma. If there is no one able to recognize these subtle signals, the trauma can suddenly become very visible, when its influence and the damage it brings – which could have been avoided – brings the team or organization to a standstill. In one of his lectures Peter de Prins, Professor at the Vlerick Management School, calls organizational trauma the Slow Killer.

When working with organizational trauma, it is useful to bear a number of things in mind:

- The interplay between the three faces of the Trauma Cube.
- As trauma infects an organization, it can have its effect slowly, quietly and invisibly but still impact many different dimensions.
- Trauma is rarely restricted to one part of the Trauma Cube.
- make itself, and its need for healing, visible.

If you intend to dive deeply into working with organizational trauma, then it is crucial that you learn how to look at an organization systemically.

## Zooming in and zooming out

Although identifying individual trauma requires training and experience, it remains much easier than identifying organizational trauma. And what makes this even more difficult is, first, that organizational trauma often manifests through an individual and, second, that from our earliest schooling we are trained to zoom in rather than to zoom out. 'Zooming in' originates in mechanistic, reductionist thinking driven by the deep-seated belief that you can only understand the functioning of the whole by breaking it down into increasingly smaller parts. This approach has achieved marvelous things, such as unraveling the secrets of DNA, upon which so much of medical science hangs its hopes. But if we apply the same approach to working with organizations, we are inclined to reduce the functioning of an organization down to the behavior of individuals. For example, many organizations view burn-out as an individual issue, which limits the approach to individualized care and guidance, which often stigmatizes the burned-out employees. If the problem seems to affect only one department, then it's time to zoom out.

**Zoom in (= analytic perspective)
means deconstructing something
in order to understand it.**

**Zoom out (= systemic perspective)
means understanding something
by placing it in the context of the larger whole.**

Fritjof Capra

To zoom out means looking at the world with a different frame of mind than most of us have learned to use. Neither way of thinking – analytic or systemic – is better or worse. Being aware of both allows us to consciously choose the framework appropriate to the situation. The systemic perspective invites us to look at relationships. Between people, teams, departments and so on. This way of looking also invites us to take into account the history, and destiny, of groups and organizations. The present can feel supported by the past but the past can also put weight on the future. Another – albeit conceptual – form of belonging: we relate not only to people but also to concepts, ideologies, values, colors and emotions. In practice, this means that the space around what we can see and touch is, literally, full of relationships. Looking with systemic eyes means having less attention for the familiar, tangible reality and more for how things relate to or connect with each other. For example, if someone has the tendency to be aggressive, that person will continue to suffer from this tendency until he changes his relationship to it. When a team, piece by piece, loses its resiliency and flexibility, it might be worthwhile examining how that team relates to its environment. Rebuilding the team's internal resilience might need some intervention that addresses how the team and the outside world relate to each other. Zooming out means that you try to understand the behavior of an individual or a team by examining how they relate to their surroundings, especially other teams, professionals in other organizations, and society. So you can consciously choose to zoom in or zoom out. The following table gives you some guidance.

| Zoom in (= mechanistic) | Zoom out (= systemic) |
|---|---|
| Focus on the individual. | Focus on the system (team, department, organization etc.) and the relationships between the parts of the system. |
| Identify the problem – identify a single cause – solve the problem. | Identify and work with patterns and dynamics. |
| Origin has just one root cause. | Something unfolds through the combination of a set of circumstances and an interaction between several factors. |
| Look for individual responsibility and attribute the cause there. | Work with shared responsibilities. |
| Emphasis on individual behavior. Anything pointing to the surrounding context (team, organization, family of origin etc.) is best ignored. | Focus on the interaction between behavior and the structures, systems and values of the organization. |
| The organization can rectify the individual/team's dysfunctional or undesirable conduct without recognizing its own role in the problem. | Individual dysfunction is seen as a reason to (re)build the whole. This applies just as much to the individual as to the greater whole. |

| It is expected that eventually – with appropriate support and guidance – the individual will adjust his or her behavior. | Understanding symptoms, patterns and dynamics leads to approaches that strengthen the whole and make it healthier. |
| --- | --- |
| Focus on individual or isolated behavior. | Focus on connectedness and circularity, or how one affects the other and vice versa. |

**When you zoom out, what are you looking for?**

Every year, air shows are organized all over the world. Fans of these events look forward to seeing new aircraft but, perhaps even more, to the spectacle created by precision aerobatic teams from different countries. Britain's Red Arrows for instance, or Australia's Roulettes, or the Patrouille de France. Naturally these teams boast their nation's best pilots, but that is not enough. There is also something special about those pilots as a whole, something they spend months, even years, working on. If one of the pilots leaves, he cannot simply be replaced by a new pilot. What existed between the initial pilots, the level achieved together, must be rebuilt. Hence the statement: *"You can't just learn to fly in formation"*. What has been built up between those pilots is something that can't easily be explained. It has grown into something almost magical. Unfortunately, just like magic, it is difficult to manage, to guarantee, to photograph or to grasp.

Work in the industrial age was divided into very basic, simple activities. Then came work process design, the brainchild of some very bright minds. In those days, once the process design was completed, you could pull just about anyone off the street and put them to work on the assembly line. However, work complexity has increased dramatically, making it almost impossible to split a process into simple, separate tasks. More so, the quality of an organization's service or products increasingly depends on the interplay between different employees, disciplines and departments. When the complexity of a task transcends a single individual, the answer is to invest in developing the relational wiring between them. This is necessary to nurture collective intelligence in teams and between disciplines. Many organizations give too little energy to this invisible aspect between people while it is this potential that can make the difference between being ordinary and being exceptional. Just because a team has the required number of members, it does not mean that the team will be successful. Chances are, though, that you'll hear a manager in an organization say: *"There's a capable person filling every function, so why is the team still not performing? There are other teams that are performing better with fewer people".*

Many organizations find that collaboration between departments is poor: they have become silos. And some feel that they will never have happy customers until the walls that make the silos are demolished.

> *One of the largest logistics organizations in the world made many acquisitions over many years. Freight transport possibilities grew. First their own bikes, then moving on to vans, trucks, trains, cargo ships and even their own airplanes. The point came when the organization had all of these options at their command. But internal competition had arisen between the different divisions (silos). Customers found the promise of combined and integrated transport options very attractive, but they noticed – especially in the beginning – that this didn't work out so well in practice. Fortunately, the organization understood that their real added value lay in the healthy interplay between divisions and so they invested in developing this. The various departments learned better how to fly in formation.*

### Technical problems versus adaptive challenges

The authors of *The Practice of Adaptive Leadership The Practice of Adaptive Leadership* (Heifeitz, Linsky, and Grashow, 2009, [16]) argue that an important aspect of leadership is the ability to distinguish between technical problems and adaptive challenges (aka wicked problems). Each requires a totally different approach. When you're dealing with a technical problem – repairing a machine for example – zooming in will help to find the cause and develop a plan of action. With adaptive challenges there is often no single, unique cause. More often it is a combination of factors that affect each other mutually. A step towards a possible solution might need a change in how some, or all, of the parts interact. These changes in interaction would cause changes in the relationships and consequences of these parts and so on. This asks for a new and dynamic choreography to be created between all concerned. This solution only becomes visible when you zoom out and look from a systemic perspective. Trauma is absolutely an adaptive challenge. Unfortunately, both organizations and society approach the vast majority of adaptive challenges as if they are technical problems. Leadership goes hand in hand with the ability to zoom fluently from in to out to meet changing circumstances.

### An eye for the invisible

What turns an 'ordinary' business into a high-performance organization is a constantly-evolving issue. As the world becomes ever faster and more complex, we find ourselves at a tipping point where it is clear that the classic top-down model of organization is reaching its limits. The attached diagram, inspired by the work of Art Brock *Wealth a Living Systems Model* (Brock, 2014, [6]) and Dave Snowden *"Decision Making. A Leader's Framework for Decision Making"* (Snowden and Boone, 2007, [26]) , shows an overview of where to look for the potential in organizations. The higher you go in the diagram, the more suited a living system will be to thrive in a fast changing, complex world.

**The future belongs to those
who prepare for it today.**

Malcolm X

Emergence    Emergence: To what extent can the organization, being a living network of (sub) systems, gain advance understanding of what is going to happen in the market? And to what extent is this living network succeeding in adapting and developing, in tailoring itself to the unfolding future? So it is about the ability to feel into and anticipate, so that the organization creates the market rather than experiences it. Self-regulation – which is an expression of relational flexibility – appears to be an important condition for realizing this potential.

Relationships    Relationships: How qualitative are the relationships between the (sub) systems? Is it a well-connected, flexible network? To what extent is the organization able to transcend existing silos? We see that the interplay, the choreography, between departments or disciplines is as or more important than individual talent; it is not always the country with the best players that wins a World Cup.

Output and performance    Output and performance: What does the organization do with the (sub) systems at its disposal? This is about how similar organizations can achieve different results with more or less the same means.

Properties    Properties: What are the particular characteristics of the organization's people, machines, tools, systems etc.?

Ownership and numbers    Ownership and numbers: How many and what kind of people, machines, tools etc. does the organization have?

Knowing that organizations operate in a VUCA-world defined by its ever-increasing Volatility, Uncertainty, Complexity and Ambiguity, it is mainly the first of the above table's properties – emergence – that makes an organization fit for such a VUCA-world. Emergence naturally results from pre-existing, established properties, seen lower in the diagram. These properties, which include a sense of being connected and the relationships between people, teams, departments and disciplines, are therefore not nice-to-haves but must haves.

**The more complex a network is, the more complex its pattern of interconnections, the more resilient it will be.**

Fritjof Capra

That invisible aspect gets a lot of different, sometimes overlapping, names: organizational culture, relational wiring, organizational web, white space, social capital, field, third entity, relational fabric and so on. Just like a rubber band this relational wiring can be elastic (resilient) or brittle. Based on what is happening to and with this fabric, it can bounce back to its original state, become distorted and so lose some of its elasticity, small cracks can appear or it can split right down the middle. Zooming out means, above all, learning to look at the quality of this fabric, the warp and the weft, and at the resulting dance between the parts of a living system. And so, we arrive at a usable definition of organizational trauma. A definition that emphasises that relational wiring.

**The health of the relational wiring creates the ground for emergence.**

## 2.4 Organizational trauma, a definition

When we investigate the phenomenon of trauma, using every face of the Trauma Cube, we see a number of repeating patterns that offer us a more-comprehensive definition of organizational trauma:

> Organizational trauma results from a major event, a series of drastic events or ongoing conditions, that are experienced as toxic or threatening to the survival, the coherence or the healthy functioning of a living system (team, department, group, organization etc.) because the ability to confine the intense, emotional charge that comes free, is overwhelmed. Often, this leads to an unhealthy dynamic that, suddenly or step by step, infiltrates the dynamics of that living system to the extent that its normal, resilient functioning is impaired.

This exerts pressure upon the spiritual, mental, emotional and physical health of the employees who are part of that living system.

And this brings us to a sharper definition:

> Organizational trauma is caused by a major event or series of events, or by persistent, toxic conditions, that have an overwhelming effect on a group, family, organization and/or community, impairing the ability of the whole to function on balanced physical, emotional, mental and spiritual planes.

## 2.5 The Trauma Trap

Tracking down organizational trauma is best approached by zooming out, while looking at the relational fabric. If you do this in different organizations or within different departments or teams, step by step you'll begin to come across some differences. So we arrive at the Trauma Trap.

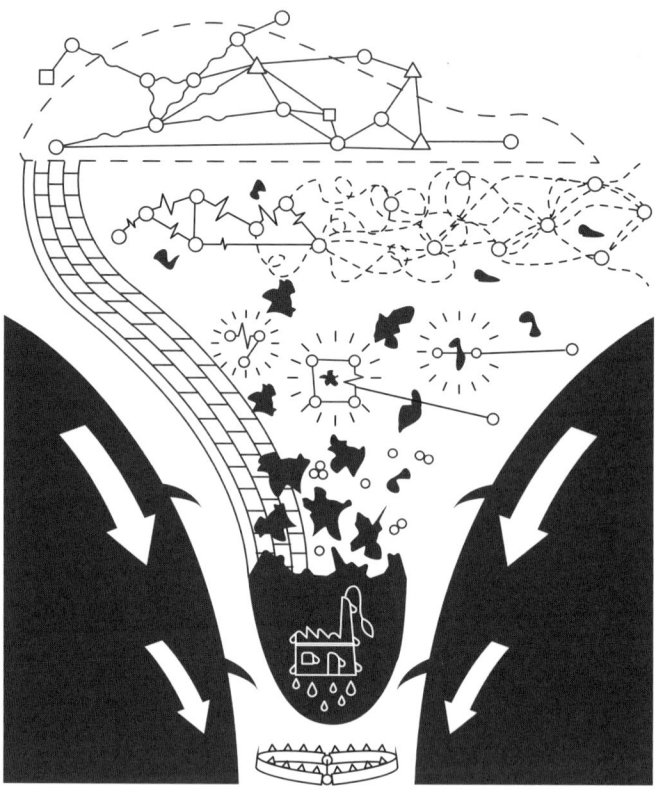

*Figure 11: Trauma Trap – Full view*

Let's look at how the relational wiring of an organization evolves as it sinks into the Trauma Trap. Extreme events can force the organization to the bottom of the Trauma Trap in one stroke. Continuous toxic conditions can cause an organization gradually to slide deeper into the Trauma Trap, making the relational fabric increasingly vulnerable until, ultimately, the organization is so badly damaged that it gets stuck at the bottom of the Trauma Trap.

**Resilient: far removed from the Trauma Trap:**

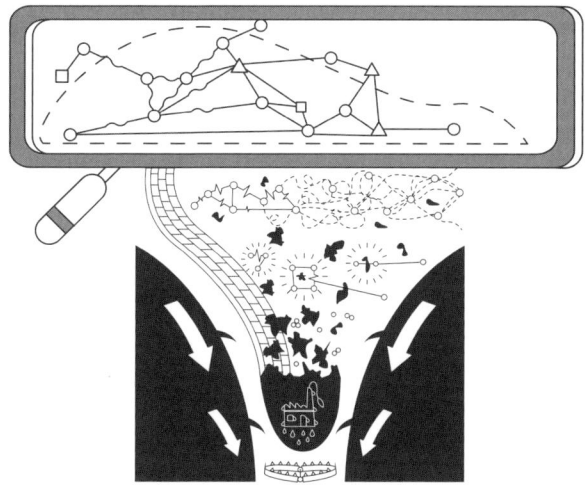

*Figure 12: Trauma Trap – Resilient phase*

- The fabric of a living system is healthy and enjoys healthy, support-ive connections.

- Wherever intense cooperation is necessary, the relational fabric is much finer (= clusters). Smooth collaboration and exchange sup-ports the development of collective intelligence.

- These clusters, or subsystems, are the opposite of isolated silos. They are connected with other clusters and exchange occurs freely between the clusters when needed.

- Whenever this living system is challenged, by a change in the market for example, it easily and quickly creates new connections that bring new interactions within and between the clusters that continue to evolve. New clusters form easily when needed.

- The organization is an integrated whole of which the clusters are parts. This means the clusters are interdependent in their functioning. This is made possible by the framework of the whole system, the organization, which functions as a kind of platform (instead of a pyramid).

- So, in addition to healthy interaction between clusters, we also see smooth interaction between clusters and the organization. Specifically, we see that a cluster can influence the course of the whole. Not all guidance comes from the larger whole because that would be top-down control.

- The responsiveness of such an organization – in which more and more features of a healthy living system begin to show – is particularly large, allowing a need for change to be picked up and channeled, through the healthy relational fabric, to the place (or cluster) where something meaningful can be done with it. Think back to the metaphor of the bird flock we encountered earlier. Some believe the development of the internet increases the potential for people to experience and learn from this type of experience.

- Nassim Taleb – author of *The Black Swan* (Taleb, 2008, [31]) and *Antifragility* (Taleb, 2012, [30]) – calls this kind of resilience 'antifragile' because any cluster can pick up and pass on an internal/external call or need for change. This ensures that an organization can navigate unchartered waters because there is plenty of resilience. And, just by being in this turbulence, resilience grows; a self-reinforcing loop. Less resilient organizations will incur damage if they try to sail these turbulent waters. They are much more vulnerable to organizational trauma.

- In a resilient organization there is a large degree of self-regulation. We deliberately avoid the term self-steering. Self-regulation means that every cluster has a clear role within the organization and that each cluster gets the space to fulfill that role, while adhering to the goals and values of the organization, the larger whole. Self-steering would increase the chance that clusters set their own course, without taking due account of the whole. The clusters would then, step by step, take the upper hand and the whole could be lost. This would erode the connection between the clusters. If those connections were suddenly needed to respond to a new challenge, they would be less able to respond with speed and agility, just like a muscle that for years has not been trained.

- Clusters enjoy healthy functioning with each other with regard to internal organizational relationships. Exchange is also good with the outside world. And yet there is a palpable difference between internal and external. This is because part of the organization is formed from shared values, rituals, traditions and customs. The clusters get their identity from their membership of the surrounding organization.

- If a cluster becomes 'sick' or has become redundant, the surrounding network is strong enough to carry that and, in extremis, to dissolve the cluster, possibly letting staff go, but always in a sensitive and proper manner. Desperately holding on to something, that no longer functions or has no function, can be a symptom of dysfunction.

When an organization finds itself at this level of health or integration then there is the possibility of emergence – the quality, much-coveted by organizations, that we mentioned earlier. It seems like a dream and yet it is possible. It takes a high level of maturity in the leaders, managers and employees, yet there's also a kind of naturalness in this kind of organization. Common sense tends to take center stage. And, more and more, it becomes clear that many classic management approaches hinder the development of emergence in organizations. Emergent functioning, however, is only feasible if the organization is built on trauma-wise foundations. In particular, this ensures that care is taken for the overall health of the organization, and also ensures that damage occurring in potentially turbulent waters is addressed in a timely manner. Thus, the chance for organizational trauma is significantly minimized. That's how the relational wiring of a resilient living systems looks.

Even such an organization can suddenly be confronted by an overwhelming event so that the relational fabric is torn apart and the organization is thrown immediately to the bottom of the Trauma Trap. The structure of this model, however, invites us to descend step by step. And with each step we increase our understanding of how an organization can unknowingly become increasingly vulnerable to organizational trauma.

**The first signs of distress**

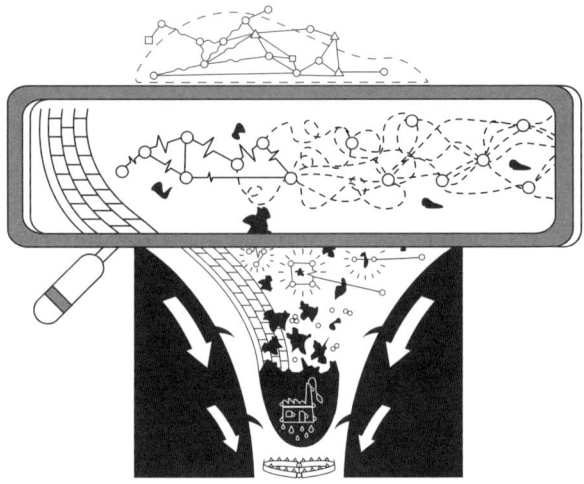

*Figure 13: Trauma Trap – First signs of distress phase*

A healthy living system manages the need for change – whether it originates internally or externally – in a timely and meaningful process that translates it into one or another adjustment or intervention. However, if the force of the change exceeds the ability to process it, initial signs of stress (chaos and/or rigidity) might arise. Here is how these might look:

- Healthy inter-cluster exchange comes under pressure, with clusters putting themselves first rather than the whole. The permeability of the walls between clusters, subsystems and the whole (just like the pores of our skin) reduces. This makes relationships between clusters more rigid – at the expense of the sensitivity and responsiveness of the overall organization. In this way, internal stability is monitored and protected. In particular by keeping change incentives 'outside' to avoid too much internal pressure or friction. This makes the system more 'robust', but on the other hand it becomes more 'rigid' too, and begins, as it were, to exclude the outside world. Unfortunately – especially in a rapidly-changing world – this can easily and quickly become a damaging mistake.

- There might also be a reverse movement: relationships with the outside world become stronger because borders are now more porous. In this case, focus turns to the outside world at the expense of internal interaction and internal stability. Internal diversity then increases until it becomes a negative quality; internal connections suffer and we see the beginnings of fragmentation or silos. The ability of an organization to produce integral or holistic solutions is snowed under. For many organizations, this is their daily reality, because they never have or had the time and space to find the tools needed to build an integrated whole.

An organization at this level can still be working efficiently but has to manage a lot more friction. Addressing this friction can help the organization to develop in the direction of more resilience. Unfortunately, if this friction is not contained it can interfere with good functioning at any moment. In any case, a result is that the organization's resilience is weakened and the probability of emergence decreases. In a subtle way, conservatism seeps into the organization and little by little it becomes more risk averse. This reduces the courage to navigate in uncharted waters and will limit the development of antifragility and contribute to diminished resilience.

One of the reasons why a healthy organization can get stuck in this state, and this might initially sound paradoxical, is because the organization no longer maintains a healthy balance between acceleration and slowing down. Perhaps a sports analogy will help: too little exercise (coping with turbulent waters) causes your body to become lazier. Too much exercise makes it impossible for your body to recover sufficiently, increasing the risk of injury and lowering your performance ceiling. Organizations are living systems, not machines. The profit imperative asks that you run your machines 24/7. Living systems are extremely sensitive to the law of diminishing returns and, at a certain moment, become dysfunctional. Unfortunately, many organizations are operating exactly on this edge.

**When distress becomes chronic**

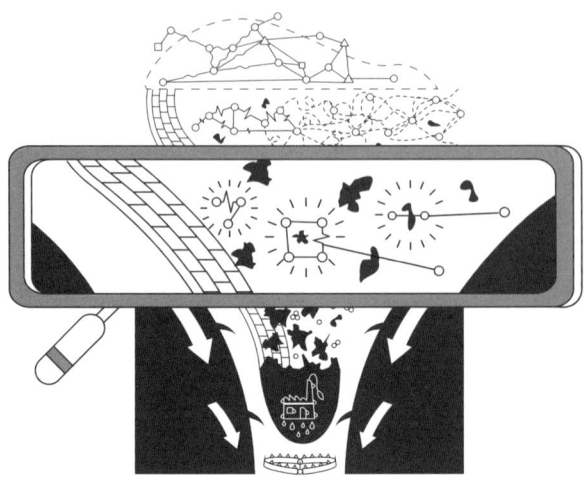

*Figure 14: Trauma Trap – Chronic distress phase*

The Trauma Trap can be an intuitive measuring device to keep the relational fabric of organizations in good health. The prior state – initial distress – is then a kind of early-warning phase. 'Early' because there are no pronounced signs of dysfunction. There are only silent signals. The friction showing at this stage could be an indicator that intervention with the 'whole system' is needed before any cracks appear in the relational fabric. Compare this with a conflict. There is a phase in which there is still room for constructive conversation, but there may also be a phase where all the bridges have been burned. A lot of organizations, unfortunately, make significant interventions and changes and expect immediate recovery. These organizations are neglecting the fact that an organization is a living system (vs. a machine). The organizational image held by the management or board will be decisive in the choices they make at this stage. And be aware that the members of a board are often trapped by forces or situations over which they have no control: acquisitions, mergers, shareholder-power and more.

In this phase, distress is no longer contained so, of course, it increases. Negative emotions begin to pile up, hence the blackness and gray mist that begins to loom, down in the Trauma Trap. All the mechanisms, needed to keep the living system fully healthy, begin to falter. Signals that intervention is needed – the cries for help – are lost in the damaged relational fabric. Information that might facilitate a breakthrough, no longer flows freely through the organization. Ownership and taking responsibility make way for us-versus-them dynamics. People say "*Yes*" and do "*No*". The gap between strategy and execution widens. The process of disintegration has begun and, as the relational fabric loses its integrity, the first cracks begin to show . . . but no one seems to be awake.

Once the process of disintegration has started, the quality of relationships between the clusters decreases. This means that certain clusters are still connected, if needed, with other clusters. But, between some clusters walls begin to go up. Clusters which are no longer well-connected or fail to influence other clusters or the whole, naturally lose the ability to respond if an opportunity/challenge/danger – a call for change – emerges. This can seriously impact the organization's adaptability.  Compare it to a tower guard who sees danger looming on the horizon but is unable or willing to warn the residents of the castle. An organization in this state is particularly vulnerable to 'unexpected' events.

We noted that, on several occasions, the need to change or adjust had already existed, and had been noticed and action suggested. Despite this, it often took far too long before anyone took action, because either the need was ignored or the channels for action were completely clogged-up or broken. Being unprepared makes an organization vulnerable to organizational trauma. And some forms of it could be avoided.

An organization with static or positional hierarchy is particularly sensitive to becoming stuck at this stage of the Trauma Trap. Let's build on the comparison with the tower guard.  In a healthy organization someone would hear his voice. In a classic top-down organization there's a big chance that his 'signals' would be ignored.  In rough and uncharted waters this could be especially dangerous: if one cluster starts influencing the whole too much or is too one-sided, it diverts focus, from the outside world and the whole, towards that individual cluster. In this case, it is not the relationship with the market, the customer or each other that is most important, but the relationship with the management (the steering cluster). On the one hand, this is a greater responsibility for the steering cluster but, on the other hand, this makes it completely blind or insensitive to relevant stimuli that come from elsewhere in the system. Think back to our tower guard.

In short, this is an extremely dangerous zone to be in. Looking at the Trauma Trap you could argue that, in this case, the organization can still recover from the situation. But if the organization sinks even further, whether suddenly or slowly, the damage could be substantial, even irreversible. By irreversible, we actually mean that healing is still possible but can no longer be complete: more-complex care and support will be needed and, in most cases, there will be permanent scars. Here the Trauma Trap turns into a sucking vortex. An organization in this zone is incredibly vulnerable and fragile (as opposed to antifragile). Sadly, this is where many organizations call 'home'.

**The first symptoms of organizational trauma**

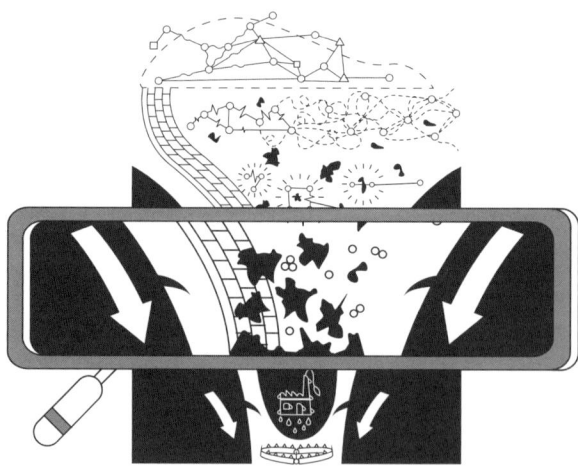

*Figure 15: Trauma Trap – First symptoms of organizational trauma phase*

The point comes when being connected is predominantly experienced as troublesome, or negative, or disruptive.  Then you might hear comments about internal relationships like: "*If that department would just get on with their work we would make our numbers*".  This attitude can be expressed in relation to the customer or the internal client.  In practice this means that, for example, employees can no longer open up to the needs of others.  The 'other' has become a burden.  Many aid workers, or employees in the healthcare sector, at some time in their career end up at this point.  They are emotionally spent, no longer able to care or be sympathetic.  Many organizations in the healthcare sector have lost the balance between speeding up and slowing down because the management focus is on productivity, costs, efficiency and so on.  In such a context, people are unable to work to their full capacity and, eventually, fail.

The previously positive qualities of interaction, exchange, cooperation and connection lose their energy-giving potential and start to cost energy. The relational fabric suffers, becoming weaker and ever more fragile. The apparently 'healthy' connections that are still visible, are often between sick or damaged clusters, and function only to support each other or to complain about the state of the organization. These kinds of connections do not help the organization escape from the Trauma Trap. The dragging-down forces are stronger than the pulling-up forces. The resilience of the organization is lost, totally. We are now past the point from which a living system can naturally recover. If an organization, or a part, ends up here, it would find the doors of the Trauma Trap standing wide open. It is already extremely difficult, probably impossible, to get out of there without doing even more damage to the relational fabric. Downward dynamics color the organization's functioning; barbed hooks await, lining the bottom of the Trauma Trap.

**Organizational trauma**

*Figure 16: Trauma Trap – Organizational Trauma phase*

In this phase, the relational fabric is now in rags or has become a conduit for negativity. Yiannis Gabriel *"Organizations and Their Discontents: Miasma, Toxicity and Violation"* (Gabriel, 2005, [13]) (University of Bath School of Management, Division of Strategy & Organization) employs the term. 'miasma' from the ancient Greek meaning 'pollution'. According to him, an organization is in a state of miasma if its environment or atmosphere is characterized by an extreme amount of stress and negative emotions. Within the concept of the Trauma Trap this would manifest as either absent or painful relationships that lead to full structural dysfunction of the organization. He compares this to a city that is afflicted by the plague. In such a city nothing and no one is immune to the disease and, step by step, this ensures that the inhabitants totally lose confidence in their sovereign, their institutions, their identity, their neighbors and their future.

No matter how hard people try to protect themselves, the downward spiral of anxiety, depression, shame, humiliation, desperation and sadness, slowly sucks all the vibrancy out of the organization. The downward spiral appears irreversible. Healing is possible: but often only if the cause of the tragedy is faced and recognized and space is given for the accompanying emotions. When this does not happen, the soul of the organization gets stuck or lost. There is no longer an attractive future perspective, and so the energy for work, for building the future, gets completely stuck.

**In conclusion**

Emergence is a property that we all know.  As a property it expresses the integration and health of the relationships between parts of a living system. You can compare it to a football team at a World Cup, a team during an Olympic sailing race or a jazz orchestra at its best. This is a particularly high level of cooperation. It is a level that is often achieved rather coincidentally yet, at the same time, a level organizations can consciously learn how to work towards.

Using the Trauma Trap as a lens can help in understanding organizational dynamics. At its heart, however, it is a conceptual model that actually allows you to look at the relational fabric of a living system. What you consider as 'whole' or 'part' can thus evolve according to the size of the entity with which you work:

- When you're working with an organization, then the organization is the 'whole' and the departments or teams (= clusters) make up the 'parts'.

- When you're working with a team, then the team is the 'whole' and the team members are the 'parts'.

- When you're working with a community or a network of organizations and associations, that greater network is the 'whole' and the organizations and associations form the 'parts'.

So here too there is zooming in and zooming out. Compare it with the famous Russian Matryoshka nesting dolls, that fit into each other. In any case, the Trauma Trap helps you shift your attention from the material or tangible (people, teams, departments, buildings, machines, …) to the relationships between the parts. This makes the quality of the relational tissue a lot more negotiable.

Finally, a whole organization can sink into the Trauma Trap, but it can also be just part(s) of the organization that get trapped. Here, in essence, is the difference between looking more systemically or looking less systemically. Someone who has never learned to look systemically would reduce this to a problem with the 'sick' part. Someone adept at looking systemically would see this as a symptom of a sick whole. The following chapters will clarify how you can learn to zoom in and out and when it is called for. In any case, when the relational fabric of a living system loses its elasticity – suddenly or over time – it will begin to show symptoms of organizational trauma. Part II talks about the causes of organizational trauma and details a range of symptoms that point to its presence.

# PART II

## FROM RECOGNITION TO ACKNOWLEDGEMENT

# How organizational trauma arises

**3**

The Trauma Trap shows what can happen when the relational fabric of a living system comes under too much pressure. The pressure can be of external origin such as an environmental disaster, or internal such as mismanagement. The chance that now or in the future you'll have to deal with organizational trauma is substantial – whether you're an employee, the MD, an external consultant; whatever your role. There are a number of issues important to identifying and working with organizational trauma:

- Exactly what causes organizational trauma?

- How do you initially get on the scent of organizational trauma?

- How do the patterns, that ensure organizational trauma, fit together?

- How can you work with these patterns?

- How do you repair or heal the relational fabric of an organization?

- How might trauma-informed leadership help organizations to function in a healthy way while enduring the turbulence that trauma brings?

We've already seen that trauma is caused by an overwhelming event, series of events or by persistent, toxic conditions. Knowing what could cause organizational trauma will allow for earlier intervention and better ongoing guidance, should an organization be overcome by it. It would also permit the establishing of more-extensive preventive measures that would improve the resilience of the organization. It would ensure that certain, often unavoidable, decisions, such as closures or mergers, could be taken while bearing in mind the possible impact on the relational fabric of the organization. In short, trauma-informed leadership is an important condition for getting the best out of organizations and their people.

In the context of organizations, we can subdivide the origins of organizational trauma into four parts. These will be briefly discussed and clarified using specific examples. Then follows a series of insights and approaches that are critical to really getting to grips with organizational trauma.

So we come, again, to the difference between trauma with a small 't' and with a capital 'T'. As you move through the examples, you will notice that the subjective, less-tangible dimension, as shown in the Trauma

Cube, increases.  In this case, it is often very difficult for organizations to recognize that something is going on or wrong.  Ways of recognition, that now exist in the area of individual trauma, are still largely unexplored in organizations.  Often organizational trauma is just laughed-off or falls under a blanket of silence.  This approach can appear to work – as long as business results are good – but, meanwhile, something damaging is developing under the surface (= 'The Slow Killer').  Covering it up or ignoring it – as with unmourned grief – simply makes the problem more complex and working on it more difficult.  Trauma patterns can also become entrenched in a system.

## 3.1 Origin 1: Sudden and external

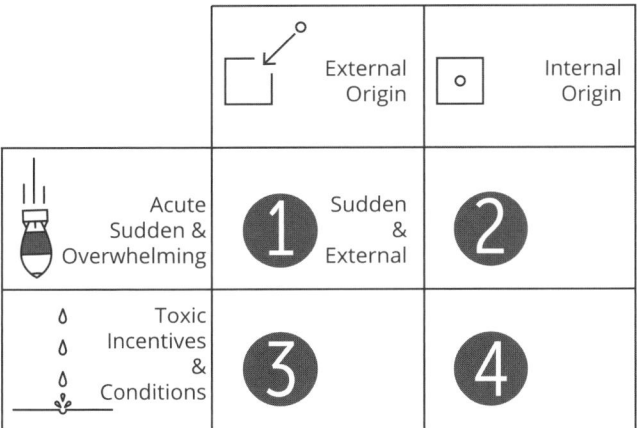

*Figure 17: Sudden and external origin of organizational trauma*

Some of the events, that cause organizational trauma, can be traced to a specific moment and originate outside the organization. They are acute, sudden and dramatic (= trauma with big 'T'). Sometimes Nature can be brutal. Natural disasters, such as hurricanes, tsunamis, volcanic eruptions and forest fires, are all examples of major events that can overwhelm and seriously damage a family, village or organization.

The pace and level of human development has also given us the capacity to do massive damage to people, places and the planet. Atomic bombs, terrorist attacks, nuclear accidents or oil spills can turn the world upside down in an instant. Here are some recent examples:

> *September 11, 2001 was a wake-up call for the whole world: two aircraft were deliberately flown into the WTC, aka the Twin Towers, in New York. Local communities, organizations with offices there, family members of those who died, the whole world in fact, were deeply affected by this terrorist attack.*

This major event touched, and touches still, the families of all the victims, but also the relational fabric of the organizations involved. 9/11 is an extreme example of the damage man can do. It can be useful to track this example across the faces of the Trauma Cube and see just how widely it is spread.

There have been other examples from the world of aviation; a series of recent disasters involving aircraft.

> *In 2014, Malaysia Airlines lost two passenger aircraft with a total of more than 500 passengers on board. One plane disappeared in the Indian Ocean, the other was shot down over Ukraine during fierce battles between the Ukrainian armed forces and pro-Russian separatists.*

> *A year later, Germanwings co-pilot Andreas Lubitz flew a passenger plane into the side of a mountain in the French Alps. It was a very costly suicide: Lubitz took 150 passengers with him to their graves.*

That these drastic events had a heavy impact on the airlines involved is clear. But what we don't know is what kind of indirect effect this had. On each of those flights were business people, sometimes several from the same company. So you could say the passengers and the airlines were the primary victims and the passengers' employers, as they were not directly involved, were secondary victims. This applies, too, for the families of all the people who perished.

In the Netherlands, from where most of the victims of the Malaysian Airlines flight came, exceptional attention was given to the aftermath of the disaster, including an official national war commemoration service. But how and what place the two airlines gave to the disaster remains unclear. When something like this happens, organizations often close themselves off to the outside world.

Wars still cause a lot of suffering. Terrorism – once relatively rare in the Western world – is now a frequent and global threat.  In recent years, the world has seen a host of large-scale terrorist attacks: 9/11 was the first deliberately-public attack of that size, and the domino effect continues, apparently unabated.  There was the attack on the French satirical weekly magazine *Charlie Hebdo*; the shooting at the Paris concert hall *Le Bataclan*; the recent attacks at Brussels Airport and on the Brussels subway and, in Nice, France, the truck driven into the crowd celebrating Bastille Day. The list gets ever longer: Berlin; Stockholm; London; Paris; Manchester…

A final, and far less-distressing example in this category, is when an organization unexpectedly loses essential funding.  If money or support, that was fundamental to future plans, suddenly becomes unavailable, then there is nothing immediately ready to fill that gap.  This can lead to bankruptcies or painful layoffs, especially in small, start-up companies, or in institutions – such as hospitals, cultural centers, schools and so on – that often depend on subsidies for funding. Some organizations make the best of such situations and find the strength to persevere, while others are so deeply affected that they either never fully recover or they cease to exist.

## 3.2 Origin 2: Sudden and internal

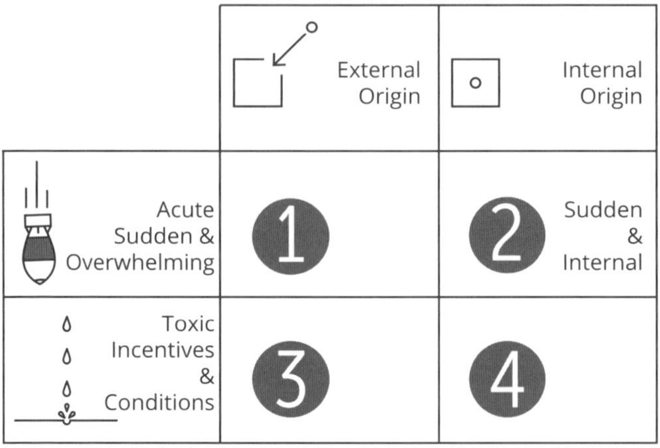

*Figure 18: Sudden and internal origin of organizational trauma*

Major events can also occur via an organization's everyday operations. In practice, this means also that the origin of the pain, the proverbial perpetrator, is a part of the organization or even can be the organization itself. Experience shows that this often sets loose a totally different dynamic, one that makes the road to recovery a whole lot tougher. This occurs more regularly in certain industries due to the nature of the work. Employees of hospitals, nursing homes, psychiatric institutions and other care-giving bodies often face situations that are profoundly difficult for their patients, clients or family members. When employees have to face this kind of situation – even when it is not actually about them – it still affects them and the relational fabric of their organization. As mentioned earlier, in these cases, we use the term 'vicarious' trauma to describe the way it seeps into, for example, aid workers and carers, through the 'emotional' pores of their skin.

Whether it happens to someone suddenly or it seeps in over time because employees are constantly dealing with others' suffering, a person working in a hospital's emergency department, an on-duty doctor for example, has to face death every working day. Critically-ill patients come under his care: some survive – he 'saves' them – and some do not. During such a career, a doctor might be intimately face-to-face with 1,000 or more people who die in or soon after his care.  And just like this emergency medical practitioner, there are many professions that are constantly confronted with this kind of deeply-affecting situation.  The professions call this 'compassion fatigue': the psychological damage suffered by carers who are constantly confronted with illness, dying and death.  It is worth noting that, in such cases, there is no organizational trauma; more likely there are multiple employees with individual trauma.  This has, to some degree and at some cost, to be carried by the relational fabric of the organization.  And so we come to our next example:

No matter how carefully and precisely everything might take place in a hospital, things do, inevitably, go wrong.  And medical errors can lead to deaths, such as Catherine's newborn baby (see preface).  Sometimes it is very clear that a medical error was made, and sometimes it is not.  But clarity doesn't necessarily help: either situation can completely paralyze an organization.  Such a sudden event injures a team or organization to the core and, in one blow, smashes the relational fabric to the bottom of the Trauma Trap.

Often the quality of the triage, the immediate reception and care of people and groups, is crucial to reducing the chances of individual and organizational trauma developing.  However, in practice, we see a different way of responding to major internal events that come from within the organization – compared to external.  With a physical attack, the origin is clearly external.  Having a visible, external enemy often seems to motivate, connect and mobilize victims and aid organizations.  We see a similar phenomenon in terrorist attacks.  People are more selfless, they look out for each other.  Recovery activities, events and rituals are organized together.  It is easier to find care and shelter.  The relational fabric is, to a degree, reactivated and this provides support and recognition.  Mind you, in spite of this, victims are often still left out in the cold.  What we determined earlier, is that an internal event causes much deeper damage and paralysis within the organization.  In addition, a completely different dynamic is triggered when there is a need to identify exactly what went wrong, and who might have been negligent.  At the exact moment that healing action is necessary – to restore the relational fabric – this 'blaming' dynamic gives precedence to legal and insurance issues, blocking what is really needed.

*In a hospital, a medical error occurred, leading to the death of a teenager. Pressure on the department where the error was made was particularly high for several years, making the resilience of the relational fabric particularly fragile. The parents started a legal battle that lasted five years and, for those five years, time stood still for the medical teams involved. Only after the official report was published was there even a little bit of safe space for people to talk about the events with each other. Some people had already left the hospital. The split between certain people, teams and departments had grown so wide it had become irreparable. Meanwhile, shame and grief had nestled deeply under the surface and teams were stuck in an obstinate 'blaming' dynamic.*

Over time, we have learned that the safe space needed, to reduce the risk of organizational trauma, can be completely eradicated if one starts looking for a guilty person, process or event. Doing so tends to cause total paralysis. It is possible for this approach to work, but it requires extraordinary levels of maturity in all concerned.

Industrial and workplace accidents that are fatal or cause permanent disability also take a severe toll on the victim, colleagues and family. This is another clear example of a major internal event which, in the absence of appropriate guidance and response, can cause organizational trauma.

*An organization was faced with two fatal accidents and a suicide (which the deceased's colleagues had seen coming) over a period of fifteen years. There followed a judicial inquiry. To avoid persecution and negative press coverage, very little was communicated. There was much shame and fear of prosecution with all involved: the management, the executive and the colleagues. These choices, however, gave no room for emotions to be naturally expressed and worked through.*

*Years later, an organizational coach was hired because the management was experiencing a lot of resistance from employees. During exploratory interviews it became evident that this 'resistance' had its roots in a bilateral lack of respect and confidence. In addition, there was a bullying problem among the employees. Once there was clarity around the organization's history, it became obvious that the issue was organizational trauma. Rather coincidentally, the coach had experience in dealing with organizational trauma. This opened the door for dealing with the unhealed trauma that had its origin in a combination of easily-identifiable major events, that had not been addressed. It was these events that pushed the organization into the Trauma Trap.*

Because the scale of these examples is narrower – it's not about multiple people as with a disaster or a terrorist attack – what happens will be forgotten sooner. But the chance is high that the event will continue to affect the family members, the parties themselves and the colleagues in one way or another. What is important in these examples is the fact that exactly by not dealing transparently with the various deaths or accidents, an unhealthy dynamic is established, in the culture of the organization that, step by step, starts to impair its daily operations. However, it doesn't always need a serious incident. Here's another example of how an organization might find itself in the Trauma Trap.

*A recently-established foundation had a particularly open and participatory culture. There was a deep trust in and between employees and good work was done with and for the clients (people with mental handicaps). The foundation was also embraced by the local community. One day, however, an accounting error was found. A large sum of money had disappeared and, due to the blind-faith culture, no perpetrator could be identified. The fact that people who had always worked in an atmosphere of transparency and trust suddenly ended up in an atmosphere of distrust and suspicion caused an immediate, deep wound in the organization's fabric. You could call it a shock to the organization's soul. Fortunately, the managers were committed to providing space for everyone to exchange and air their views and grievances. The organization lost something through the incident, but also learned something. During the recovery period, clearer agreements were made on a number of issues and more control was built into a number of processes.*

For certain organizations, such an incident would have had little or no impact. In this organization, the impact was exceptional for various reasons. First and foremost, it had a direct impact on the core values of the organization, exacerbated by the fact that the organization was very dependent on grants and donations. The incident threatened its basic functioning and core values. This example emphasizes that you cannot simply create a list of what might or might not lead to organizational trauma.

The following is worth bearing in mind when discussing the internal or external origin of organizational trauma, especially sudden, unexpected, overwhelming events:

- A clear-cut, profound event that is not properly addressed at the moment itself can cause organizational trauma.

- It might, however strange it might sound, also provide growth and development (= Post-Traumatic Growth), provided that one addresses it right away. When the origin is external, this chance that something positive ensues, seems to be greater.

- In practice we provide appropriate care and intervention before legal and/or insurance requirements impair the chances for recovery. When we do not act in time, the organization can spend an extended period of time stuck in the lower layers of the Trauma Trap, ensuring that organizational trauma becomes imbedded in the dynamics of the organization, making eventual healing significantly more difficult.

Our definition tells us that organizational trauma need not always be of acute origin. So we come to the following two categories.

## 3.3 Origin 3: Insidious and external

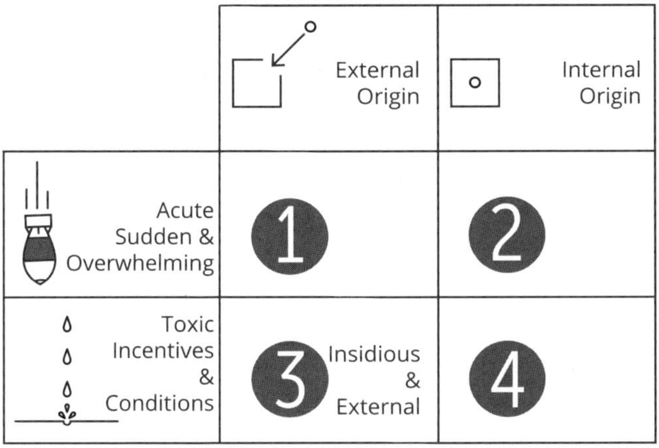

*Figure 19: Insidious and external origin of organizational trauma*

Organizational trauma can also develop in a more subtle way (The Slow Killer), through a combination of seemingly minor events (= trauma with small 't') or ongoing toxic conditions which ultimately can have the same destructive impact.   These events too can push an organization down to the bottom of the Trauma Trap. We are now moving into the area of the invisible and elusive aspects of groups and organizations, which we encountered as we deepened our understanding of the Trauma Cube. The more-subtle these are, the greater the awareness needed and the more-challenging the task of spotting them.

A perhaps unpleasant, but nevertheless excellent comparison, is the classic Chinese torture technique of gradually letting water drip onto the forehead of the victim until he breaks mentally. Unless you knew of this as a torture technique, you would never believe that a tiny drop of water on the forehead could drive someone to madness. In a similar way, it might seem unlikely that certain working conditions could have a similar effect until you find yourself working in such a traumatizing situation.

In any case, persistent (emotionally) overpowering, toxic conditions (aka allostatic load) can cause a group of people – a living system – to lose its balance, or the mechanism that should ensure balance, to become completely disrupted. This is currently being discussed in more and more organizations. The impact of ongoing stressful circumstances can thus be as great as the impact of a single, overwhelming event. Certainly, if you want to draw attention to this kind of organizational trauma, it is essential to give people insight into the cost of certain negative dynamics or behaviors.

These overpowering conditions can originate in the outside world of a company. In that case, we are not talking about a single overwhelming event such as a terrorist attack, but about persistent stressors or circumstances from the environment to which an organization is constantly exposed, like the 'Chinese' water torturing. This threat might arise independently of the organization's involvement, but the initial trigger or the cause, could equally be from within the organization itself, as shown in the following example.

> In the mid-1950s, a particular drug was often prescribed to counteract nausea in pregnant women. This drug was found to affect the fetus, causing more than ten thousand children to be born with birth defects. When the link between the abnormalities and the drug was demonstrated, the producer immediately removed it from the market.

> Like many organizations who find themselves in such a difficult situation, the producer initially stayed silent. A silence only broken 50 years later with a statement from the CEO wherein he expressed his personal apologies and those of the company as a whole. His statement was accompanied by the erection of a bronze statue of a malformed child in the organization's headquarters. It took half a century, he said, because the company was in shock and did not know how to respond.

> For years, the company had denied any claims for compensation by stating that it acted according to the current standards regarding drugs testing. It was precisely this (lack of) action, that affected the parents and children because it did not give them the recognition they asked for. Consequently, they continued to besiege the organization for years with claims for justice … and this caused constant tension on all sides.

The example shows a tendency in some organizations not to respond to a major event. Partly because the organization is in shock, but partly to avoid compensation claims. This ensures there is no completion for all involved and so the organization continues to be haunted by its past. This guarantees a constant, latent unrest. Whether intentionally or not, as long as an offender avoids responsibility for the consequences of his or her actions, the healing process gets stuck in its earliest stages. There might be no financial compensation, but there will also never be any peace. It is similar to a hit-and-run traffic accident, and it brings similar dynamics.

If new management is in place, it is often thought that the company can then turn over a new page. But this simply does not work. Just as trauma in families can be passed down from generation to generation, so can organizational trauma. When there is denial instead of recognition, the event, the issue, cannot find rest. In organizations where there is organizational trauma, an important responsibility falls on the leadership. It is in such moments that greatness might show itself. As a leader you must learn to recognize, allow or create these essential opportunities for recognition and healing. After all, every time such an opportunity is missed, the fires of denial are fuelled again, reinforcing the power of the Trauma Trap. We often see this in organizations that deny the effects – intentionally or otherwise – of the damage caused.

Denial can take many forms:

- Years of silence (internal and external), based on rational, legal thinking.

- Pass the (responsibility) buck by relying on legislation or legal constructions.

- Avoid costs by ignoring compensation claims.

- Ensure no authentic contact with the victims by channeling all communication through mediators, lawyers and so on.

- Any recognition of what happened should be formal not personal in order to protect the organization's image. For example, via the media instead of face to face with the victims.

Such events often involve a mechanistic illusion. Initially, it seems that the organization (as an institute) and the victims (as a group) are the only players. Secondly, it seems that something gets 'left behind' in time, like turning over a page. However, the inside and outside worlds cannot be separated. The chances are that the dynamics of the relationship with the outside world will color the internal dynamics of the organization. The chance is higher that similar patterns will unfold inside the organization: covering-up of failures, sticking exactly to procedures, avoiding authentic connection, refusing to take responsibility for errors and so on. Like a fractal the repeating pattern contains and reflects everything that arises in the organization's relationship with the outside and ensures it manifests in the dynamics of the organization.

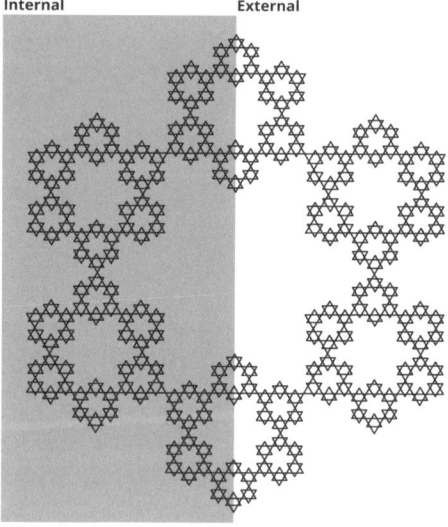

*Figure 20: Fractal: as inside so outside*

If you're new to systemic thinking, the example above is worth taking time out to consider, with the Trauma Cube and the Trauma Trap 'at hand'. Examine what happened, what followed once the negative effects of the nausea-drug became clear, who was involved or impacted and in what way, the dynamics inside and around the company, the actions and interventions, the effects pre and post any healing intervention. The following steps started to open up the path to healing:

- The public apology by the CEO. Even though it was fifty years late and made by a CEO who played no part in the tragedy. This was the first public recognition of the event.

- The organizing of an inauguration ritual for the statue at the head office. Rituals and symbols have been used for centuries to complete certain stages and transitions or to mark certain events in history, in such a way that those phenomena can no longer be made invisible by denial.

- Sitting down with the victims in a more authentic, problem-solving way, to work towards a correct settlement and/or compensation.

- The matter was given formal recognition in the history of the organization, including a comprehensive account on the company website.

Finally, it is important to point out that this affair had a positive consequence too: it brought about a total overhaul of pharmaceutical testing and marketing regulations. When the causes of trauma are recognized, the chances of growth and development increase.

At present, healthcare organizations in most countries are struggling with challenges in several key areas: budgets, growing demand on scarce resources and extreme quality requirements. Whole organizations are only just keeping their heads above water. More and more people, in vulnerable target groups, are falling by the wayside. Employees often compensate, for example, by working longer hours at their own expense, at the cost of their own resilience. At the same time, it becomes clear that a sick or depleted organization cannot really offer quality care. And the soul of such organizations, the wellspring of the inspiration they need, runs dry. Unfortunately, care without soul is not care at all. Many organizations in the industry operate within very narrow margins. Let's hope that this forward-looking, budget-oriented stampede will eventually be reined back and find balance again.

## 3.4 Origin 4: Insidious and internal

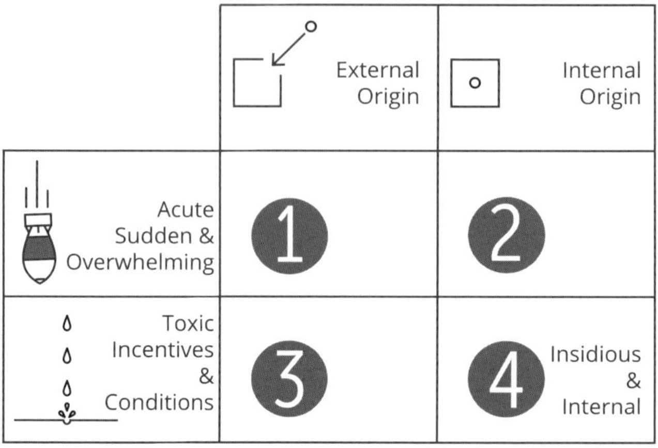

*Figure 21: Insidious and internal origin of organizational trauma*

Ongoing toxic conditions can also originate in the company. Below is an example of this quiet, creeping form.

> *A consultancy firm, founded by three independent profession-*
> *als, with a handful of employees, struggled with some tricky or-*
> *ganizational issues of their own. So they hired a coach. During*
> *exploratory interviews a pattern emerged. The common theme,*
> *in every conversation, was trust or lack of it.*
>
> *Step by step an important event was revealed that had not been*
> *given a place in this young, dynamic organization. Initially,*
> *each partner had shared all their contacts and networks with*
> *the other partners. In just the first year, one of the partners*
> *– despite agreements to the contrary – left, taking all the con-*
> *tacts and information from the other partners. This action was*
> *deeply in conflict with the values that the founders wanted to*
> *cultivate in their organization.*
>
> *Although the partners experienced this event as very disloyal*
> *and unethical, they had no idea it might have an impact on the*

*future functioning of the organization. They did not 'process' it and so it kept on working, down in the hidden dynamics of the company. What seemed to be an issue for the partners alone, over time became a sticky dynamic affecting the whole organization.*

People who are not initially involved often are kept out of such a situation or incident. Either because it really does not involve them or because the people concerned do not want to hang out their dirty laundry. Often enough, there are solid, rational reasons for these choices. But, unfortunately, this rarely ensures things stay private, even when they are never mentioned. We have seen that what is not spoken out can subtly accumulate in an organization's dynamics. With the right kind of sensitivity you can 'feel' it, just as you can feel the tension between two people, even though they never speak of it.

What shows here is a particular mechanism by which living systems try to stay healthy: when something that is not healed stays neglected, it often manifests symptoms in other places. Looking systemically at organizations means knowing that certain symptoms might well be cries for attention by what is – as yet – unhealed.

The fabric of an organization or a team can also become brittle, or even tear, through a damaging or inappropriate management style.

*A small team was completely stunned by an unfortunate change of circumstances. The company was in a highly-competitive market and pressure on employees and resources was intense. Due to the fairly high cost structure, there was no spare capacity: employees had to respond very promptly and correctly to questions and complaints from customers. Any mistake made by the team was immediately passed on to the sales director. The team manager was himself a perfectionist, allergic to emotions, and led the team in an extremely rigid way.*

*In addition, it was not always easy to plan for (normal) absences such as holidays or medical appointments, as all the employees were part-time and it was essential that a certain minimum number were present. Coincidentally, all the employees had painful, personal histories, giving them little individual re-*

*silence. Every time there was a problem with the team's perfor-*
*mance or if someone made a mistake, tension increased.  As a*
*result, the manager gave the team less and less space to man-*
*age themselves. Willingness to step in for each other decreased,*
*mutual rancor grew and collaboration became extremely rigid.*
*The whole team had fallen into the Trauma Trap.*

Hyper-sensitive employees, combined with a manager who cannot tol-
erate or process any emotions, make for a deadly cocktail.  Just like a muscle must be trained, the ability of a team to manage emotions requires
practice.  Without this, the relational fabric of the team is disrupted by
the slightest 'injury'. Rigidity increases in a counterproductive attempt to
avoid being re-stimulated. Unfortunately, the more rigid a living system
is, the more sensitive it becomes to disruption.  It is a vicious circle that
opens the doors of the Trauma Trap as wide as possible.

In the context of the two insidious types of trauma it is important to
remember the following:

- It is not only drastic/overwhelming events that lead to organizational trauma;

- The vulnerability or position of an organization in the Trauma Trap,
  however, allows particular, seemingly trivial, stimuli to have a particularly adverse impact;

- Facing-up to internal sources of organizational trauma will be even
  more difficult for organizations;

- For certain, organizations working with vulnerable target groups,
  and especially when the pressure on those organizations and employees is too high, will no longer be possible in a qualitative, sustainable manner.

These four categories – sudden and external, sudden and internal, insidious and external, insidious and internal – give us our first impression
of the possible origins of organizational trauma. In Part III we take a closer
look at the role of traumas' origins in helping or hindering the healing process.

To close this part, there follows a brief list of fields in which people are investigating organizational trauma as described in the four categories discussed above. This accurately reflects the breadth of current research.

Take a moment to link the following examples with one of the four categories:

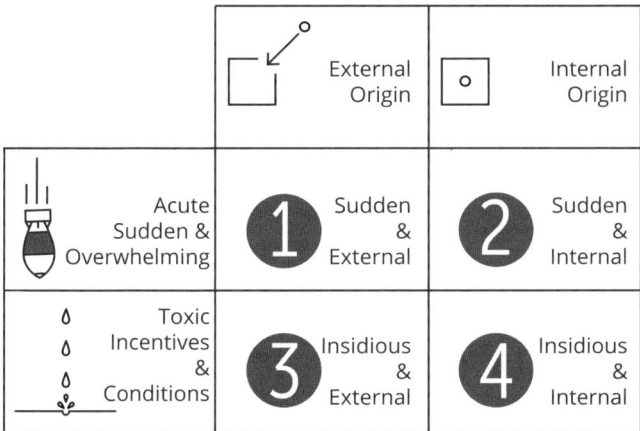

*Figure 22: Overview of origins of organizational trauma*

- Adverse effects of organizational processes such as procedures, management and governance;

- Scandal, theft, fraud, ethical issues, environmental damage, damage to the community;

- Inappropriate treatment of employees such as bullying, mobbing, discrimination, toxic working conditions both physical and mental;

- Major organizational changes such as mergers, acquisitions and downsizings;

- Unpredictable, turbulent market conditions within a particular sector;

- Human or organizational mistakes;

- Deaths, serious injuries, hostage-taking of members of the organization;

- Workplace accidents, security issues, high risk situations;

- Technological disasters, explosions, environmental disasters and serious accidents such as train and airplane crashes;

- Professions with stressful work and working conditions that negatively-impact employee resilience, such as the fire service, police, hospitals, the military, aid workers operating in dangerous locations or with dangerous diseases;

- Natural disasters such as forest fires, floods, earthquakes and tsunami;

- Epidemics like the Ebola and Zika viruses and any crisis in the field of public health;

- Financial and economic crises;

- Political persecution/oppression and (civil) wars;

- Terrorist attacks, mass murders.

# Insidious and lethal for organizations

**4**

What you do not know or know of, or know how to see, you cannot perceive. Awareness that there is something called organizational trauma, how it arises (fast or slow), and how you can recognize it, is becoming a necessary prerequisite to work with organizations. It ensures that you rapidly notice that something negative is going on, so you can be on the ball immediately. After all, the deeper a living system collapses into the Trauma Trap, the more persistent the problem will be. In this chapter we provide a number of tools more specific to the kind of slow-developing organizational trauma that seeps, unnoticed, into an organization; the kind that is the hardest to recognize.

## 4.1 Recognize in order to acknowledge

When you talk to executives working in an organization suffering from organizational trauma, it's interesting to observe closely how they respond to the concept. Reactions range from ignorant to empathetic and everything in between.

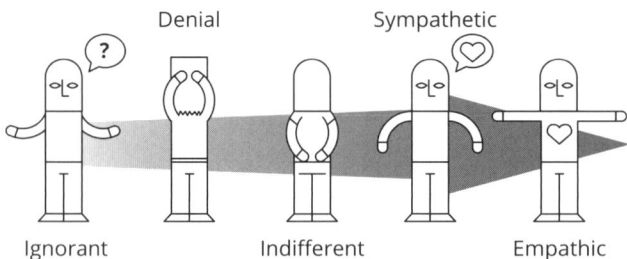

*Figure 23: From ignorant to emphatic*

If an organization's leadership is unacquainted with the phenomenon of trauma, the possibility of healing is incredibly small, and the pain is often pushed even deeper into the fabric of the organization. Organizational trauma does not heal when the position taken is that it is just the way things are (aka Business as Usual). Contrary to popular wisdom, time does not heal this kind of wound. Very often managers and directors – at least within the context of the organization – choose to react rather distantly and rationally. If they cannot, will not or may not make contact with their own feelings or vulnerabilities, then the barrier to sharing emotions is enormous for others. This also creates an imbalance in relationships, with one appearing strong and the other feeling weak and ashamed. This imbalance erodes the self-worth of individuals and groups. Often people must undergo a personal crisis before they get in touch, often for the first time, with their own emotional world. What we repeatedly see in managers, who function well with fears and feelings, is that they have learned how to create space for other people's pain and emotions because they can feel their own uncertainty and vulnerability.

There are many reasons why someone does or does not acknowledge something. You can assume that if a person is not open to certain emotions, sensibilities or injuries in themselves, they are highly unlikely to be able to recognize and accept them in others. Besides, an organization can be so surprised by a certain event that the entire organization – including the people trusted to respond appropriately – are paralyzed. If the directors themselves are paralyzed, they cannot help or guide the rest of the organization. When this happens the absolute priority is for the directors to get whatever is needed for them to feel the ground under their feet again.

## 4.2 It's about more than just overwhelming events

In Chapter 3, we began to develop the concept of a major event. Think back to the distinction between trauma and Trauma: a clearly-defined major event isn't always needed for an organization to find itself caught up in the Trauma Trap. Therefore it is worth keeping an eye out for ongoing toxic events or conditions that might be pushing a group or organization into the Trauma Trap. When a group starts heading down into the Trauma Trap, the fact that it is getting no attention just makes things worse.

The following formula can help you to map the position of an organization (or part of an organization) in the Trauma Trap, at a certain moment in time based on what happened before that moment. Working with the Trauma Formula will help you as you dive into the history of an organization.

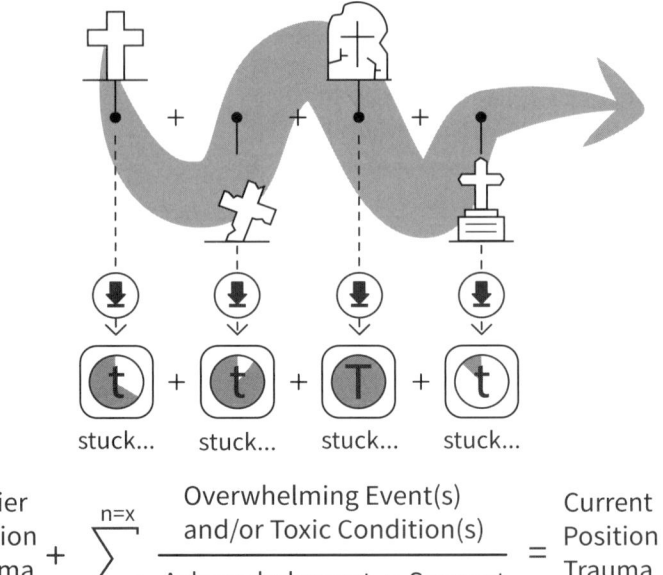

*Figure 24: Trauma Formula 1.0*

Let's run through the different elements of the formula so you can start using it. At the end of each new chapter, I'll refer back to this formula and in Chapter 8 you'll learn how to use this formula when working with organizational trauma.

$$t_x = t_a + \sum_{n=a}^{n=x} \frac{OE(n) + TC(n)}{Ack(n) \times Sup(n)}$$

The Trauma Trap is composed of **5 different positions** as represented on the following visual:

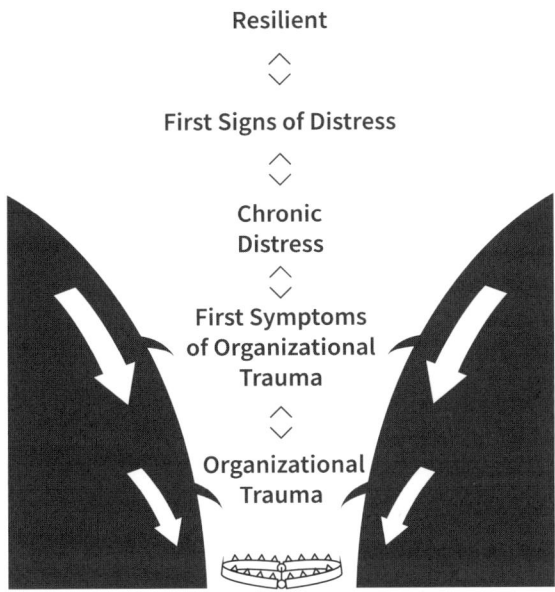

Resilient

First Signs of Distress

Chronic
Distress

First Symptoms
of Organizational
Trauma

Organizational
Trauma

*Figure 25: Trauma Trap with the five phases*

When you start working with an organization that shows symptoms of organizational trauma, you can use this formula to map its **Current Position in the Trauma Trap** (= $t_x$).

Most of the time, you refer to an earlier moment in time where the organization (or part of the organization) was more or less doing well or not yet impacted by overwhelming events or toxic conditions.  Then you'll try to figure out what happened between that moment in time and today.  This **Earlier Position in the Trauma Trap** (= $t_a$) of the team, group or organization with whom you're working is important. It gives you a feeling for what the state of resilience, preparedness and resourcefulness was at that specific moment.

Then you can work through that specific period of time – from $t_1$ to $t_n$ – and map the Impact of one or more **Overwhelming – potentially traumatizing – Events (=OE) and/or Toxic Conditions (=TC) during that specific**

**period** (= the numerator of the formula). At the end of this book you'll have a clear representation of what kind of events or conditions contribute to the development of organizational trauma.

It's important to know that it's not only an overwhelming event, or the aggregation of toxic conditions, that force an organization deeper into the Trauma Trap. What happens during and after those incidents will have a huge impact. That's why the next factor, **Acknowledgment (=Ack) and Support (=Sup)**, (= the denominator of the formula) is linked to each of the threatening or potentially overwhelming incidents and/or toxic conditions. So when mapping a certain period – for example from $t_a$ to $t_x$ – the final result can be either negative or positive. When negative, the relational fabric will be more damaged than earlier and the system you're working with will be deeper in the Trauma Trap. But you could get a positive outcome too. This would mean that the entity could have become more resilient, through having survived particular events. This is what we call post-traumatic growth.

The distinction between '**Acknowledgment**' and '**Support**' shows that support without acknowledgment, and vice versa, can have little effect or even be negative. Acknowledgment without support does not help people in their healing process. So both elements of the denominator can either reinforce or neutralize each other.

Practice teaches us that victims of traumatizing events tend not to enter into a healing process unless or until the organization (if the organizations is considered to be the perpetrator) accepts its share of the responsibility. This is a frequently recurring, often unconscious, pattern between perpetrator and victim: *"I'll hold onto my pain until you face and acknowledge your role in causing it. If I would heal my pain, then you would – without cost or effort – walk away innocent"*. Often people refuse even to consider accepting any support offered by an organization that does not acknowledges or denies its part or its share in creating the problem. Applying a similar logic to naturally-occurring traumas, such as hurricanes or earthquakes, we see that they are accepted and integrated more easily and fully than traumas caused by humans.

> *For many years a team – including its team leader and department manager – was stuck in a toxic dynamic that eventually forced them deep into the Trauma Trap. Over the years, various*

*interventions were attempted with that team, without success, and the organization continued to turn a blind eye to the destructive influence of the (failing) chain of command. In the end, out of desperation, the manager of the department resigned, but kept working while the company sought a new manager for his position. In the same period – triggered by the leaving of the department manager – the team leader had to leave the company because of the problems in the team.*

*Within a week the team leader was replaced, but very soon the new person was pulling his hair out in desperation, trying to deal with this same, toxic dynamic in the team. He asked for someone to come from outside and coach the team. The company engaged a team coach and, during the intake interview, the coach felt that working with the team was not what was needed. His assessment of the situation was that apology from the organization was necessary to free-up the situation, because the failing chain of command had allowed such a toxic working environment for much too long.*

*Once this key to getting out of the Trauma Trap was defined, the coach tried to identify, with the team leader's help, who would be the right person to make the apology and ensure the correct sense of acknowledgment was conveyed. It was clear that the right words from the wrong person would carry no power and have no effect. It had to be (at least) one of the managers who were part of the failing chain of command.*

- *It's clear that the new team leader apologizing would have no impact.*

- *His predecessor had to leave the company. He wasn't the one to blame for the fact that this situation wasn't dealt with for so many years. (His competence is not relevant here).*

- *The same reasoning applies to the department manager who resigned but was still in the company waiting to be replaced. He was ready to apologize but it was clear that he was no longer appropriate to represent the company.*

*The buck finally stopped, so to speak, at the door of the Divisional Director who had overseen the whole debacle for years. He was the principal person who could and should apologize on behalf of the organization, but he was not willing to do this. The team coach was very aware of the impact this would have on the healing process of the team but was not able to influence the rigid position of the Divisional Manager; a clear case of support without acknowledgment, the two elements of the denominator canceling each other out.*

This example gives you a feeling for how you can identify what would be an appropriate form of acknowledgment (or intervention) as shown in the formula above. Putting yourself in the shoes of the 'victim(s)' can help you to feel the impact of an intervention. This is a critical competence and attitude to be able to work with organizational trauma. More about this in the third part of this book.

## 4.3  Where organizational trauma first shows up

Around fifteen years ago absenteeism started to appear on the agendas of organizations. One reason was government pressure to make organizations more accountable for the costs society bears for employee absence. In parallel, the concept of safety at work had expanded to include psychosocial security, underscored by the ever-increasing frequency in the media of stories about burn-out.  The tendency for organizations to treat people as replaceable tools is now frowned-upon in the West, with the workplace expected to contribute to people's and society's wellbeing.  More and more, business leaders are accepting that they have a responsibility to provide for the mental health of employees.

All organizations can find value in considering the following questions:

- Is our workplace emotionally safe, encouraging development and self-esteem? Or does it fuel fear and uncertainty?

- As an organization, are we maintaining the stigma around mental health problems or do we give space to less conspicuous feelings such as insecurity, vulnerability and sadness?

- Do our executives and managers show their vulnerability or do they give people the feeling that this is a sign of weakness?
- Do we have focus and interest in the relational fabric between people, departments and disciplines or is our focus limited to production and profit?

Exploring these questions could reduce the stigma associated with mental health and vulnerability in the workplace. After all, it's exactly this stigma that creates the denial of organizational trauma. Removing this stigma would go a long way towards sensitizing organizations to look for help, before getting stuck in the Trauma Trap.

> **Do we dare to see people's well-being as an early-warning mechanism for the organization's overall health or would we rather wait until organizational trauma 'appears' in the share price, the profit forecast or customer turnover.**

The emphasis is on the staff, since the effects of organizational trauma, especially if not addressed, are felt initially by employees and only much later in the results or in the board. The company's directors, and its performance, are 'carried' by employees' resilience up to the point at which they can no longer cope. In the short term, an organization can ignore this phenomenon, for example by replacing 'failing' workers. In the long term, however, when organizational trauma is becoming a fact, it becomes a persistent and wicked problem. I believe that how employees feel is an excellent indicator of an organization's health.

## 4.4 Trauma is rarely an isolated phenomenon

Trauma can rarely if ever be traced back to one person. Anyone who is involved can be affected by what happens to someone he is associated with. When an individual is hit, he is connected to other colleagues. That means an apparently-individual trauma can push a team, a department or an entire organization a little or a lot deeper into the Trauma Trap, as a consequence of an event that seems, initially, to affect only one person.

Being fired, for example, is usually considered to be an issue between the organization and the individual. Some cultural 'law' ensures everyone respects confidentiality, often making it impossible to explain or understand why someone was fired or forced to retire. The remaining colleagues (of the person leaving), receive no special attention or treatment. So they find their own, by coming up with an explanation for the decision: *"You had better not be critical in this company, because if you do, you'll get fired".*

And unconsciously, the hidden loyalty to the colleague who was fired turns them against their organization or line manager. A dismissal always has an impact on the relational fabric of a team, department or organization. So it is best to approach this kind of decision from a number of perspectives:

- Of the company;

- Of the person who was fired;

- Of the relational fabric that enveloped and extended from that person.

Often the person fired is still connected to many of his or her colleagues, indirectly souring the team's environment and process. The relational fabric can also become stronger (and more resilient) around the person fired – even though he is no longer present – than with the organization. What we are dealing with here are issues of loyalty. They might be invisible, but they determine the hidden dynamics in organizations. Unbounded by time or space, their impact on the functioning of an organization can be immense.

Finally, people can usually handle one resignation or dismissal if their organization handles it with care, but when there are several, that can knock the stuffing out of them. And of course, there are so many events – besides dismissals – that can push and pull at an organization's relational fabric. Eventually, as all the small wounds stack up on each other, a stubborn knot of negative potential forms. In short, trauma that goes unnoticed or unhealed persists, and is felt independently of time and space. It weakens the relational fabric of a company.

*Figure 26: Toxic conditions*

## 4.5 What makes organizations vulnerable to trauma

Pat Vivian and Shana Hormann refer to three major factors that make an organization more vulnerable to organizational trauma in *Organizational Trauma and Healing* (Vivian and Hormann, 2013, [35]) . You could compare it to the relationship between the solidity of a house and the scale of an earthquake. A ramshackle house will collapse more easily during a minor earthquake than a sturdy house.

*Figure 27: Factors that make organizations vulnerable to trauma*

**The work itself**

- Some professions are more frequently exposed to death, disease, human suffering, crisis and trauma, increasing the chances that they will experience vicarious trauma or compassion fatigue;

- Sometimes work can be so dull, boring or lonely that it is impossible for employees to derive any energy or self-esteem from it;

- Some kinds of work are abusive or lack respect towards other people, animals, society or nature;

- Some people do very tough and demanding work that rarely leads to a lasting product or result.

  *People who work with drug addicts, often invest days, weeks sometimes years of their lives to help someone kick their habit or detox, only for the client to fall back into the old dependency within a few weeks. We often call this kind of work soul-destroying: where does a person find the energy to start over with the same client again and again?*

Something similar applies to teams working with vulnerable or difficult target groups such as young offenders, the homeless, foster children, the elderly and so on. And it becomes even more severe when their work difficulties are compounded by cuts in funding and resources. As an employee, how do you maintain your boundaries, stop yourself crossing the line into giving too much time, energy or money?

**Vision, mission, culture and structure**

- The design of an organization, and the way in which the work is organized, can be supportive of teams, but often things are the other way round: too little support, too little 'wiggle' room, too heavy workloads, micro-managing, standards too high, continuous stress. Even potentially nourishing work can be experienced as stressful if conditions are poor or toxic.

  *Some time ago a manager was working with a team that had been stuck in all kinds of conflict and tension for years. The organization's view was that work was needed around cooperation and collaboration. After a few discussions it became clear that the team members had two conflicting processes running. The success of one half of the team usually came at the expense of the other and vice versa. This relational conflict was an expression of a process conflict. In addition, the team's manager was 'absent' because he hid behind his support for self-regulation. His attitude meant the team remained saddled with the situation and could see no solution. This situation alone was enough to devastate the team's resilience.*

- Some organizations fill up with what are called double-binds. These are situations in which whatever pleases somebody, displeases somebody else. You rarely experience a sense of peace or satisfaction. What you do right for the customer, turns out to be wrong for the organization. To please your manager, you must contradict the organization's values. When you do it right for your employer, you damage your family. To get ahead in the organization, you must deny your core values. Such situations cause people to feel alienated from themselves, and they develop a kind of psychological 'anesthesia' in order to survive. When this is the nature of an organization's environment, it is just a small step away from slipping into the Trauma Trap. Healing an organization that's filled with double-bind situations, is like a detox cure. It might be a tough journey, but without this purification there is little chance that an organization will ever really excel.

- The quality of the leadership – that ultimately is an expression of the culture of an organization – has significant impact on its relational fabric. The relationship with one's line-manager constantly arises as a key reason for burnout and absenteeism.

- During the start-up period of an organization, its mission is defined. This will deeply influence how the company unfolds. Sometimes, a kind of vulnerability is already embedded in that mission statement. Some organizations are born out of pain, disappointment or misunderstanding, and that associates their origin directly with a certain kind of woundedness. Imagine a victim of abuse, bullying or fraud who then starts a victim-support organization. The organization's foundations are built on an injury, and it is likely that it will attract employees who feel a bond with that kind of injury or have experienced something similar themselves. Because that organization goes on to work with victims, its employees will be affected again (compassion fatigue and vicarious trauma). This really stretches people's resilience and the relational fabric of the organization. Often, emotions spin out of control – in such an organization – whenever certain stories or situations are in the media, when new laws are proposed that affect victim's rights or if there's a threat to funding and subsidies. When people identify themselves too much with their target audience, they become too sensitive, and their resilience suffers.

• A living system is healthy if there is coherence and consistency with the soul or 'raison d'être' of the organization. Some organizations change direction, vision, values and leadership so often that all coherence is lost. Then the organization has nothing worthwhile to offer. What it does 'offer' is the likelihood of disorientation and tension in and between teams; throwing open the doors of the Trauma Trap. First and foremost because the soul of the organization has been lost and, second, because this ignores the fact that the employees are involved precisely because they chose for that specific purpose or mission. Being a member of the company was a way to realize their personal mission or purpose. People do not always have the strength or the courage to leave the organization, and so they give up some of their dreams, hopes and beliefs in order to stay onboard.

• Organizational trauma can arise because (a part of) the soul of an organization is lost – as mentioned when the Trauma Cube was introduced. This loss is very subtle and at the same time very profound. The soul (or part of it) must be sought and returned by the ritual known as soul-retrieval. And, sometimes, we have to say adieu to the original mission or purpose. Detaching from it will be necessary, if we are to attach to something else.

*An organization's strategy changed, for very legitimate reasons, from premium quality to cost-effectiveness. Nobody suspected there might be significant, invisible consequences to this change of values, and so, after due business process, it was implemented. However, many teams had achieved their excellence by delivering top quality in both products and services. The new strategy was at odds with their values. Teams started spiraling down into the Trauma Trap.*

*Frequent changes of leadership made managers unaware of what was happening. They were not connected with the history of the company, so they could not understand from where and why these negative emotions and dynamics arose and so they labeled them as resistance-to-change. This opened the doors of the Trauma Trap even wider.*

*Corporate rituals and ceremonies (more on that in Part III) could have helped the teams to transition into this new reality. Such an opportunity is seldom missed by managers who are sensitive to the relational fabric of a company.*

**The type of people that are attracted**

- We already pointed out that certain people have strengths that actually originated as a survival mechanism. You can recognize this when you notice that, underneath the survival behavior, there is, for example, a kind of anxiety, cramping or unhealthy form of uncertainty. Some people are perfectionists because they cannot cope with failing. Others do whatever is necessary to feel loved and their helping often has no healthy boundaries. It is really worth learning about certain frequently-recurring hurts that shape people's behavior. Bear in mind that those, or maybe most, people arrive into a company with a backpack full of their own emotional baggage and that this can easily be triggered by something as mundane, for example, as the everyday operations of the organization. It is key that leaders understand this.

- Mission-driven organizations, such as NGOs and charities, often attract mission-driven people. While such organizations are committed to helping the vulnerable and disadvantaged of the world, they do not always get the (financial) recognition and support of society. Even worse, sometimes the problem that is being corrected or solved, exists precisely because of the way our society functions. Often, employees will over-identify with their target groups, especially if they or a member of their family have been victims of exclusion, bullying, abuse, neglect and so on. If employees with this kind of history have not healed their personal traumas, it is likely that the work will eventually burn them out, because they cannot maintain healthy boundaries between their work and personal lives.

- Identification can also arise because employees work exclusively with the same target group. They start to manifest the symptoms and behaviors of their clients. Aid workers, for example, who work with vulnerable young people might, when they are in front of the executive board, feel just as vulnerable as those young clients while, in reality, they are absolutely not that vulnerable. In Chapter 3, I showed how certain dynamics can subtly seep from outside the organization into the relational fabric. Trauma-informed organizations are much quicker at noticing when patterns from the target group are being transmitted to the organization and often know how to deal with this. These organizations are constantly tracking the quality of the relational fabric because they have learned that it is exactly the state of the fabric that creates a healing or supporting context for their clients. A sick system will not be able to support the healing of others.

Finally, it is important, also, to consider the larger society that gives organizations place and meaning. Not one of the three factors above exists in a vacuum.

- Organizations that depend on grants for their existence, or are strongly regulated by the government, are a lot more vulnerable to organizational trauma.

- Each society has unconscious assumptions, values and beliefs that can block the development of resilience. If such a society experiences any kind of substantial injury or damage, trauma can follow.

Certain countries or cultures view failure very differently than others. Business failures such as bankruptcy, for example, are approached very leniently in the United States compared to most countries in Europe, where it often conveys a deeply-felt shame. In family businesses, especially, later generations can struggle to succeed without ever understanding why.

- A less obvious phenomenon, also in terms of assumptions, that causes much stress, frustration, anger and fear – but also inflexibility – exists in organizations and is supported by social legislation. It has its roots in an employment model that, in most developed countries, is no longer appropriate or (in general) possible. Up till about twenty years ago it was normal that your whole working career would be with the same company. This created a deep sense of connection, a bond between employer and employee that felt to both parties as being part of a family. Employees were loyal and gave their working lives to the organization, sometimes across several generations. In turn, organizations took responsibility for the welfare and quality of life of their employees. To resign or be made redundant was rare. When, as is sometimes inevitable, it did happen, it was felt by all concerned as something very painful. Many practices that we know today are rooted in this age-old structure: age-linked salaries, immensely-high termination-of-employment payments for employees with many years of service, massive payments to senior executives irrespective of the reasons for their departure, extra benefits that an employee loses if he or she leaves (e.g. savings plans, insurance, shares options, and so on). Such frameworks give a totally different perspective to common modern-day events like dismissals, career changes or radical organizational change.

Political leaders should also be aware of the mental models they keep installing in our society. As already mentioned, some of them don't support the development of resilience in people, companies nor on a societal level.

This brings us to an extra factor – the vulnerability factor – first seen here in the Trauma Formula introduced earlier in this chapter. Practice shows us that giving consideration to the quasi-inherent vulnerability of an organization – based on the factors above – is important for both senior executives and external facilitators. Awareness of organizational vulnerability should inform your strategy when you are first invited in to help.

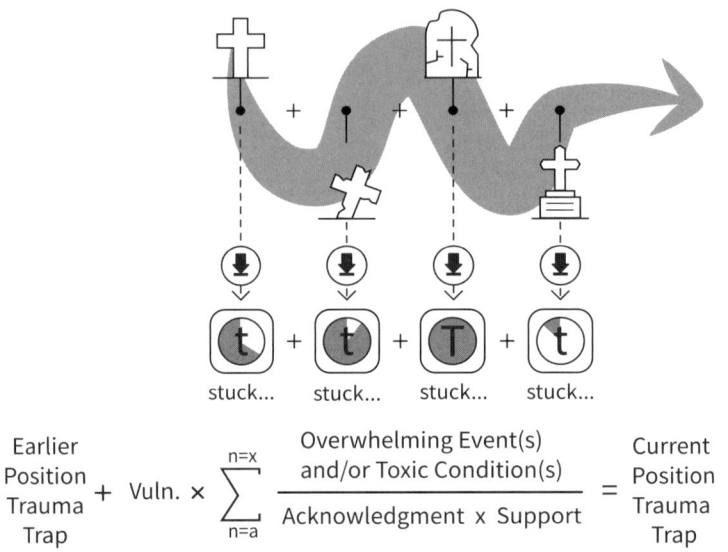

$$\underset{\substack{\text{Earlier}\\\text{Position}\\\text{Trauma}\\\text{Trap}}}{} + \text{Vuln.} \times \sum_{n=a}^{n=x} \frac{\text{Overwhelming Event(s)}}{\text{and/or Toxic Condition(s)}}{\text{Acknowledgment} \times \text{Support}} = \underset{\substack{\text{Current}\\\text{Position}\\\text{Trauma}\\\text{Trap}}}{}$$

*Figure 28: Trauma Formula 2.0*

Based on what is explained above, organizations that are clearly vulnerable for organizational trauma are most in need of trauma-informed management. This applies to a lot of fields of business and society. At this moment in time it's a critical issue in the care sector.

# How to recognize organizational trauma

**5**

In the previous chapters we had our first look at how to detect organizational trauma. This chapter broadens and deepens this theme by making the symptoms more concrete, which is crucial to identifying trauma in organizations. Mind you, for many organizations this is still a perplexing issue. Anyhow, understanding is essential to identify trauma and deal with it. Let this chapter inspire you.

Be aware of the fact that, even if your perception is trauma-informed, relevant signs or symptoms can accidentally pass you by. Let's look at some of the major reasons we sometimes do not see what we are looking for:

- People in the organization are not always aware that there has been an overwhelming event or they are unable to see the link between the current comings and goings in the organization and an overwhelming event in its near or distant past;

- The impact of one or more overwhelming events on the organization is denied or negated because the organization is still in shock, investigating related legal issues, busy showing a positive public face etc.;

- People don't feel safe enough to show their vulnerability and share emotions;

- Employees who witnessed the affecting event have left the company or have learned that it's best not to talk about it;

- There was no clearly defined event, but rather constant, toxic conditions which are much more difficult to link to organizational trauma;

- Unhealthy dynamics within and between groups, teams, departments, hierarchical layers or disciplines are traced to relational and/or personal issues without considering the structures, procedures or reward systems that play a role;

- The (organizational) trauma manifests in individuals. Via burnout and absenteeism, for example, but also through the more-recent phenomenon of presentism (= the practice of coming to work despite illness, injury, anxiety, etc.), often resulting in reduced productivity. Wherever it shows up, it can look as if these problems belong with the individual.

By becoming familiar with the symptoms of organizational trauma, you'll more-rapidly see that 'something else' needs consideration and be able to zoom out as and when needed. The Trauma Trap is a crucial concept, as it gives a good overview of the dynamics to look out for.

Besides recognizing and pulling the symptoms together, one needs to keep an eye on how they are spread throughout the organization. This indicates how widely the trauma has affected the organization. It can be very isolated, perhaps just in one team, it can be affecting every employee and every process, or it can be spread throughout the organization, but be found only in a specific group of employees.  Imagine that a department gets closed down; the employees are not fired, but are placed, without having any input, into other roles across the company. Many organizations have, somewhere, a department where employees – who neither know each other or have much in common – have been relocated to work 'together'. In that situation, the chance of organizational trauma increases significantly. It might seem like an isolated situation, but it is actually a direct reflection of the capacity to let people go, or reassign them, in a good and healthy way.

When working with organizational trauma, you run the risk of being confused, entangled or dumbfounded by what has contaminated the dynamics of an organization. In a way, you become actively involved (without realizing it), and feel like savior and victim at the same time.  In that case, it becomes more difficult for you to create a safe setting for all involved.  It is easy, and can be shocking, to find that you have become a part of the problem. This is when, crucially, you fall back on your intuition and your gut feel. Your body picks up signals much faster than your 'normal' senses: you get stomach cramp, your shoulders tighten up, you feel something bothering you. Or, when you come home, you are much more emotional than usual. Body awareness and self-knowledge are essential to detecting organizational trauma. We call this looking inward, somatic exploring. The more sensitive you become, the better you can distinguish when (a part of) the organization is in the Trauma Trap.

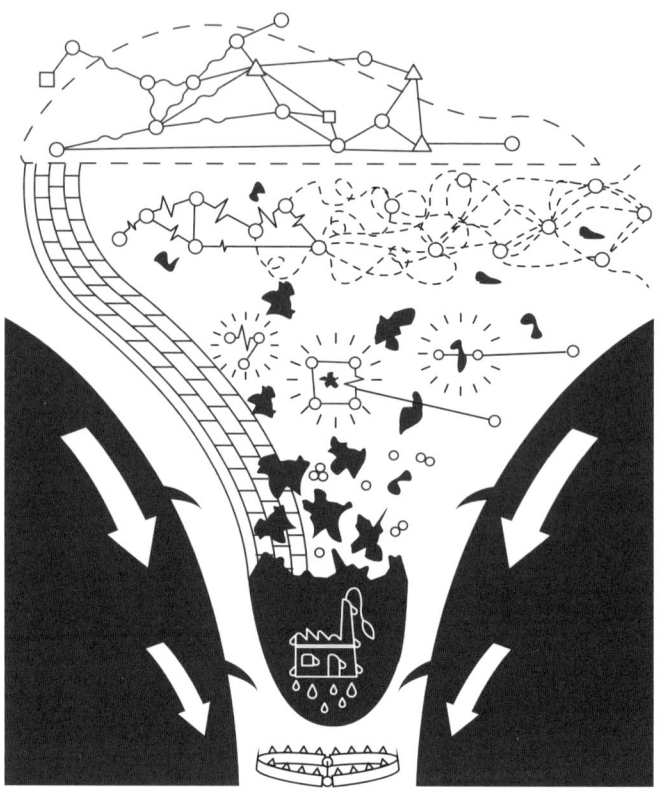

*Figure 29: Trauma Trap – Full view*

## 5.1 Properties of healthy living systems

Looking far above the Trauma Trap, we see a high degree of integration. This concept is central to interpersonal neurobiology, an emerging discipline that searches for patterns between different disciplines such as biology, cybernetics, linguistics, neuroscience, anthropology, psychiatry, mathematics, psychology, medicine, physics, sociology and chaos theory. The work of Dr. Daniel Siegel 'Siegel2010' is instrumental in the development of this discipline. When applied to the field of trauma, the discipline leads to much new insight. In this context, integration is the willingness and ability of every part of the system to work together and to do so in a dynamic, fluid manner. This ability and will are reinforced by giving space to the unique qualities of all parts, essential to realizing the added value of diversity. Only then is there room for emergence.

In this case, there is a dynamic tension between chaos (too much difference, too little connectedness) and rigidity (too little difference and suffocating closeness). An organization can go in both directions. In our initial discussion of the Trauma Trap, rigidity and chaos were cited as the first indicators of agitation and stress. Integration, however, manifests at the point where the added value of both connectedness and difference unfolds.

Siegel compares an integrated organization with a choir. Each member makes a unique contribution, but at the same time adjusts to the chosen piece, producing music that gives you goose bumps. The extremes would be cacophony (chaos) or a choir where no blending or interplay can be heard (rigidity).

Integration is, to a living system, what flow is for an individual. It can be identified by the following characteristics:

| | |
|---|---|
| **Flexibility** | The ability to adapt to adverse circumstances and then return to a previous point of stability. This ability is an important distinction between stress and trauma. A traumatized system can no longer return to its stable former state. |
| **Adaptability** | The ability to find a new point of stability based on changed needs. |
| **Coherence** | Healthy cohesion, consistency, connectedness and harmony. |
| **Energy** | Vitality, the power to act, lust for life, drive |
| **Stability** | A dynamic form of balance, rest, groundedness and alignment. |

A living system, at its best, displays these characteristics. Their presence implies emergence, the seemingly-spontaneous arising of new qualities or attributes through the interplay or choreography between the different parts of a living system. You cannot plan for, make or enforce the unfolding capabilities. They arise through the right conditions being created. The group or organization seems to transcend itself; the whole is visibly more than the sum of the parts. These are also the conditions that support the development of collective intelligence that is much needed in organizations nowadays.

Organizations where command and control is central, are actually working against this inherent ability of living systems: not only is self-regulation made impossible, but also the magic of emergence. Denying itself the innate qualities of living systems, the organization becomes more vulnerable to organizational trauma, operating – perhaps just surviving – on the edge of the Trauma Trap. There is a total lack of flexibility, adaptability, consistency, energy and stability. Not because these are impossible, but because the conditions they depend upon are not being created.

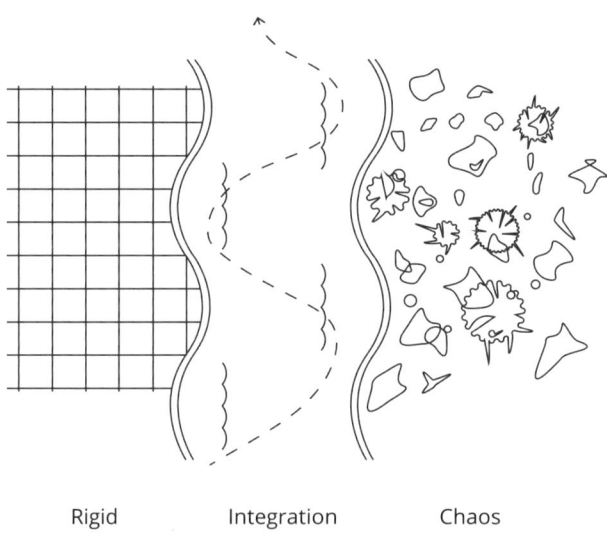

Rigid            Integration            Chaos

*Figure 30: River of integration*

A metaphor – also introduced by Dr. Dan Siegel *Mindsight The New Science of Personal Transformation* (Siegel, 2010, [25]) – that can help here, is of a river. The deep central channel of the river symbolizes the place where an organization is at its best and the above-mentioned qualities of integration can unfold. Clearly this is far above the Trauma Trap. Stress can push such a well-functioning organization out of this channel but, for example after a rest period, it contains the power to return. But an overwhelming event or persistent toxicity can knock the organization 'of course' into one of the riverbanks, where it can become stuck. One bank seems rigid and inflexible – because space for differentiation and creativity has gone; the other bank looks chaotic – due to loss of connection and alignment.

If an organization becomes more vulnerable to being agitated and distressed and, at the same time, its ability to recover is weak, then it is probably on the edge of sinking into the Trauma Trap. The free-running channel becomes narrower and narrower as the banks of chaos and rigidity encroach. Then the following symptoms appear:

- Past events have had no completion. People find that they are still suffering from something in the history of the organization (dismissals, closures, accidents etc.).

- A kind of heaviness permeates the fabric of the organization;

- Certain essential skills seem to be unavailable or are trapped in certain teams or departments.

- Certain places or activities are being avoided.

- People, teams, departments, disciplines and hierarchical layers start acting in isolation instead of connectedness. That is an expression of damage to the relational fabric and the start of distrust.

- Feelings are never or rarely shared or expressed. People seem disconnected from their emotions, which shows as splitting-off, denial, numbness.

- There is increased irritability or continuous underlying tension. Employees react more emotionally than appropriate. For example, reacting with disproportionate anger to a decision to change something.

- There is a permanent sense of agitation, of worry, which is a coping strategy to avoid feelings and emotions.

- Everything seems perfectly in order; it all seems just too good to be true. This can be a form of rigidity. Notice what happens when something is going wrong.

- People seem to no longer to connect with the organization, they seem to have no pride anymore.

- When particular themes are mentioned, conversations seem to tail-off or you feel a change in the energy in the room.

- Failure, staff turnover, resignations and complaints increase.

- If people open up to you, you'll encounter shame, fear, insecurity, sadness, anger, loneliness, insolence, exhaustion and despair.

- Often, there is denial that anything is wrong.

*Some time ago we worked for a department in a large organization. As our work progressed, it became apparent that they needed to collaborate better in order to succeed in implementing a new strategy. At the same time, and unexpectedly, our facilitation started to feel gluey and syrupy. Our boat seemed to have run aground on the bank of 'rigidity'. We had touched on something connected with cooperation. Something was stuck in the system.*

*When we dived into the history of the department, it became clear that its survival had been severely threatened a couple of years earlier. The department had become so powerful that other, related departments felt threatened. When a manager from one of those 'threatened' departments was promoted to a senior position, he immediately started a witch hunt against the department with which we were now working. He wasn't able to destroy the department, but he seriously damaged its core mission, or soul.*

*It seemed that, under the radar, a survival mechanism was at work. It coupled the new strategy with the feelings from the period of the witch hunt. Becoming strong again could mean the*

*end of the department. Our work seemed to be reactivating old*
*pain and fear in an unconscious way.*

## 5.2 Toxins begin to pile up

In *The Search for Leadership An Organizational Perspective* (Tate, 2009, [32])
, author William Tate uses a particularly powerful metaphor that fits well
with the framework of this book. He compares an organization to a fishtank, where the managers and the employees are the fish. All the other
elements that make up the fishtank are factors which have to be considered or dealt with. The fish should be able to survive in that water because
it has all the necessary nutrition. Of course the water is rarely 100% clear
but, as the water becomes increasingly cloudy from the 'waste products'
of personal and business activities and interactions, it becomes increasingly difficult to show consideration for each other, the other inhabitants
and relevant factors in the fishtank. This can lead to agitation and disorientation, which in turn creates irregular currents and flows, leading to
even more confusion and stress. More 'waste' comes loose until, after a
while, the fishtank's environment has become a thick, toxic, soup (= the
bottom of the Trauma Trap). In such a situation, no one feels responsible for the toxic mess and no one feels responsible for cleaning up the
fishtank. Everyone points the finger at someone else, while the soup gets
thicker and more poisonous. Removing fish from the aquarium, changing
the fish or cleaning the fish will never bring the water back to health. The
whole system needs attention.

Every living system creates toxins. Painstaking attempts to avoid them
– another form of rigidity – will not succeed and certainly not in a world full
of challenges and changes. Resilient organizations accept that toxins exist and regularly process them. But this requires a different organizational
design than what we might call a 'classic' organization. Constantly changing or adjusting releases toxins and/or difficult emotions such as sadness,
frustration, insecurity, embarrassment, anger and fear. They can arise in
different ways:

- A project that a group of employees has been working on for months
  is canceled because signals suggest changes are likely in the market.

- The strategy rolled out last year is radically modified because essential subsidies are withdrawn.

- Recently-hired employees are fired due to poor company performance.

- A new, promising manager leaves the organization to accept a better offer from a competitor.

- The most experienced teams are continuously used to train young employees to work on new assembly lines. Once the trainees are competent, they move on and a new group of trainees are brought in, and the old hands repeatedly have to start from scratch with new people.

- How reporting takes place changes due to more and tighter controls.

- The make-up of the team is frequently changed to meet changing market conditions.

An ever-faster changing world makes for faster cycles of attachment and detachment, which isn't necessarily significant, but it might be a good idea for organizations to give it some consideration. Many people have already had to deal with the effect of these accelerating cycles:

- By experiencing more change than they can cope with;

- Because they never learned to deal with the accompanying emotions;

- Because these types of processes receive limited guidance in organizations;

Learning to deal with this phenomenon will be necessary to keep organizations healthy. It's as logical as regularly cleaning a fishtank.

| *Aspects of the third dimension of the Trauma Cube:* | **Detaching** | **Attaching** |
|---|---|---|
| Physical | Letting go of familiar tools, machinery, applications, workplaces etc. | Learning how to use new tools, moving into a new workplace, integrating new practices and processes |
| Emotional | Letting go of trusted colleagues, managers, customers etc. | Connecting, again and again, with new people: managers, customers, colleagues, team members etc. |
| Mental | Letting go of certain beliefs about quality, service, precision, clarity etc. | Embracing new values, principles, beliefs in the field of work and (role) identity etc. |
| Spiritual | Letting go of initial mission goals, of social recognition for how and what the organization contributes etc. | Embracing a new mission and new values, opening up to new practices, adapting to changes in the market … |

Detachment is, almost always, accompanied by some degree of mourning and/or processing and often it precedes energy-intensive learning and change. If the toxins released are not processed, an organization becomes more vulnerable and edges much closer to the point at which it is in danger of plunging headfirst into the Trauma Trap.

For an organization to stay healthy, it is necessary to map where and how toxins accumulate and to have a plan for how they can be minimized and/or processed. Such a plan is an excellent sign of trauma-informed leadership. Unfortunately, in many organizations, due to excessive performance pressure or an inability to deal with emotions, there is insufficient space and time to process accumulated toxins. So, they are transferred onto the next manager, who is neither conscious of this nor prepared for it. This toxic recycling takes its toll on the resilience of a living system, just like an over-acidic body can no longer perform in a healthy way.

It is important to know that unprocessed toxins do not disappear, even though they might no longer be 'visible'. They actually become encapsulated and nestle down in the deeper layers of the organization, slowly and remorselessly eroding the resilience of an organization. We call these encapsulated toxins Trauma Capsules. These start showing up on lower levels of the Trauma Trap (check-out the diagram of the Trauma Trap). A useful comparison is with pharmaceutical soft capsules, whose contents only come free when the capsule enters the small intestine.

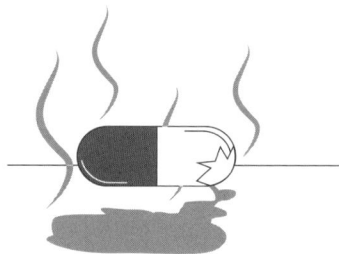

*Figure 31: Trauma Capsule*

Trauma Capsules also have a 'cell wall', constructed and maintained by denial, suppression and/or splitting-off. This wall can become extremely thick if the people and their surrounding organization are unable, in some way, to face the emotions that have built up over time, or from one overwhelming event. Sometimes this wall is gossamer-thin, because emotions have been building exponentially since the event.

Unfortunately, we are not very good at mourning or allowing space for emotions, which means, of course, that they do not get processed. Modern perception of mourning sees it as an individual event; in the past, however, it was a family and/or community activity. There is much that westerners can (re)learn from indigenous cultures, who maintain numerous rituals and ceremonies that care for the relational fabric of the tribe (= keeping their fishtank clean).

## 5.3  A living system has annual rings

There is a special link between trauma and time. People tend to think of time as being linear; we talk of what was, what is and what will be. Un-healed trauma, however, is not limited by time. Something that, according to linear logic, belongs in the past, can appear to be happening right now, in this moment. Trauma is a phenomenon where time exists like the annual rings of a tree: older layers are still a part of the present.

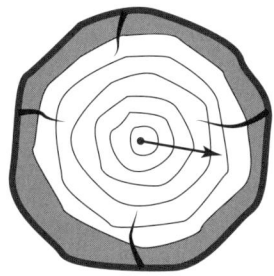

*Figure 32: Annual rings of trauma*

No matter how old the tree, the scratches and cracks that have developed in earlier tree rings are still part of the tree. The rings grow up and out, but they are there to be seen – if you look in the right place. The same goes for living systems. Advising someone to 'just let it go' is usually well intentioned, but not particularly supportive, especially for people who are struggling with intense sorrow. Even if something has healed it might still be sensitive, and this absolutely applies to trauma. Its marks remain, long after it has 'gone'.

So can you, as a colleague, manager or facilitator, bump into a Trauma Capsule. When that happens, there is often resonance or re-activation. This means that the previously unacknowledged emotions, from the past, have come free. A change process, for example, that suddenly begins to run out of control – see the example previously mentioned – might have 'bumped into' a Trauma Capsule. In this way, people try, unconsciously, to avoid feeling old pain again. Usually because no one knows how to deal with the old emotions. Indeed, an avoidance reaction distances the person from acknowledgment and healing. By keeping the emotions encapsulated and avoiding Trauma Capsules, re-activation can be avoided. The upside is that even more toxins are not created. The downside is that the encapsulated emotions remain ready to explode at the slightest stimulation. The greater the emotional encapsulation the lesser the ability to deal with emotions.

In concrete terms, this means that an individual or a group has, at that moment, partly or completely, lost their link with the here and now. When this happens, a situation that seems totally innocent to an outsider could feel threatening to the people affected. Those involved are often pulled back to an older annual ring, because there is a kind of subtle resonance for them between what is happening now and the original overwhelming event.

> *On New Year's Eve the loud bang of a firework throws a police officer, who has PTSD, back into a war situation where he and his platoon came under fire and suffered serious injuries.*

> *An employee who, years ago, survived an explosion in a chemical company goes completely into panic when he hears a normal, hissing noise or smells something that reminds him of the old explosion, and reacts as if there is real and present danger.*

> *A soldier who lost a number of colleagues in an ambush during a military operation in Afghanistan can no longer find peace or rest. He is permanently on guard. If his partner caresses him unexpectedly, his whole body cramps up and he resists her, as if his life is at stake.*

> *But so can mass hysteria and complete chaos break out. Think back to the panic in Turin's San Carlo Square during the 2017 Champions League final. With the upsurge in terrorist attacks, an unexpected firecracker has a totally different effect to a few years ago. No one knows the material and lasting effects this will have on our society and, at the same time, most governments and leaders are at a loss to know how to respond or deal with this.*

In these cases there is a stimulus or trigger that causes an individual or a group to be thrown back in time. Trauma means that people frequently and unexpectedly feel overwhelmed by something that actually lies behind them in time. A part of them, large or small, has split-off and is stuck in the past. This costs enormous amounts of energy.

But each time there is an encounter with a Trauma Capsule, there is also an opportunity. If space is allowed for processing the toxins that the encounter releases, then the old wound can begin to heal.  If that does not happen, and denial continues, then the toxicity of the Trauma Capsule increases. Therefore re-activation is an important indicator for dealing with trauma. You need to learn how to discern the difference between re-activation and re-enactment:

- Re-activation is triggered by something in the environment that bumps into a Trauma Capsule that belongs to, for example, a traumatized team. In that case, the team is triggered from the outside.

- Re-enactment is when the traumatized team drags its environment back into a trauma dynamic, often in an unconscious attempt to find healing.  In that case the trauma dynamic is activated by the people still suffering from trauma. Compare it with retarting a fight and hoping you'll win it this time.

In either situation, it will seem like time is standing still or a group seems to be stuck in an old annual ring. And of course, the passing of time makes it even more difficult to change something. A cluster of these signs lets you know you are on the path of organizational trauma. As a coach, you will learn to discern, more accurately, whether the released toxins are new or old. Learning to embrace this kind of intensity is an important prerequisite for working with organizational trauma.

This is how your trauma 'radar' develops and it will help you identify Trauma Capsules. Your body awareness, in combination with your existing  experience and skills in working with organizations, organizational trauma, emotional processes and groups will all be needed.  We cannot emphasize enough: the extent to which you can help your clients process these kinds of emotions, is proportional to how much you have worked personally with your feelings, your emotions and your traumas.

*In her teens Marie endured a terrible bereavement. It took her many years to process it, through which she developed a special sensitivity for unresolved grief and mourning. Later she became a counselor specializing in this area. She learned how to differentiate between her own, unhealed pain and the pain she can feel when counseling others. She was conducting an intake interview with a team and she felt sadness. Carefully, she looked into the history of the team, using her particular qualities of perception, and discovered that something was still at work in the dynamics of the team. At that time, the team had a temporary manager. Their formal manager had been absent for a long time due to life-threatening cancer, but he remained in touch with the team. He regularly read and sent emails to monitor or update business. Naturally, this caused confusion within the team, but nobody dared to say anything about it out of concern for the sick manager. This also clarified why the temporary manager was unable to effectively manage the team. In a way this team was mourning their formal manager and so were not yet available to a new manager.*

Be careful though. You will not always be received with open arms if you notice and mention issues like this. If you report that 'something' is still at work in the dynamics of the organization, you're likely to hit a brick wall. A wall that has been created because people do not want to 'waste' time or because they really do not know how to approach these issues. Ignoring organizational trauma does not make it disappear. In any case, you'll learn, from the reaction you get, how a particular organization does or does not deal with trauma, and that will be very useful information.

The following example shows how you can bump into a Trauma Capsule when you've only just started exploring a situation. Before long you'll be able to feel the energy wobbling, pointing you to something being touched in the deeper layers of the organization. It is not necessary to name it right away but you'll want to keep it in mind.

*A meeting was organized with a management team and an external coach after one of the directors announced her departure. The rift between her and her department had become a chasm. They discussed different approaches to working with*

*that department and what they might be looking for in a possi-
ble successor.  There was also talk about working towards creating self-regulating teams, because they feared that a new director  might  find  herself  in  a  similar  situation.  The  department's personnel were known to be particularly autonomous,
you could say allergic to authority.  During the discussions, the
coach picked up on something that prompted him to ask a number of focused questions about the department's history.  The
conversation became very emotional and a number of things
became immediately clear:*

- *The  department  had  previously  been  an  independent
  company, and had been taken over by the current, larger,
  organization.*

- *Saying goodbye to the founder of that smaller organization, which had been very successful in the early years,
  had been painful.  Although people had tried their best to
  handle this well, there was still a lot of pain in the organization and in the founder, with whom some employees
  still had contact.*

- *The current director, and a number of people in her department who had also announced their imminent depar-
  tures, had been recruited by the founder.*

You might suspect that year rings only affect the people who were personally involved in a particular overwhelming event.  But here we see what
is really special about living systems.  Unhealed trauma seeps inside the
relational fabric and gradually becomes part of a group, a family, an organization or a community.  It is not only in the people but also between the
people.

Even when none of the original people remain in the organization, old
trauma can still seep across generations.  This is important because the
argument that "*it happened decades ago*" is often used to sweep organizational trauma back under the mat.  And, if you are working with a family
company, be aware that an interaction (we could even say 'infection') can
arise between old family issues and the organization.  The following is an
illustration of exactly this.

*Years ago a local organization chose to develop its business in foreign markets. The plan created a lot of positive energy and at the same time carried significant risk. However, it turned out to be a fiasco for the organization and their adventures abroad cost them almost their whole company. The organization re-covered and, after a while, was doing well again. None of the people who had been involved in the 'adventure' were working there anymore. And for the 'new' people it seemed a very logical step to expand abroad. But this remained only an idea: the bur-den of history ensured nobody would take that risk again. Nat-urally, competitors and newcomers to the market – who didn't carry this burden – saw the same opportunities and built up a competitive advantage in these emerging markets.*

For this reason, it is always important to develop a sense of the organi-zation's history. You might suspect the presence of organizational trauma or notice that, although the capability to achieve specific strategic goals is available, everything seems stuck, and for no apparent reason. Then the chance is that something is negating those capabilities and 'replacing' them with old pain. It is crucial that you shine some light on that pain.

And so we come to a frequently-recurring pattern that eventually will help you – when starting to work with an organization – identify trauma. A Trauma Capsule has two parts. One part contains the toxins and the other contains the capabilities, which were damaged by an overwhelming event and whose development stopped at that point in time. The process of healing a Trauma Capsule not only releases old toxins, but also reopens a space for those capabilities and assets, that were frozen in time, to thaw out and become productive again. You might already have noticed the connection between this and the ancient Soul Retrieval Ritual we men-tioned in Part I. Healing starts the clock ticking again for the assets and capabilities that were stuck in one or more years gone by.

*Figure 33: Trauma Capsule with capabilities, stuck in time*

Apathy – which is not uncommon in organizations – is often actually wounded desire or damage to the inner motivation of those employees who have been affected by an overwhelming event. Passion fuels the energy, creativity and enthusiasm of workers at all levels. But passion is also vulnerable. If people suffer too often, they unconsciously rein in their passion, to avoid additional damage. You can see this in relationships, in personal ambitions, but also in the areas of professional or shared ambitions.

## 5.4 Trauma Capsules

One of the Western pioneers in the field of trauma in groups and systems is Wilfred Bion *Experiences in Groups* (Bion, 1968, [3]) . Much of the, albeit limited, literature around trauma in organizations is built on his findings. For example, he found that in an optimally functioning group, most of the energy and attention goes to accomplishing the real work. The more toxic an environment becomes, the more an organization begins sliding into the Trauma Trap. Energy and attention are drawn towards the emotions and dynamics and away from the work. Certain aspects of organizational trauma can be seen in how a group seems to avoid, or circle around Trauma Capsules, rather than getting on with the work at hand. It's like a group that must focus on a specific task while trying to avoid being hit by a heavy, swinging ball (a Trauma Capsule) that randomly attacks them. Chances are high that the assignment will never come to fruition or it'll take much more energy than necessary.

When the hidden dynamics determine the dance – and that's what is happening when an organization gets caught in the Trauma Trap – the efficiency of teams, departments or the whole organization decreases exponentially; professionalism is eroded and the work costs extra energy. In organizations the pressure, from within an organization, to perform is often extremely high. While under this pressure people must deal with the needs of colleagues, customers, patients and so on. When hidden, dysfunctional dynamics are at play employees try harder and harder, but only become less and less effective. In teams that are very result oriented, damage to the relational fabric needs to be severe before it begins to show up in the bottom line results. And it is exactly this characteristic that ensures toxins are passed on, unconsciously of course, from manager to successive manager. If you have inherited a team or department that is already at the bottom of the Trauma Trap, you're in trouble. You've inherited the harvest of short-term thinking. Here, again, we can learn something from indigenous peoples, who base their decisions on long-term perspectives. They always try to take into account the impact of their choices on the following seven generations.

If you often work with groups, you'll know how quickly you can notice the existing 'river banks' of a group. At the start of the first meeting everyone sits neatly behind the table. Contact tends to be quite reserved and you are seen, primarily, as an external facilitator. You might also have experienced the disruption caused to some groups when faced with a circle of chairs. In some cases, that's already enough to push people into the bank of rigidity. If you see this – when working with a group of people that have known each other for a while – take it as an invitation to listen a little closer to your trauma radar (although this behavior does not always point towards organizational trauma).

Then, once the group begins to feel more at ease, you could give them an assignment that needs little regulation or coordination from you. With appropriate care, you throw the group in at the deep end – or so it might feel to them. This is a good way for them to find their way to the other side, the bank of chaos. Often people start talking across each other, interrupting. Some try to get their approach to the fore, others withdraw and some sit wondering why you do not intervene or give more instructions. After a while, the participants will regroup, somewhere between the riverbanks of chaos and rigidity, where they can begin the process of becoming more integrated. So if you are working with groups, it's worth keeping these 'banks' in mind. It helps you to adjust the process to the resilience or degree of self-regulation the group already has. However, if you want to take a group a little further – as a facilitator – it will be necessary, at times, to take them out of their comfort zone and/or set boundaries, especially if your instincts suggest the possibility of organizational trauma. Part III will give you some more tools to deal with this.

In these kinds of situations you can see the difference in experience of the leaders or facilitators.

When the group begins to sense that you are picking-up these cues, they will feel a growing sense of safety: an essential prerequisite to working with organizational trauma.

Less-experienced leaders are often so preoccupied with a predefined approach that they do not see what the group is reflecting back.

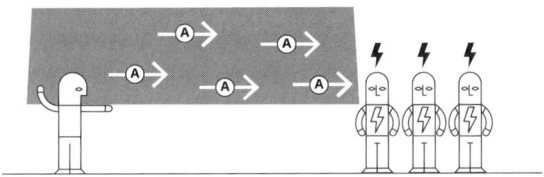

*Figure 34: Focus on action*

As a result, they often miss valuable signposts on the path, that point to helpful ways to support the development of the group.

Those with more experience will work with the group's subtle reactions and implicit feedback.

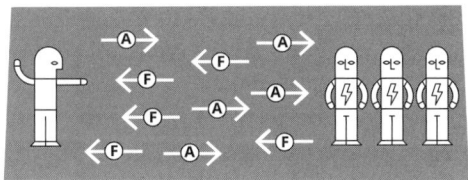

*Figure 35: Focus on feedback*

Because we are talking about hard, emotional labor, feeling healthy and well personally is crucial when you are doing this kind of work. As an individual, you too can be on the edge of being affected by trauma or you can just be exhausted or too occupied with your own stuff. This aspect of wellbeing is extremely important for everyone who works with other people and especially when working with vulnerable or wounded groups. If you're too tired or too stressed, you won't be able to open up for others. When your body is over-stimulated it makes it difficult to tune-in to others. That's why managers who are concerned about the health of their organization should, as much as possible, start with the health of their employees. And doubly so if their organization is working with vulnerable or traumatized people.

When you are fit, your body awareness is good. You need that to be able to accurately tune-in to other people and situations. It enables you to scan the dynamics of a group while facilitating. This is called 'deep listening', an aspect of phenomenological work. It's a fast way to tune-in to a particular situation or group. For example, if you feel, while working with a group, that you have begun walking on eggshells, chances are high that you are reacting to a group dynamic. What arises in the relationship between you and the group is often a reflection of (one of) the group's hidden, unconscious patterns. Organizational trauma often manifests as a mess of syrupy feelings, rigidity or chaos. The following symptoms – based on Bion's work *Experiences in Groups* (Bion, 1968, [3]) – are expressions of hidden dynamics taking over. Consider these as alarm bells or indications that the organization is now either at the edge of the Trauma Trap or has fallen into it.

**1. When people seem to be very dependent**

*Figure 36: Symptom of organizational trauma: people seem dependent*

This dynamic is noticeable in the following ways:

- People quickly and frequently ask for help and advice about trivial things.

- There will be glorification and idealization. Most of the authority will be passed to the Executive Board, the leader or the expert. This can show up as blind or passive following.

- People appear totally dependent on someone from whom they expect 'salvation'.

- You meet an unhealthy parent-child dynamic in which the leader will unconsciously try to be the perfect parent and will try to remove all the group's discomfort in order to avoid being rejected.

- An obviously unhealthy form of dependency seems to conceal a great deal of fear and uncertainty.

- Fear of making mistakes, leading to rigidity.

*A young, dynamic organization was acquired by a multinational. A few years later, the inspirational founder left the company, angrily, and with bad blood between him and the new owners. 'His' people at the original offices felt deserted, like orphans. Since then, every time a new director or ambitious new employee joined the original branch, he or she was burdened with all the hopes and needs of the existing employees. However, for the new person, this was pretty soon buried under all the problems in the branch, both new and built up over the years. So, each new manager was quickly overwhelmed by the situation. Unable to turn it around, he or she was eventually swallowed up by the deeply ingrained helplessness that permeated the people and the location. Whenever one of them tried to point out their responsibilities to their colleagues, he or she quickly lost the position of promising newcomer and was rejected. The consequence was that a persistent, rigid situation was maintained, for many years, which eventually pulled the business down into the red.*

In order to experience safety and stability in these kinds of situations, a group tends to suck people into a particular role. A group that cannot deal with the toxins associated with mistakes needs a scapegoat. This is the way a group getting stuck in the riverbank of rigidity deals with being over-stressed. Who might end up as the scapegoat? A new employee, a new manager... an external consultant?

In the case study above, the group is trying to stay in their familiar state of helplessness and victimization. As a result, the group saddles the new person with the role of savior until he or she fails, although the only real solution for the group is to look at their own role or responsibility in the problematic situation. If not, idealization tends to morph into rejection. A lot of managers and consultants will have experienced this already.

When the hidden dynamics take over a group or situation, it is really a cry for help from the living system, inviting you to care and attend to the relational fabric. So, working in a trauma-informed way means learning to see these kinds of seemingly irrational dynamics as signposts, as alarm bells from the relational fabric.

**When you hear an alarm,
don't look for the off-switch,
look for the fire.**

**2. When fight-and-flight behavior**

*Figure 37: Symptom of organizational trauma: fight/flight behavior*

This dynamic is noticeable in the following ways:

- You notice that people tend, quite quickly, to withdraw.  They are cautious or make themselves 'invisible'.  Conflicts are evaded or kept at arm's length, if necessary by acting as if nothing is going on at all.  You see a lot of avoidance behavior.

- Or you notice – and often this and the above behavior alternate – a highly conflict-sensitive dynamic.  People quickly take sides in conversations, disagreements happen rapidly and are cutting, humiliating or personal.  This is fighting behavior.

- Attacking and withdrawing lead to pronounced, rigid positioning, or a war-of-principles which totally foils any chance for collective intelligence to develop.  And that leads, of course, to everyone, tacitly and unconsciously, agreeing to avoid conflict.  The result is a crippling perpetrator-victim dynamic.  Once a group gets caught in this, any statement or act by one party is misunderstood or misrepresented by the other.  Every exchange simply adds to the toxic load and fuels the fires of distrust and dislike.

The dynamics outlined above can become a fertile ground for perverse behaviors such as bullying, exclusion or scapegoating.  Although it often seems to be about one individual, it is mostly the result of something unhealed in the relational fabric.  In these cases, the individual employee represents something that the group is suffering from, or damage it has incurred. Zooming-out is crucial here. What can be helpful is trying to get a feel for the quality – which, out of necessity perhaps, is exaggerated – the 'victim' is expressing. Often this is a quality that, at some time, damaged the relational fabric, and/or a quality that has ended up in the organization's 'shadow'.

*In a small organization, the behavior known as 'mobbing' was taking place.  In practice, this means that several people are bullying one person rather than one person bullying another. What struck us most was the fact that the person being bullied was one of the only employees who dared to really challenge others.  The rest of the employees radiated harmony.  As facilitators, we noticed that the development of the organization was faltering because they were trying to arrange everything, as it were, through harmony.  There must have been a link with the way they tried to handle conflict in the organization's history because the ability to handle conflict was sealed off somehow, probably in a Trauma Capsule. Except for that one person who was able to be critical, and so was attacked. The tendency of the group was to exclude whoever disturbed harmony. But the path to true healing was one of embracing constructive conflict, knowing that it was conflict that had once caused serious damage within the organization. Only by diving deeper into the history of the organization did this become clear.*

## 3. Hope is laid at the door of two parties

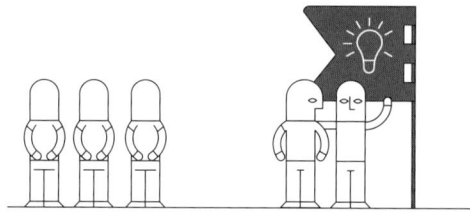

*Figure 38: Symptom of organizational trauma: all hope at the door*

Here again you see an expression of unhealthy dependence, not focused on one person but on the interplay between two people (or entities).

You see that people in the organization seem to be waiting for a point in the future where everything will click together, restoring stability and peace to the organization. Actions and decisions are postponed because things will work themselves out soon(er or later). Groups project, so to speak, their expectations on two or more people who will come up with the perfect solution that will make everything okay (again).
Because people wait for direction and action to come from someone or somewhere else, this pushes decisiveness and leadership to the back burner.

When tension in the relational fabric is affecting a group or an organization we often see a split into camps, each trying to impose their vision without this ever really being made explicit during meetings and gatherings. Origins of this kind of dynamic are diverse and can often be linked to something in the system's history (for example a poorly-managed merger). If this clash doesn't get resolved it will be expressed through two members of this group as if it's their conflict. You might see the rest of the participants starting to lean back in their seats away from the mini-system of the two protagonists hoping that, if they just keep out of the way, the two will solve the problem (for the rest).

This can also play out on a larger scale, throughout the whole organization. It can put an entire organization into 'standby mode'. Waiting while, for example, two directors argue endlessly with each other, instead of moving on, making everyday decisions as part of the firm's daily operations. The question that might come up here is: *"What happened in the past to the capability to resolve disagreements in a good way?"*.

## 4. No longer a middle way

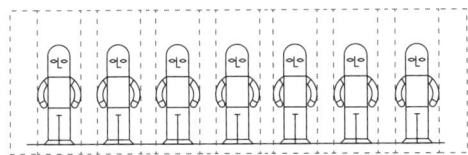

*Figure 39: Symptom of organizational trauma: no middle way*

Symptoms one, two and three are linked to the work of Wilfred Bion. This fourth symptom has a more-recent origin but it is likely you will be familiar with it too. In a healthy living system there is fluid interaction between the parts and the whole. As we saw earlier, this is an expression of integration. When a living system collapses into the Trauma Trap, this fluidity gets lost. People see-saw constantly between unity – one big, happy family – and an emphasis on individuality, boundaries and differences.

This kind of shifting can happen several times in the same meeting, which might confuse you as a facilitator. The dynamic that shows up is often the opposite of what you are trying to establish or need to move on: you might be attempting an exercise in connecting – like building a common vision – only to see the group emphasizing what is different and separate about them. And if you choose to zoom in on the differences – identifying specific qualities or expertise – the group seems to take the opposite tack, as if there are no real differences.

This confusing relationship between parts and the whole can play out between the members of a team but also between the departments of an organization. The dynamic seems to be 'one or the other' or 'for or against' irrespective of the context. Being fixated on the idea of 'we without differences' is often an unconscious attempt to prevent exclusion. After all, being 'different' can lead to being or feeling excluded. And vice versa; sticking to one's individuality ensures that differences continue to exist and that one is not swallowed up by the whole. Instead of condemning such dynamics, you can use them to better understand the group you're facilitating. These kinds of questions can help you to explore this strange, but very interesting, dynamic:

- Who or which people were different and so were excluded?
- What kind of difference was openly or covertly punished?
- What was merged, while actually being quite different?
- What was lost by being merged?

Looking back over these four symptoms, which often can be a kind of soup, it is important to highlight that *not every organizational issue is an expression of organizational trauma*. The purpose of this book is not to give this label to everything that seems strange at first sight. This book is an invitation to look a little deeper by learning to recognize these kinds of symptoms and see them as pointers in your attempt to uncover unhealed organizational trauma. Keep in mind that the cries of a living system are often silent, vague or ambiguous.

## 5.5  Learning to hear the cries of a living system

A living system is characterized by its desire to develop and unfold towards survival or its destination. Self-regulation, self-healing and emergence appear to be innate capabilities of living systems. The universe, and life on this planet, have been developing for 3.8 billion years through these capabilities. They ensure the survival of living systems within their particular contexts and they manifest as a natural urge to adapt and re-organize when necessary. This is as natural as gravity and not something that has to be learned. Working in a systemic way is more about freeing up a situation so life energy can flow again. In concrete terms, this means that if the parts of a living system are allowed to self-regulate – within the framework of the whole – they will naturally find the best way of working together to ensure survival. Understanding, honoring and using these capabilities is a key difference between working mechanistically or systemically.

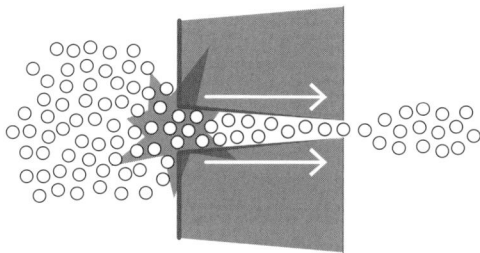

*Figure 40: Emergence and self-regulation*

*The human body is a beautiful 'product' of the evolution that results from self-regulating subsystems. An adult body needs a certain amount of water to function and to discharge accumulated waste and toxins. To this end, a body develops thirst signals, one of the primary ways it stays healthy. If you consistently ignore those primary signals, your body will start sending a hunger signal. This is just a secondary attempt: to extract liquid from the food. If you start drinking water regularly again, the primary thirst signals will be reactivated because you answered this subtle request from the body.*

This is revolutionary for people who are used to approaching organizations as machines. A machine-like organization is centrally controlled and has little or no capacity for self-regulation or adaptation. Primary signals are chronically suppressed which causes symptoms, eventually, to show. Approaching an organization as a living system leads you to see these symptoms as cries for help. In organizations where people have some understanding of systemic principles, they have developed eyes and ears for these subtle signals and learned to respond to them sooner rather than later, thus reducing the chance of persistent symptoms or louder cries. This makes such organizations particularly resilient.

If you want to work on organizational trauma, it is crucial that you work with the living system and not against it. Learn to rely on the system's embedded wisdom. You have nothing to repair; just identify the blockages that are negating its inherent capabilities and remove them, reinstating normal flow. It has much more to do with listening or letting the living system show you the way. Symptoms can be seen as cries from the relational fabric. They are unsuccessful or interrupted attempts of the living system to stay healthy.

> An organization, employing mainly manual workers, engaged a facilitator because there was a big disconnect between management and employees. It ensured that most management initiatives failed in the face of hardline resistance. During a number of exploratory interviews, the coach felt a kind of hardness (= fight dynamic) in every contact instance, which caused him, from time to time, to feel unsafe. Little by little it came to light that within the organization there was a serious bullying problem.

> To address the problem, cameras had been placed in many areas since some time ago. However, they were regularly destroyed or covered, creating a real cat and mouse game between employees and managers. Step by step it became clear that the bullying was mostly directed at new employees as a kind of initiation rite. That unsafe feeling, the hardness and the bullying of new employees seemed like a pattern. But what was the system trying to bring to the surface?

*It turned out that, several years earlier, an interim employee 'accidentally' died in suspicious circumstances. It had never quite become clear what exactly had happened and who else had been involved in the incident.*

*Since then there had been a wall of suspicion and anger be-tween management and workers. The management was – by law – responsible for the incident although they had never been able to really address the bullying problem. Based on that, there arose, within the executive board a kind of paralysis and shame because they felt powerless to find any kind of solution. It was this unresolved incident – unhealed trauma – that was continually putting pressure on the whole organization.*

In short, if you encounter one of the four dynamics presented earlier in this chapter, start exploring.  As a facilitator, be aware that there is a real danger of being sucked into these dynamics and becoming trapped in the dance. As soon as you become party to a conflict, you lose objectivity and the chance is high that you'll begin to fuel the dynamic you are trying to solve.  Learning to sense that you are being sucked-in is a crucial skill if you want to work with organizational trauma. But how do you notice this happening?

- You are seen as a savior and, if that's an unconscious pattern of yours, you could be easily seduced into that role.

- You become the confessor. All the organization's ills are brought to you, but mouths shut as soon as any manager appears. People who feel they are victims might try to get you on their side.  If you are the type who has empathy for 'victims' or if you like to challenge hierarchy then you need to be very careful about such an 'invitation'.

- You can also become a scapegoat or a bringer of bad news for the board of directors, so that nobody has to take responsibility if a strategy does not work or feedback isn't received well.

- The collaboration, between you and the person who brought you in, can put the organization into standby. As if it is waiting for the two of you to decide what is needed to solve an issue.

- If you find it difficult to step into a leadership role or to confront a group with their part in a problem, then it is very likely that the group will begin playing cat and mouse with you, frequently changing shape and becoming impossible to pin down.

These dynamics are usually unconscious. Yet it asks a lot of you to stay out of them. It can help to bring a colleague along. If you cannot, then make sure you have arranged for regular professional supervision because this kind of dynamic will drag you under from time to time.

## 5.6 Triggers are irrational and yet very real

The dynamics we've discussed will push a living system deeper into the Trauma Trap, which makes the relational fabric more fragile and more sensitive. You might be treading very carefully, but chances are high that you'll meet these dynamics somewhere. Trying to avoid Trauma Capsules or toxins will lead to rigidity and will make a living system even more vulnerable for change. Exactly the opposite of what companies need to thrive in a fast changing, complex world. Rigidity and toxin avoidance will, in the end, fail as a coping strategy. Only facing and processing toxins – no matter how old – will help develop resilience.

> *A living system that is cut off from the outside world, resisting renewal, endlessly searching for plans without risks, giving interconnectedness less and less attention, going into survival mode (fight, flight, freeze, please) at the slightest disturbance will, eventually, fall apart.*

If the hidden, unhealthy dynamics determine the dance, the emphasis is no longer on effectiveness or development, but on avoiding difficulties or chaos.

Work on Trauma Capsules requires insight into what we call 'triggers'. Triggers are situations, memories, sounds, sensations or events that provoke reactivation of unhealed trauma that is still present in the annual rings of the living system. Those triggers can be very subtle and stay as long as the trauma linked to them is not healed. The following examples should help you understand this better.

*A team was downsized by 50% a few years ago. The redundan-
cies were communicated one at a time, person by person. If you
were next in line, your phone would ring and you'd be called.
The first time a phone rang it had no 'special' effect but, from
then on, everyone knew what the sound of a phone could mean.
It took months for the sound of a phone to become something
normal again even for the employees who were not made redundant. For some of the employees who left, the sound of an
unexpected phone ringing filled them with unrest for years.*

In essence an unpleasant experience can also be a mechanism by
which people learn.  Usually it is enough to burn your fingers once on a
hot stove; then, when you see a hot stove again, you don't panic. This is a
healthy form of learning.

If the effects of an overwhelming event persist for more than a few
months, you can assume that you are chronically attached to the event
This might cause you to suffer from a post-traumatic injury and avoid situations which might reactivate that 'old' wound. This could indicate that
not all of the energy, built up in your body at the moment of the event, has
been processed. This makes you vulnerable and, in certain circumstances,
it does not take much to push you into survival mode. This is how the term
'trigger' has become part of the psychotherapeutic vocabulary.

The team members and the team from the 'redundancy' example
above have indeed become a restless, fearful and even risk-avoidant
group, as a consequence of the layoffs, even if the team didn't sink very
deep into the Trauma Trap. And, of course, the employees who had to
leave also took with them that specific sensitivity to ringing phones. What
some managers might see as an individual issue can thus affect the whole
team and even impact the whole organization. When it takes residence in
the fabric of the team or the organization, organizational trauma can develop. Let's look at an example that applies more to a whole organization.

*A change in the law merged all of a country's independent aid
foundations by region.  As a result, many team managers had
to move to another location and they lost their familiar, small-
scale teams that functioned well in an inclusive model of par-
ticipation and working together. In addition, the change in the
law also impacted their established practices. For all the work-*

*ers, familiar anchors were gone and they were no longer sur-rounded by trusted relationships to turn to for help.  Another outcome of the move was that day-to-day management be-came much more difficult. All this caused confusion, anger and uncertainty.*

*Because the organization continued to grow and some smaller teams were merged, particular property leases were not re-newed. For some teams, the occasional local 'hub' was moved or even removed. With every expansion or relocation, the man-agement had to contend with a flaring-up of emotions. The whole organization was kind of triggered by these kinds of de-cisions. On the one hand many people were in constant turmoil and no longer felt they had any roots in the organization.  On the other hand, the executive board found themselves, increas-ingly, walking on eggshells – which, step by over-careful step, began to exhaust them.*

In the example above there was repeated re-activation, which further increased the toxin load in the relational fabric, which diverted the en-ergy of the workforce from their work. The management found things in-creasingly difficult because they were responding, less and less, to the real story. As a result, the whole organization was looking (and hoping) for a savior, a heroic leader or perfect parent to solve the problems once and for all. The divide between management and employees widened and a vic-tim/perpetrator dynamic established itself in the company. The moment particular people are identified with the perpetrator role, and the rest start identifying with the victim role, a very stubborn situation can arise. We'll return to this in Part III.

Being on the look out for re-activation (a situation triggering old wounds) and re-enactment (people unconsciously dragging others into a re-enactment of an old trauma) is important for anyone working with or-ganizations, especially when organizational trauma might be present. Be-fore you know it, a downward spiral can be activated: the greater the num-ber of Trauma Capsules, the more likely one is to bump into them and the greater the chance that extra toxins will be created.

Trauma Capsules have another distorting effect: they alter the percep-tion of the outside world, making it appear more dangerous, and generating an irrational form of watchfulness. The lens of the living system is, as it were, smeared. Dave Ulrich, one of the world's most influential thinkers in the field of Human Resources, explains the link between an organization's culture and how it looks at the outside world *The HR Value Propostion* (Ulrich and Brockband, 2005, [34]) :

> *A firm whose culture cannot accurately perceive and interpret its environment – the requirements of its customers, investors and  regulators, the technological alternatives it faces, the moves its competitors make – and effectively translate those perceptions and interpretations into employee behaviors will have great difficulty staying in business.*

## 5.7 Triggers are signposts

Daniel Goleman, in his 1995 book, *Emotional Intelligence* (Goleman, 1995, [15]) , was one of the first authors to take us inside the workings of the human brain. Since then, evolution in this area of research has been rapidly applied to organizations.  Rather than diving into the technical details, let's look at an example that provides clear insight into how our brain functions when triggered.  This example is especially helpful for anyone leading people and/or organizations. So let's look at one survival mechanism of horses, a herd species that has survived for more than 15,000 years.

> *A herd of wild horses are grazing on a plain. Every horse is alert to possible danger.  The inner peace of each individual horse is a reflection of the tranquility of the herd.  If a predator comes near, one particular horse will smell or hear it before the others. That horse focuses its senses on checking if there is a real risk. This immediately elevates the alertness of the whole herd.  The inner self of one horse is a stimulus for the rest of the herd.  If the danger turns out to be real, the herd flees.  If not, the herd grazes quietly on.*

To respond appropriately to danger, the alarm mechanism of the horses should work quickly and accurately.  This is true for each horse individually and for the signals they exchange with each other.  Horses have developed a particularly high sensitivity for patterns in and around the herd. Knowing and recognizing these patterns gives a kind of pre-dictability to how the herd can anticipate predators. They notice patterns by being especially sensitive to smell, movement and sound – and they do this as one, as the herd. We see that the herd has multiple sensors (each horse), connected to each other, which supports their survival. It's the wiring between the horses that makes the whole so much more sensi-tive than the sum of its parts.

This example has a number of elements of particular relevance for or-ganizations. Specifically, how quickly is 'danger' recognized and commu-nicated to the rest of the organization? Remember that danger can have several dimensions (as shown on the third axis of the Trauma Cube: phys-ical, social, mental and/or spiritual). In essence, certain dangers can, in the short or longer term, threaten the survival of an organization. A lot of organizations that did not notice market changes soon enough, ended up either in total disarray or went bust. In a rapidly changing or VUCA-world the ability to sense change early, and react with appropriate responses, is essential to the survival of an organization. Here, again, is Dave Ulrich making a nice link to the relational wiring of organizations:

> **The more an organization can do to make sure informa-tion passes smoothly to the places where people can use it, the better off it will be. And since information is much of what creates culture, organizations that can create and sustain effective cultures manage information ef-fectively. Thereby, employees clearly understand the importance of their work to customers and to the orga-nization as a whole.**
>
> Dave Ulrich

When the relational fabric is underdeveloped, that'll be reflected in the functioning of an organization. And when it is saturated by toxins or, in places, completely torn, this could be immensely damaging. Healing or-ganizational trauma is now a necessity for organizations that want to stay resilient in a fast-changing world.

And further, it's impossible to build a resilient organization if you do not embrace the logic of living systems. A living system survives because all its sensors – and the network connecting those sensors – is always poised, ready to act appropriately.  In this sense, resilient organizations see employees as sensors and the relational fabric as the network through which they can exchange – in every possible direction – just like the complex network that is a human nervous system.  Only then can internal or external needs and potential dangers be sensed, anywhere that they occur, and quickly communicated to the correct part for the appropriate response.

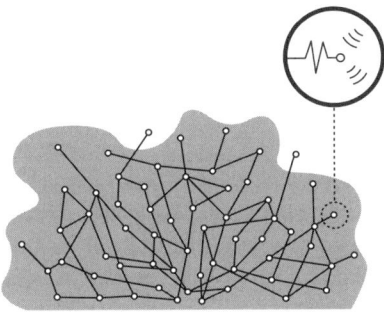

*Figure 41: Wired sensors*

Danger can come from the outside:

- For an individual: a car about to hit you head on, being bullied and so on.

- For an organization: a disruptive player in the market, the potential loss of subsidies, hostile takeovers and so on.

But also from the inside:

- For an individual: frequent migraine headaches, a torn muscle, thirst and so on.

- For an organization: quarreling between the founders which could threaten the organization, responding too slowly to changes in the market, the lack of specific technologies and so on.

The development of the internet, as an open source for knowledge sharing and communication, is showing us the growing power and possibilities of effective networks. Again, it is strange to see how much resistance old-school organizations display to become more open and transparent. Unfortunately, for them, at the expense of their own resilience.

In a healthy living system all sensors are continuously alert, sensing inside and outside in service of the whole. This facilitates optimal functioning and maintains alignment with the environment at the same time. By feeling and integrating the data collected via these sensors, a living system remains in a continuous state of development. This builds resilience and ensures survival.

When a 'life-threatening' situation arises, the initial response is one of fight-or-flight. This is a state of hyper activation that releases much more energy than normal into the body of the living system to make sure enough energy is available for an appropriate response. Also, our brain switches to a survival mode. The neo-cortex – the part of the brain wired for complexity – is short-circuited. The more reflexive and instinctive part of the brain – the brain stem – starts running the show. This part is wired to deal with danger in split seconds: because being too slow could be the difference between life and death.

What we often see when working with teams and organizations is a similar build-up of energy (and toxins) to protect the living system when it feels threatened. If this energy is not released, the relational fabric cannot return to its original state of integration. We can compare it with shaking a bottle of sparkling water: as long as the pressure is high, it's better not to open the bottle. This elevated tension, in combination with the tendency to avoid processing it, keeps the living system trapped in a hyperactive state. And when an organization is sinking or stuck in the lower layers of the Trauma Trap, the capabilities essential to surviving a complex, fast changing world will also get stuck.

When fight or flight strategies do not work, because the threat is too big or something hinders the living system's response, the freeze mechanism is activated. In a sense, this is the living system collapsing. The trio of fight, flight or freeze is well known in the field of trauma, but Marianne Bentzen in *The Neuroaffective Picture Book* (Bentzen, 2015, [2]) , introduces a fourth survival strategy, one you might also see in social systems. She calls it the 'tend, befriend or please' survival strategy; used, for example, when a person needs to calm down a perpetrator. You'll meet all four strategies in the organizations with which you engage.

> *Due to many different circumstances, the turnover of a sales organization had fallen way below targets and expectations. Because his job was at risk, the sales manager called a meeting with all his account managers, where each account manager had to present an action-plan to achieve his or her sales targets. No sooner had the first presentation began, when the sales manager started cross-examining the account manager. The meeting room turned into a courtroom. The rest of the account managers pulled back, became silent and made themselves 'invisible' (freezing) to avoid being sucked into the battle. Later, every time a meeting was planned for the account managers, they tried to find out if the sales manager would also be present. If he wouldn't, there would follow a sigh of relief. If he would be there, anxiety and tension skyrocketed. The account managers were only a shadow of their potential when the sales manager was in the room. This made him doubt them even more. A vicious circle was in operation.*

When threatened, a living system adopts survival strategies but returns to 'normal' functioning when the threat is over (remember the example of the antelope). When this feeling of being threatened becomes chronic, it begins to damage the relational fabric of the living system, making it more vulnerable. If this isn't dealt with, the living system loses its resilience and its capacity to deal with unexpected change. Increasingly, it easily feels threatened or overwhelmed. Necessary capabilities get stuck, toxins pile up in Trauma Capsules and the channels for releasing tension and toxins get congested. The deeper in the Trauma Trap, the more difficult it becomes to arrest this downward spiral.

What could help? Nature can be our inspiration. As soon as animals feel safe, they release that peak energy. They do this through a natural shiver-response. We humans suppress this natural response – both individually and collectively – and that unreleased peak energy forms or fills Trauma Capsules, as it must go somewhere. When releasing is blocked, the next option is storing it inside the system. But this corrodes the relational fabric and elevates the alert-state, because weaker systems become more vulnerable. Stressors and challenges must be avoided in two ways:

- Outside threats and challenges must be avoided because the capabilities to deal with them are no longer available.

- The same happens inside. The capabilities to deal with the Trauma Capsules or to release the stored toxins are also inhibited.

Spotting triggers is a good way to develop your understanding of what is going on. As you have seen, they can be particularly annoying or prohibitive but – at the same time – beneficial, because they try to limit further disintegration of the individual or group. They show the living system's efforts to survive and show you where healing is most needed.

**In conclusion**

Let's take all of the insights mentioned in this chapter and incorporate them into our Trauma Formula:

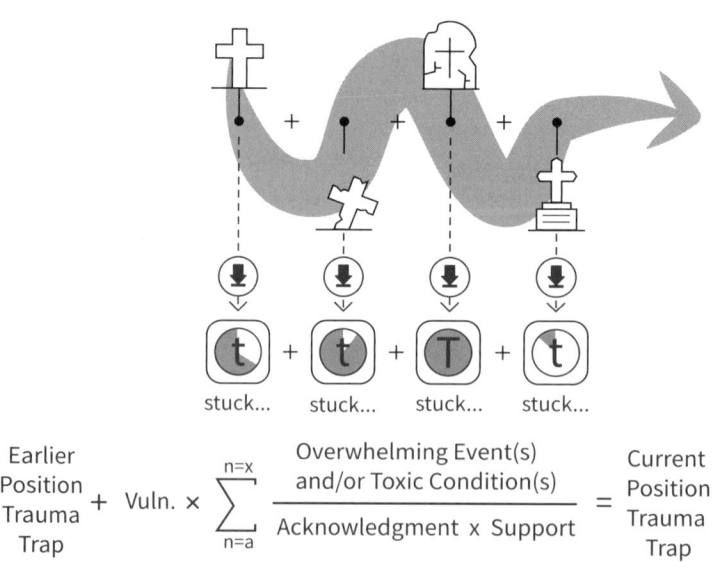

$$\text{Earlier Position Trauma Trap} + \text{Vuln.} \times \sum_{n=a}^{n=x} \frac{\text{Overwhelming Event(s) and/or Toxic Condition(s)}}{\text{Acknowledgment} \times \text{Support}} = \text{Current Position Trauma Trap}$$

*Figure 42: Trauma Formula 2.0*

We have learned that overwhelming events and also chronic, toxic stressors weaken the relational fabric of an organization, if the built-up energy is not acknowledged and released. This begins the process of sinking into the Trauma Trap.

When this happens, the bandwidth to process challenges (resilience) becomes narrower, and re-activation (via triggers) occurs more rapidly. The lower an organization falls in the Trauma Trap the more energy it consumes to maintain its internal stability and remain aligned with the volatile environment (e.g. the market) of the organization. The fear of being in 'chaos' is experienced more quickly, which leads to greater 'rigidity'; a key indicator of organizational trauma.

When you notice this happening, it's a good idea to start getting an idea of how an organization might be more vulnerable to organizational trauma. Perhaps via the type of employees it takes on, the nature of the work, the culture, its management practices or the organization's design. If so, try to figure out if enough practices are in place to detect damage to the relational fabric, and also check if the bandwidth for processing toxins at an early stage parallels the manner and amount by which they increase. If not, the risk of organizational trauma is very real.

Irrational dynamics will show up as:

- People behaving in very dependent ways

- Regular expressions of fight-and-flight behavior

- All hope being laid at the door of two parties

- It becomes difficult to find an appropriate middle way between part and whole, individual and collective.

These are invitations by the living system to listen more deeply. It tries to bring your attention and awareness to what is still not processed, not released and needs healing. Listening deeply will bring you to the triggers that are re-activating what is not healed. Only by releasing the toxins that are still stuck in Trauma Capsules can you free up the organization's capabilities. If not, the past (annual rings) will continue to influence the present. Healing is needed so that time can start running again.

So, timely detection and processing of toxins and Trauma Capsules is crucial. Understanding the concept of organizational trauma can help you respond to the cries-for-help from an organization. After all, what stays in the dark will wither and rot: only light brings healing. That brings us to the third and last part of this book, where we take a detailed look at what it takes to get to grips with organizational trauma.

# PART III

## WORKING WITH
## ORGANIZATIONAL TRAUMA

A world without dramatic, overwhelming events is impossible. In spite of the damage and the suffering that can occur, it is also important to accept that some things are improved or addressed through these same events. Conflict and trauma contribute to development, both individual and collective. Earlier, we referred to the term post-traumatic growth as the other side of the post-traumatic stress syndrome. However, there is a certain degree of trauma-understanding needed to turn overwhelming events into growth and development for individuals, groups, organizations and even entire communities. While Parts I and II laid the foundations for learning how to look at organizations from a trauma-informed perspective, Part III shows how to really work with organizational trauma. Based on the literature and our experience in working with organizational trauma, we identified four different domains or approaches to organizational trauma. These are schematically represented on the Trauma Diamond. Practice has taught us that these four domains are equal in value, are inextricably linked to each other, and can influence each other either positively or negatively.

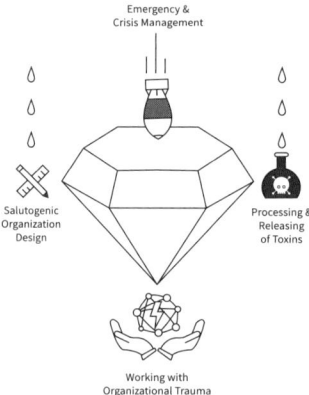

*Figure 43: Trauma Diamond*

These four domains are represented by the following four questions:

## Being prepared for potential traumatic events

Being prepared for potential traumatic events makes an organization much less likely to be overwhelmed or destabilized. If it does happen, a prepared organization will be more resilient and damage will be limited. Practice shows, so far, that the sooner the appropriate response the more problems can be avoided. So the answer to this question falls largely within the field of Emergency and Crisis Management, which will be discussed in Chapter 6.

## Processing toxins

A rapidly evolving, increasingly complex world makes for unseen, stealthy stressors that cause toxins to build up in organizations, making them more vulnerable. This is why it is important to detect and process toxins as soon as possible to prevent an organization from becoming more vulnerable or sliding – step-by-step – into the Trauma Trap. Classically-designed organizations appear to be oriented towards stability rather than development, which is a double-edged sword. On the one hand, it makes the organization vulnerable to accelerated toxin build up. On the other hand, such organizations are not as well equipped to release or process this build-up of toxins. So the toxins sink down and settle in the relational fabric of an organization. Fundamentally, processing and releasing toxins has to become a regular and accepted organizational function. This is discussed in Chapter 7.

## Still being dragged down

In many organizations, organizational trauma is slumbering. Just as an individual can struggle on, year after year, carrying an overly-heavy backpack, so too can organizations. And successive generations of management get caught up in this 'game'. However, the time always comes when that backpack, finally, feels too heavy. For an organization this moment can be triggered by seemingly normal challenges, such as changing market conditions or a major restructuring. In such situations, the organizational trauma is triggered and comes to the surface in a more visible and felt way. Dealing with those changing conditions often cannot work without first healing the organizational trauma – because the necessary capacities are still stuck in Trauma Capsules. Only if the people facilitating the change processes are trauma-informed, will they take this into consideration. Working with organizational trauma that has settled in the deeper layers of the organization will be dealt with in Chapter 8.

## Organizational trauma by design

The level of stress within some organizations is enormous. This is apparent, among other things, from the rising number of people who drop out or are burned out for long periods. The performance-bar is set particularly high for white-collar workers and teams. Therefore, it is vital that organizations are structured in ways that support the functioning of teams. Guiding or coaching them will be much more effective than micro-managing and measuring them. Too often we realize that it is not the job itself that feels stressful, but the way the work is organized, or how the organization is managed or designed. If the work itself is already stressful, the design of the organization must not make the work even more difficult. More and more we are seeing that the design of the organization can put more pressure on the relational fabric, making it unnecessarily weaker. That's what drags an organization, in a subtle way, down into the Trauma Trap. Sadly, in some organizations, we even speak of 'trauma by design', which brings us to the fourth domain of the Trauma Diamond: Salutogenic Organization Design, discussed in Chapter 9.

# Emergency & Crisis Management

**6**

Nothing or no one is totally immune to the impact of overwhelming events. After the event, as human beings, we like to put the blame somewhere, on a person or some fault in the system. After every disaster you'll hear or read about many different issues:

- *"Why were the emergency services so late?"*

- *"Coordination between the various emergency services was a disaster and caused even more chaos."*

- *"Reports detailing this risk had existed for a long time. Why hadn't something already been done?"*

The search for a scapegoat is a way to separate oneself from the guilt and the cause, but also to give a place to the emotions that have built up (indignation, anguish, sadness etc.). But that is usually not the most effective way to process the effects of such events. On the other hand, it is worthwhile to use the lessons learned from such incidents to improve responses or, even better, avoid experiencing such an event again. As we all know, the devil is in the detail and in the art of responding. For example:

- If something happens to you (or someone from your family), can others easily find the details of those who need to be contacted?

- If something drastic happens at your workplace, do you or your colleagues know what they should to make themselves and others safe?

- If you witness a serious industrial accident, do you know what you should or should not do with victims?

Emergency and crisis management are important factors within the framework of trauma prevention in organizations. The purpose is initially to be ready for risks, to prevent them when possible and to deal with them if they occur. In organizations, prevention is usually the responsibility of (the department of) Health, Safety & the Environment and/or Human Resources. How employees and executives respond during an evacuation exercise is a good indication of an organization's preparedness. One could devote a large book to just this issue. In part, because organizations have significantly improved their operations in this area in recent years, we have chosen to give a relatively short overview of this topic.

The link between organizational trauma and the origins of trauma is clear: we talk about disaster when a group of people, an organization or a community is overwhelmed by a specific event that blocks their ability to respond adequately, often creating chaos.  And if that happens, what can people fall back on? To what level are they trained to respond appropriately? How is external assistance initiated? How is the event communicated, internally and externally? In short, in such a case there is a need for sustained, external assistance.  Because the risk of trauma is high, it is vital to limit damage by rapid, accurate interventions and quickly isolating, shielding or eliminating potential hazards such as explosives, dangerous machines, fallen power lines, unstable buildings, gas leaks, etc., in the moments immediately following the event.  The following steps would help create an effective emergency and crisis management plan:

1. Mapping possible **risks and vulnerabilities**;

2. Identifying deficiencies and requirements, based on **scenarios**;

3. which should include how **individuals and groups** are cared for. The recovery process should also be part of the plan;

4. Briefing, training, practicing, implementing measures, purchasing materials: a good plan does not always mean one is **fully prepared**;

5. **Refine the plan further** using experience-based insight.

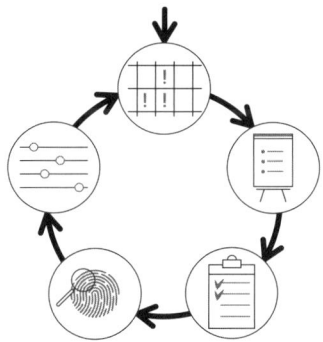

*Figure 44: Steps for an effective emergency and crisis management plan*

In practice, working together on the above contributes to the overall health and good functioning of an organization. It makes people more aware of potential dangers and more alert to danger signals. Antifragility, a concept already mentioned in this book, and resilience can be trained into individuals, groups and organizations.

It is also true that after a major event we often hear that several signals had already been noticed or that several reports had already been submitted about a particular problem. Working together on targeted prevention can therefore be seen as a practical (versus an administrative) audit, a first step in prevention. It would identify weaknesses, ensure the development of resilience and engagement, and even support what links people, teams and departments: the relational wiring. This process always starts with risk mapping.

## 6.1 Step 1: Mapping risks and vulnerabilities

In order to prepare an organization and train people, the potential risks and possible consequences must first be mapped. Here it is useful to keep an eye on every dimension of the Trauma Cube, but it's equally important to take into account the various possible sources of trauma: acute vs. drop-by-drop, internal vs. external. Too often, prevention measures are aimed one-sidedly at the physical aspect or at matters that were previously acute, while there may also be a psycho-emotional or even spiritual component in the development of organizational trauma. Because each type of organization has its own specific risks or vulnerabilities, this kind of work has to be tailored to the specifics of each organization:

- If your business involves hazardous substances (chemicals, nuclear power plants, waste disposal etc.) you must, at the very least, be prepared for leaks, contamination and explosions.

- Transport companies (aviation, shipping, rail, tram, metro, bus etc.) must consider serious accidents, complex technical problems, extreme weather conditions and so on.

- Organizations located in areas vulnerable to natural disasters (earthquakes, floods, hurricanes etc.) or terrorist attacks (e.g. embassies, airports, stations, shopping centers etc.) must have an action plan for mass evacuations and mass fatalities.

- Organizations that process foods or medicines must be prepared to trace and neutralize harmful ingredients and, if they have found their way into products, remove these from the market and reimburse the purchasers.

- This also applies to events where very large numbers of people gather (concerts, annual markets, religious events etc.) whether or not in the open air.

Again, in recent years, we have seen incidents and attacks with many fatalities. This is a high price to pay for the increases in prevention and security that follow such incidents. Preparing a threat/vulnerability matrix is an excellent first step. You first start by evaluating the relative likelihood of occurrence for each possible threat. Once the plausible threats are identified, a vulnerability assessment must be performed. The vulnerability assessment considers the potential impact (minor – noticeable – severe – devastating) of all different threats mapped earlier. And don't forget that it will need regular updating to keep pace with the speed at which our world is changing.

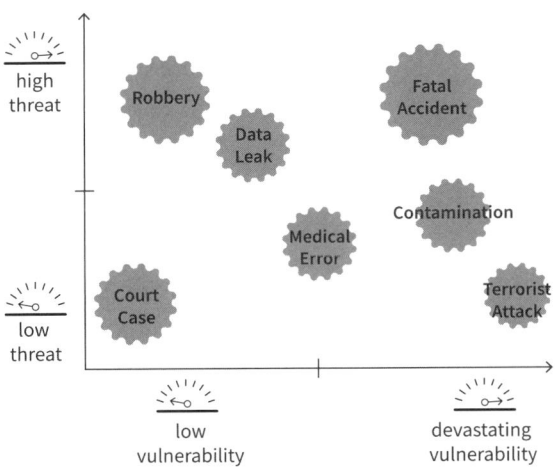

*Figure 45: Mapping risks and vulnerabilities*

## 6.2 Step 2: Identifying defects and requirements

Scenarios are useful in determining how prepared an organization and its employees are for specific events. The following questions help in this context:

- What plans and scenarios do we have and how do we find them if, for example, there is no electricity? What do they look like? Where are they kept? Who is trained to work with them?

- Are those tasked with first response trained to initiate all necessary processes? Who is responsible in each context? Do they fully understand their responsibilities? Who is trained to intervene in crisis situations (first aid, psychological care etc.)?

- Is it clear how those people can be contacted? Is there any backup if certain people are not available or are victims?

- Do employees and visitors know what to do or where to go when there is danger? Are there alternative places if the first designated places are too risky? What evacuation routes are there? Are they also accessible to people with disabilities?

- Are there clear contact lists of, for example, family members and emergency services (police, fire department, flood prevention etc.)? Are these constantly updated? Are they easy to read in a stressful situation? What if electricity, the internet or the mobile network are temporarily down?

- Is it clear who is responsible for communication? Internal and external? Via which channels? Using what languages (Many companies recruit multinationally. In times of crisis people react quicker and with more understanding to their native language). Are the responsible people trained in how to speak about such an event?

- How will information be handled, knowing that there may also be insurance or legal consequences associated with certain kinds of incidents? And by whom, and how, will incoming information and requests for information be processed? And certainly, if victims are to be traced, it is important to be able to begin directed searches as soon as possible.

Based on this step, it becomes clear what kind of gaps exist in the preparedness of an organization. This is the input for the next step.

## 6.3  Step 3: Developing a response and recovery plan

How people and groups are cared for – immediately after an overwhelming event – and how they are followed up, largely determines whether individual trauma and/or organizational trauma will develop. Within this framework, the extent to which an organization's key personnel are trauma-informed makes a particularly big difference. The response and recovery plan should be a very clear expression of this competency (or lack of it).

> *Let's take a step back and look again at how animals naturally deal with acute stress. Understanding this is often the first step to developing the capacity for trauma-informed work. If an animal feels threatened, large amounts of energy are released to defend itself or the group (fight) or to escape (flight). For example, if an antelope is being attacked by a lioness, the antelope builds up a mass of survival energy in order to get away. When the antelope feels safe again, she disperses the accumulated excess energy through vigorous shaking. That way, the accumulated energy is released from the body and the animal returns into balance. If that energy is not worked-out or released, for example because the animal is restrained in some way, then this intense energy will continue to circulate, never coming to rest. Precisely because animals do not suppress their natural reflexes, trauma is extremely rare in the wild . . . but very common in zoos.*

Humans also have this natural reflex but we tend to suppress it, albeit unconsciously. By the way, emergency workers – police, firefighters, paramedics, etc. – who have not learned about this reflex, often respond incorrectly to it, confusing it with either shock or cold, and preventing the natural bodily response of accident victims, their spontaneous shivering. Trained healthcare professionals, on the other hand, know what to do to calm a victim's over-excited nervous system without blocking the body's natural response. A key aspect of the post-traumatic stress syndrome is that the over-stimulation of the nervous system continues as if it is still in crisis, even though the danger is long gone.

The renowned trauma expert Peter Levine describes this process in his book, *In an unspoken voice* (Levine, 2012, [19]) . He portrays his experience as a victim of a traffic accident, with one rescuer increasing the stress to his nervous system by communicating in a hurried, over-excited way, and another rescuer being calm and quiet despite Levine's injuries. Thanks to his years of experience with trauma victims, Levine was able to perceive this very consciously and self-regulate his own reactions to this exceptional event.

The work of Erik de Soir *Redders in nood* (Soir, 2013, [27]) , a renowned crisis psychologist, taught me the squirrel method that many firemen and ambulance nurses are now trained to use. In an accident, if someone gets trapped in a vehicle it's very possible that next to him or her are relatives or friends who are seriously injured or even dead.  For that person, it is virtually impossible for their nervous system to stabilize when they are immersed in and overcome by the terrible new reality of the accident's aftermath.  The squirrel method is proven to accelerate medical and psychological stabilization and prevent or substantially limit residual shock and trauma.  An important component of the method is how psychological stabilization is achieved by using 'hypnotic' communication and relaxation approaches.  This demands a great deal of professionalism, understanding and training from the emergency services.

In every situation, if somebody cannot be brought into a restful state, she remains in a constant kind of hyper activation which, eventually, can lead to a variety of complaints and problems.  Increasingly, it becomes clear that immediate, appropriate care, after a disaster or overwhelming event, can significantly reduce the possibility of post-traumatic stress injuries.  Fortunately, there is a growing focus on providing this training to emergency services personnel.  But, unfortunately, the people who often get to the victims first – especially in the case of major disasters – are often neither trained nor trauma-informed.  Therefore it could be a consideration – for organizations and/or the government – based on specific risks, to widen the First Aid Training given to employees to include basic information about trauma. However, in order to really start this kind of training or raise awareness about this matter, we need to become collectively more aware that certain interventions, no matter how well intentioned, can be traumatizing, both for individuals and groups.

Following an overwhelming event, attention and initial measures must always be for individual victims first, rather than for any groups, departments or the organization as a whole. The following steps are relevant here:

- Triage: ascertaining the current physical and emotional state of the victim and orientating them to the most necessary support, such as Emergency First Aid. In this phase the immediate environment is screened for potential hazards.

- If possible, make contact with the victim and return them to psychological stability.

- Identify what is happening for the victim right at that moment and listen carefully for feelings and emotions. It helps to offer some context about what exactly happened and what the next steps might be. This helps the victim to come back to the present, from where he can provide information about the event. For example, where there might still be victims.

- As the most intense emotions are processed – which can take a long time – and the victim becomes more grounded, you can discuss with them what is going to happen next. You check whether someone can move on without assistance or if, for example, relatives can come and/or what other help a person might need. Finally, you ensure the victim is regularly checked and has the necessary contact details should he or she need ongoing support. Some kind of helpline should be arranged before victims are allowed to leave.

These interventions must, first and foremost, ensure that people are treated individually and receive appropriate medical and psychological assistance. Within 24 hours, debriefing and defusing, a critical step in the recovery process, should also take place and not as a one-time intervention. Most of the time, this step is performed by an external party, trained in post-disaster care. If this is the only support provided, it can have a counter-productive effect because, most of the time, more support and follow-up will be needed to fully process a potentially-traumatic experience. Therefore, people in the organization must assume responsibility for ongoing support if the external provider falls out of the picture.

In addition to keeping in touch with primary and secondary victims, debriefing and defusing will help everyone involved to reconstruct a coherent story of what happened and to voice the emotions triggered by the event. Without this, victims are often left with a fragmented view of what happened and the quest for understanding can haunt them for years. When the debriefing and defusing is more or less complete and if it has gone well, victims feel safe again and know that the real danger has passed. In previous chapters we saw that splitting-off can be an attempt to deal with an overwhelming event. Here, the part that splits off stays stuck in the event. It is as if, for the victim, time literally stopped at the moment of the event. If this happens, it is highly likely that the person will remain wholly or partly in fight-or-flight mode which significantly increases the risk of post-traumatic stress symptoms. The final step in this phase is contacting and activating the victim's social network and providing it with the information necessary to assist in the victim's recovery. Providing the right individual care does not necessarily mean that there will be no organizational trauma. Attention for this aspect needs to come later. But – and that is what we see more and more in our daily practice – if it appears that the organization has been negligent in terms of preparation, prevention or immediate care, then a deep distrust can arise between people, teams and the organization. And this can be enough to push an organization into the Trauma Trap. Therefore the initial, and critical, phase of specialized care must be followed by a number of actions that focus more on the relational fabric and/or the prevention of organizational trauma. Being trauma-informed means also that you stay aware of the full spectrum of the Trauma Cube. Organizations tend to focus more on the individual and physical than on the collective and non-physical (emotional, mental and spiritual).

Key actions include:

- Providing comprehensive aftercare,

- Identifying and monitoring the impact on victims, witnesses, relatives and rescuers.

- Systematically re-examining, with as many as possible of those involved, and as often as needed to get a complete picture, exactly what happened. We call this laying-out the puzzle: putting together, piece by painstaking piece, the story of the event. It is likely this will have to happen several times with the same individuals and with people who went through very different experiences.  Through this we identify who is emotionally stuck, what could be done to be more prepared, should this happen again and what further support is needed.  This 'puzzle' work must take place in a psychologically-safe setting. Be especially careful, when debriefing, that your focus remains on the psychological perspective and does not slide into stories of responsibility or liability. No matter how important these might be from a legal perspective, going into them at this stage will obstruct the laying out of the puzzle and will completely block any processing of trauma.

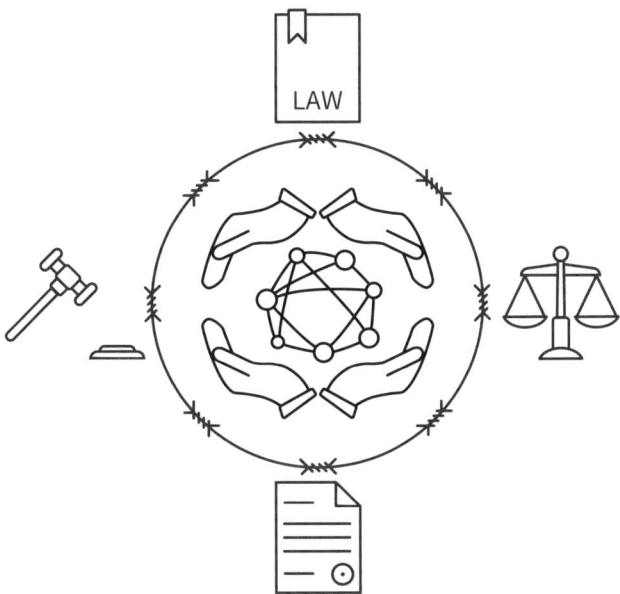

*Figure 46: LORE protected from LAW*

In practice, during the laying-out of the puzzle two different, but equally logical, processes can come into conflict with each other. We could call these the 'human' (= LORE) and the 'legal' (= LAW). Practice, again, shows that the conflict inherent in their different logical approaches could have a particularly serious impact on the proper functioning of an organization after a potentially traumatic event. Almost every major incident has a legal and/or insurance/technical aspect. This means identifying if there has been negligence, who might be held liable, who might have to pay compensation and, in extremis, who might be prosecuted. Over the years, we have noticed that the legal issues can keep an organization completely in shock until a final, usually independent, report, is made public; this can take several years. When the 'legal' interferes with the 'human' – especially relational processing – it will seriously obstruct provision of proper care, guidance and eventual healing. Here are two examples of this process-based conflict:

> *In a hospital, an employee's error causes the death of a patient and an investigation begins. The department where the death occurred is in total shock. All communication becomes purely functional. Deep distrust develops between the different teams. Many feel the Sword of Damocles hanging over their heads. The department feels totally isolated from its surrounding departments and teams. After 5 years the investigation report is published and only then is there space for the healing process. At this point, the department is stuck, deep down in the Trauma Trap. In this example LAW pushed LORE out of the process.*

> *In mid-September 2014, in thick, localized fog on the A58 in Zeeland (the Netherlands), a terrible accident occurs. Dozens of cars are involved and two people are killed. There are multiple victims and enormous damage to vehicles. In an extraordinary decision, the insurance companies choose to compensate everyone involved rather than to look for a guilty party. In this example a good balance between LAW and LORE was found.*

These two examples are not intended to make a case for the 'legal' on one hand or the 'human' on the other. Wisdom and common sense are needed here, and that means, depending on the situation, the most appropriate mix of the two approaches should be used. Unfortunately, guilt, innocence, liability and damages (= LAW) seem, in our society, to take priority over healing (= LORE). Financial compensation or a legal judgement never brings rest, let alone healing, no matter what some might want to believe.  Fortunately though, here and there, more-useful and balanced approaches are unfolding, practices such as Restorative Justice.

By ongoing monitoring of people and teams, and bringing them to-gether when necessary, effective aftercare can be provided both individ-ually and relationally.  This is crucial with regard to avoiding organiza-tional trauma. This period, depending on the intensity of the overwhelm-ing event, can take between one and three months to complete.  Over-whelming events, that are not processed in this way, can push an organi-zation, a team or a group of people all the way to the bottom of the Trauma Trap.  This can drag on for years, and is what we will examine, in greater detail, in Chapter 8.

In the current chapter we want to focus not only on immediate care but also on the recovery process.  Perhaps it is impossible to completely prepare for this, but it helps if the organization can agree certain principles or a framework for a recovery process.  Below are some good – and not so good – examples from actual experiences in this field.  Keep the image of the Trauma Trap and the relational fabric in mind while reading these examples:

| Good | Not so good |
|------|-------------|
| An organizational coach in a consultancy firm needed many months off work to recover from a major illness. To enable her reintegration, one of her colleagues had maintained her relationships with her clients. This ensured that she found it relatively easy to get back to work. | An employee had been on sick leave for over six weeks, during which he heard nothing from his employer. When he returned, he found a pile of work waiting on his desk. There was hardly any time to welcome him back and, in a short conversation over lunch, he heard that his long absence had been very heavy for the rest of the team. To avoid more absenteeism, a first written warning was placed on his HR file. |

| Good | Not so good |
| --- | --- |
| A fatal accident occurred with one of the team members. The team manager took time to discuss this with the team. During working hours, team members were given time off to visit the deceased's family. Together, the team prepared a remembrance for the funeral, during which frequent attention was paid to what happened. There was a warm bond between the team and relatives of the deceased. Colleagues of other teams, who had often collaborated with the deceased, showed care and support for the team in various ways. This created a particularly intense connection. | An organization was faced with a fatal industrial accident to one of its employees. The directors were in shock because an investigation had been started to identify possible negligence by the organization. So none of them took time to face the issue and reflect upon it and its consequences for everyone involved. This created great distrust between the workers and the directors. The workers unconsciously put the blame for the death at the feet of the directors This issue was never properly aired or discussed and is still a source of stress and distrust within the organization. |

| Good | Not so good |
|---|---|
| A complete business unit was put in the shop window because the parent company wanted to sell-off their product lines. When it became clear who the new owners were, the unit director organized a two-day workshop for all his people. He gave them the space to discuss how they wanted to work together in the unit's final months. Attention was given to how to say goodbye, especially to those who would be the first to leave, and also to what people would take with them and leave behind (experiences, memories, colleagues, skills, etc.). What could have caused depression, instead gave people power and hope. | A heavy explosion caused severe damage to an organization's heavy-equipment storage area, resulting in huge financial losses. As soon as everything was rebuilt and replaced, there was tremendous pressure to make up for lost sales. The company prided itself on its safety and security but, under the pressure to recoup losses, safety regulations were ignored. The workers identified numerous dangerous practices, all due to the desire of management to increase production. Their attempts to communicate this were ignored and even called obstructive. Their commitment and sense of belonging fell below zero and an atmosphere of cynicism developed around the disconnect between the companies (advertised) values of safety and the reality for the workers. The relationship between employees and the organization had taken a damaging blow. |

Alongside knowledge and capabilities, time and resources are also important considerations when recovering from a significant negative event. Scarcity of either of these can hamper different aspects of the recovery process. It is crucial that we understand how a lack of, or not enough, time or resources can impact the people involved. When people feel there isn't enough of either, they can find little or no strength to take appropriate restorative action. For example, people under pressure are less careful with and for each other, in spite of the fact that empathy, a listening ear, space for emotions and mutual understanding are natural in all of us. Ensuring that employees have 'official' slack time or leeway in their goals and projects, and a budget for extra support when necessary, are crucial elements in helping an organization to stay out of the Trauma Trap. This is proven to add value to the normal, daily functioning of an organization. Unfortunately, organizations adhering to the principles of lean and mean have slimmed-down so much that the basic conditions for staying out of the Trauma Trap are often no longer present. In this case, there is almost no resilience, which means these organizations are much more easily overwhelmed. It is primarily short-term thinking on the part of management that causes this crucial recovery potential to be lost. An organization working under these conditions becomes fragile rather than strong and resilient.

Whatever the situation, it is vital that an organization becomes fully operational again in the shortest possible time. We are often unaware of how vulnerable our society actually is, because we are used to everything running smoothly. Only when there is a strike or a power outage, do we feel how precarious things really are. Most people only keep enough food at home for a few days. Just two or three days without electricity would paralyze our society. If the garbage would not be collected for a few weeks, we'd be, literally, in deep shit. The functioning of many organizations is directly linked to the functioning of our society and vice versa. Getting back-to-business quickly, without creating unnecessary pressure on the organization and its people, (those who are still available) are fundamentally important aspects of emergency and crisis management. This became very clear for business people and families travelling after the recent attacks on, for example, the airports of Brussels and Istanbul.

In addition to a short-term recovery plan, there is also need for long-term planning.  Once back into the daily routine, people or teams who are still (or permanently) affected by an overwhelming event, soon understand that space for their experiences – and for processing them – is getting smaller and smaller.  Conversely, while recovering there will be many lessons that can be integrated into the day-to-day operations. This can help to build a more resilient organization. This will become clear in Chapter 9.

It is important, too, that these lessons are integrated into the organization's planning for future disasters or overwhelming events. Often, in our haste, we overlook these learning opportunities.  Being prepared is not just about avoiding a fall but, in the words of Frank Sinatra, about learning how "*to pick yourself up and get back in the race*".

Over the years we have also gathered crucial insight into what happens when an organization or government is negligent in the recovery phase. In doing so, they become kind of a passive perpetrator with regard to potential traumatic events such as floods, forest fires, earthquakes, epidemics and so on.

## 6.4  Steps 4 & 5: Testing and refining the plan

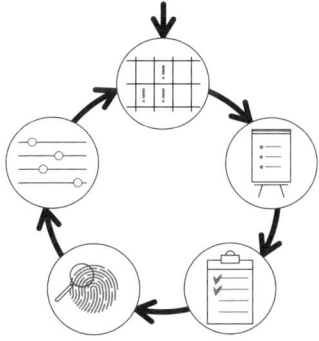

*Figure 47: Steps for an effective emergency and crisis management plan*

Once most things are in place, it's time for briefings, training sessions and exercises: to see if the plans work. Only then can it become clear how attention to the smallest details can make an incredibly big difference.

Additionally, if such exercises are well established, they have a positive effect on the overall level of collaboration in an organization. It makes the organization more efficient and resilient and strengthens the relational fabric throughout the organization.

This putting into practice will help to further refine your response and recovery plan based on new insights, new experiences and changing circumstances. Those will bring you back to the first step, the threat/vulnerability matrix.

## 6.5 In conclusion

Let's take all of the insights mentioned in this chapter and incorporate them into our Trauma Formula:

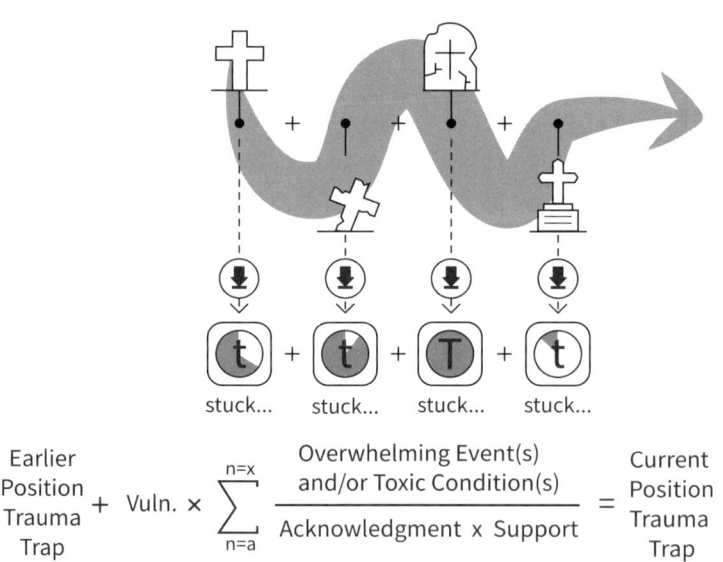

$$\text{Earlier Position Trauma Trap} + \text{Vuln.} \times \sum_{n=a}^{n=x} \frac{\text{Overwhelming Event(s) and/or Toxic Condition(s)}}{\text{Acknowledgment} \times \text{Support}} = \text{Current Position Trauma Trap}$$

*Figure 48: Trauma Formula 2.0*

- At the moment of the disaster or overwhelming event, where was the organization (department or team) in the Trauma Trap?

- In what way was the organization already vulnerable at that moment and what kind of support was missing at those moments?  If an organization neglected certain threats, it could end up in the position of passive perpetrator.

- How large was the impact (minor – noticeable – severe – devastating), taking into account that this will have been influenced by the vulnerability of the organization and its starting position in the Trauma Trap.

- Is the company capable of giving space to feelings and emotions or does 'it' prefer getting back to business a.s.a.p.?  This would block support and acknowledgement.

- Is the organization ready to provide adequate support and prepared to do the necessary follow-up (= recovery plan)?

- Is the organization open to all the dimensions impacted by a potentially traumatic event or do they only provide care for individual and physical-medical consequences?

Relevant questions.  Not to procrastinate, but to avoid adding unnecessary weight to the organization's backpack.

# Processing and releasing toxins

Earlier in the book a comparison was made between an organization and a fishtank via their shared need for regular cleaning. In this chapter we'll explore this more deeply. When reading this chapter, it is worth bearing in mind that toxins are not intrinsically negative; they are the waste products of the healthy functioning of organisms and living systems:

- After intense physical activity, the lactic acid (toxins) that has built up in an athlete's muscles is massaged away via the lymphatic system. Without this aftercare, recovery time lengthens and the risk of injury increases.

- A detox de-acidifies your body. After one, you can see and feel the difference. Part of ageing is the process of acidification.

- Spring water has a relatively high pH (more alkaline). The further the water supply is from the source, the lower the pH (more acidic). The cycles of evaporation, rain and the flow through natural mineral deposits clean and alkalize spring water.

In short, toxin build-up is an inevitable by-product, as it were, of living. The extent to which toxins are processed and released – rather then the extent to which they are avoided – determines whether an organism or living system will remain healthy. If particular circumstances produce more toxins, then more must be channeled, otherwise they will accumulate. Often we pay very little attention to what causes toxins, let alone to their processing.

## 7.1 How to deal with toxins

Trauma-informed working with organizations means that you have to learn to deal with toxins. Because of its importance, we are devoting a complete chapter to this. After all, it is toxins that make the relational fabric of an organization more vulnerable and, in the worst case, drag it into the Trauma Trap. In the accompanying diagram we can see four ways of identifying and dealing with the presence of toxins in groups or organizations:

- The horizontal axis of this diagram is about the degree to which you do or do not have a 'feel' for the invisible fabric of connections between people, groups, departments and so on. This might sound strange to you – after all, you haven't picked up this book by chance – but for some people that fabric is not there.

- The vertical axis is about how you approach toxins. Are they difficult and best avoided or a natural part of development and change. If the latter, then you can learn to use toxins as valuable information and a key to working with living systems.

This brings us to four quadrants from which you can act. Mind you, it is also common to work your way through each of the quadrants and there is nothing wrong with that. One day you might feel a bit fitter than another. Use this model to become more aware of the place from which you work and learn what you need to develop. This will help you to work from the most appropriate quadrant according to the situation you're in.

## 7.2 The four quadrants

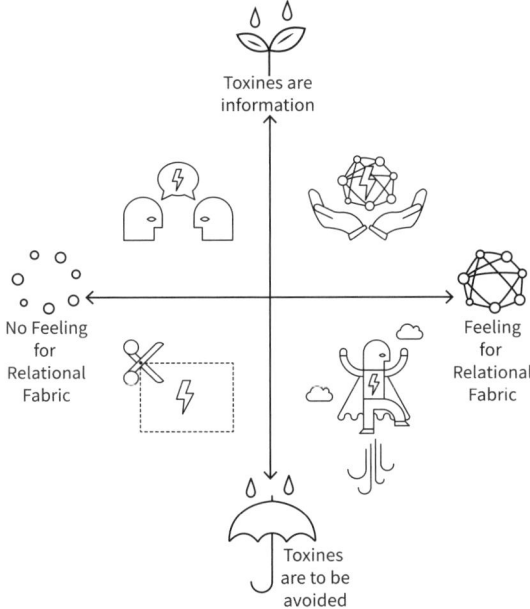

*Figure 49: Different ways of dealing with toxins*

**Q1: The Fixer**

You'll find yourself in this quadrant if you – perhaps temporarily – have no feel for, or are unable to perceive, the relational fabric and the build-up of toxins. This quadrant is not a good place from which to start working with organizational trauma. If you are stuck here, you probably need to take a break or develop more sensitivity for the subtleties of the relational dimensions of organizations.

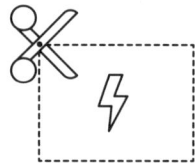

*Figure 50: The fixer*

If you work from this quadrant you are:

- Likely to want to eliminate, to resolve or, in the most extreme cases, to ignore symptoms of toxin build-up. Because you don't really care, or it's too much for you at that moment because you are not emotionally available to what's happening around you.

- More likely to perceive a critical employee as a whiner, rather than someone speaking in the interests of the whole.

- Likely to try to solve troublesome issues as quickly as possible by 'removing' the symptom rather than looking for what it is pointing at. This is like turning off the fire alarm, rather than looking for the fire. Or like approaching the issue as if it were a machine malfunction, but usually not when working with people and groups. The solving-the-problem-quickly approach tends to shift the symptom somewhere else or make it change shape and appearance.

- Lose the feedback contained in the proverbial cry-for-help from the living system. This results in toxins not being processed and settling in the deeper or hidden layers of the organization. As the saying goes, out of sight is out of mind… but still there.

**Q2: The Savior**

*Figure 51: The savior*

When you start from here, you have already taken a big step towards working effectively with organizational trauma.

- You start to recognize that symptoms can be signals or cries from the living system and you can take a broader perspective or zoom out.

- Because you see toxins as difficult for others to work with (e.g. the employees), you try to dissolve them.  Often this happens because you are either too involved, too empathetic or because you don't take your time to coach others in dealing with toxins. Hence, we call this the quadrant of the 'savior'.

- Because you act without enough forethought you run the risk of giving insufficient space to self-reliance and, consequently, you inhibit emergence.

- If you work from this quadrant, people and groups can start to become dependent upon you.  If there is organizational trauma, the chances are that you will be sucked into the role of 'perfect parent' or 'heroic leader' – as already mentioned in Part II – until it turns out that you cannot fix it either. So we see that starting from this quadrant can be a pitfall when working with organizational trauma, as this stagnates the development or healing of a group. It becomes an obstacle to self-reliance, resilience and antifragility. Only when you can allow the tension within the group to exist and, especially, resist the temptation to act, can you create a healing space for groups.

**Q3: The Healer of Parts**

*Figure 52: The healer of parts*

The big change here is the move from Fixer/Savior to Healer. Important as this is, you are still absorbed by individual issues (zooming-in) rather than the collective (zooming-out). Developing your systemic perception will be a great support here.

- Working from here, you now allow toxins to surface, but you are, as yet, inclined to associate them with the person or group manifesting them, rather than zooming-out and putting them in the larger context. A question for you might be "*Is this telling me something about the person (part) or the organization (whole)?*"

- You are able to work with a team for which a particular problem rears its head repeatedly. But, working from this quadrant, you will tend to keep looking for a solution within the boundaries of the team, while the most crucial keys might lie outside of it.

- We recognize this in the way a lot of companies deal with burnout. Sometimes, the care offered to an individual is adequate. But often, when burnout is a symptom of organizational malfunctioning, not enough care is provided. Limiting support to the individual level will not solve the problem in those cases.

- If there actually is organizational trauma and you are working from this quadrant, it might well stay under your radar.

Learning to see parts (zooming-in) and the whole (zooming-out) is the key to moving from this quadrant to the next. Often you're invited into a company as a facilitator to work on the level of a (malfunctioning) part – which could be a person, a team or a department. In that case, one of the most useful things to do is to guide your client into looking at the issue through a systemic lens.  If that person was stuck in the Fixer quadrant, then your work began in that first meeting.

> **Don't get involved in partial problems, but always take flight to where there is a free view over the whole single great problem, even if this view is still not a clear one.**
>
> Ludwig Wittgenstein

**Q4: The Healer of Wholes**

*Figure 53: The healer of wholes*

It often takes years of personal and professional development to be able to work from this quadrant.  It does need substantial amounts of equanimity – being calm and composed in challenging circumstances. Fortunately, there are more and more facilitators and leaders who see themselves as an instrument for this kind of work and, consequently, are willing to do the necessary healing work on themselves.

- If you work from this quadrant, you see toxins as information; feedback from the living system.

- You work consciously with and on the relational fabric, even when, for example, you have a difficult conversation with one individual. You understand that the effects of this conversation will spread to the employee's entourage anyway.

- As you now see toxins as an unavoidable by-product of living systems, you address them much earlier, preventing them sinking into the deeper layers of the organization.

- You are willing to engage with toxins because you've learned that they can contain valuable lessons. Think back to the chapter about the fact that there are often capabilities trapped in Trauma Capsules.

- You see emotions and toxins as neither more nor less than energy in motion, which you know becomes more toxic if ignored or suppressed. Essentially, you have let go of labeling emotions as either 'good' or 'bad'.


**Out beyond ideas of
wrongdoing and rightdoing
there is a field. I'll meet
you there.**

Rumi


An experienced facilitator is able to work from this quadrant but can, just as easily, get stuck in one of the other three quadrants if he loses his resilience. In any case, this is the quadrant from which you are most effective in working with organizational trauma. What makes you a consistently effective facilitator – for these kinds of radical processes – is caring for yourself in such a way that you are, and remain, emotionally available to anyone and everyone that is down in the Trauma Trap. Processing and releasing your own toxins, old and new, is the key to working effectively from this quadrant.

## 7.3 The difference between Healing and Fixing

There are significant differences between healing and fixing. Let's take a moment to compare these paradigms.

Fixing or repairing is ideal for mechanical/technical/technological problems where:

- There is a clear, identifiable cause.

- One or more solutions are relatively easy and quick to implement (e.g. replacing a broken part of a machine).

- Usually an expert or authority will be involved.

- There is an active party that intervenes and a more-passive party who receives or undergoes some process or intervention. There is rarely any resistance. Usually everyone involved is simply happy that the problem gets solved.

- There is no, or limited, influence from other factors or parties, making it easy to define the problem.

Healing falls more into the category of developing, coping and adjusting:

- With (organizational) trauma it is not always easy to isolate a clear, unambiguous cause, let alone to arrive at a clear, unambiguous solution.

- Healing requires psycho-emotional work such as processing emotions, learning new skills, embracing new values and beliefs.

- There is no manual. Every situation is unique. The 'art' of the facilitator goes beyond just expertise. It asks for a special way of being present.

- In this case, the people involved must do the 'work'. Nobody can do it for them. Trying, for example, to 'stand-in' for another just blocks their development and healing.

- Healing cannot follow a step-by-step plan, because you are working in a field of mutual dependence and mutual influence. There is an important relational component. For example, the entourage of one or more victims can be involved in such a way that the victim just does not want or feel free to start or try anything to start the healing process. With healing, there are often many more factors or parties that can help or hinder. That is why healing requires systemic perception.

- Healing is about searching; embracing trial and error. There are no quick fixes.

In the case of organizational trauma, if the management seems to be stuck in a fixer mindset, it is unlikely that the right type of support will be offered. And if you have been invited in as a facilitator, it is very likely that you will find yourself being sucked into the role of a fixer too. In concrete terms this could mean that after just one intervention – e.g. with a team – the management will already expect a solution. Or you could even experience that they are not inclined to see or accept their contribution to the problem situation and/or their responsibility to contribute to the recovery process. They prefer staying at a distance and letting you fix the problem. This can have a negative effect on attempts to restore balance and resilience. Victims, for example, sometimes remain in pain until acknowledgment and/or apologies are made. In the case of organizational trauma, a part of the origin can indeed rest with the management. This is also discussed in more detail in the next chapter. In concrete terms, this means that as a facilitator, you will also need to guide the relevant stakeholders into the correct quadrant. An apology from the fixer quadrant will have a completely different effect than an apology from the healer quadrant. Real healing is much more than words.

## 7.4 From Fixer to Healer

Earlier in this chapter we encountered the word equanimity (staying calm and composed in difficult situations or when faced with strong emotions). Calm and composed does not mean distant and cold. On the contrary, you are very involved and connected, able to feel into the situation without being overcome and hampered by anyone's emotions, including your own. Stephen Gilligan – in his book *The Courage to Love* (Gilligan, 1997, [14]) – calls it 'Feeling it, but not becoming it'. So, as a facilitator, you become a reliable container for strong, difficult or confusing emotions and information: able to bear or endure them through whatever it takes. Here is perhaps the most fundamental difference between a fixer and a healer. The following two examples make this difference very clear.

> *You are leaving with your family on vacation. The luggage is in the car with the rest of the family when you hear on the news that there is a massive traffic jam en route to the airport. While the rest of the family waits in the car, your youngest son tries to tie his shoelaces. He feels the agitation of the rest of the family, which does not help him to stay calm. After all, he can't do more than just tie his laces. Do you feel the tension in your gut? Can you endure it? Or does it take over. 'Forcing' you to quickly tie his laces yourself … to get rid of your own tension.*

> *You are a new team manager, chairing a team meeting. Your team has been struggling for some time with a number of difficult cases, because they are not yet trained or used to tackling them as a team. While they – in your opinion – are beating around the bush, you see a solution. Can you feel the tension arising in your body? Can you endure this tension and give your team enough room and some coaching to develop as a team, or do you just take over (complaining later to your colleagues that your team is so dependent on you)?*

As you can deduce from these everyday examples, the difference between a fixer and a healer lies in the physical or somatic dimension. If you are confronted with a problem, or something that you would like solved or put into place, tension arises in your body. Often we are not really aware of the fact that solving this problem has both an internal component (getting rid of the tension) and an external component (solving the problem). As a facilitator, you must learn to notice this internal tension and learn to accept, endure or contain it. Only in this way you can give others the space to do it themselves or to learn how to do it. As you become more skilled at this, your tension-carrying capacity increases. It is not possible to become a good facilitator without developing this ability. This is also the reason why some managers remain trapped in the fixer quadrant and stay (unconsciously) problem solvers, inhibiting the development of their employees, teams or even the whole organization.

In addition, as the facilitator working with organizational trauma, it is important to know that traumatized groups or people can activate all sorts of emotions and tensions in you.  These emotions and tensions can and sometimes will suck you into the roles of fixer, rescuer or perpetrator.  When this happens, you become part of the dysfunctional dynamic or, even worse, could make it stronger.  You won't be able to avoid this, so there's no need to be hard on yourself, you are only human.  But being aware of this is crucial to developing your capacity to hold a safe space, to create a container for the work. It starts with you.

Here is another example from everyday life that can help you to train this ability.

> *Growing children try different ways to get what they want. You had agreed with your partner to put your foot down:* "Home by midnight.  That's the deal!" *And yet, fifteen minutes later, your adolescent son or daughter manages to extend the deadline by an hour. It really isn't so difficult to influence someone if you know what his or her sensitivities are.*

We see, again, that when you're working with organizational trauma, it is particularly important to be in touch with what is happening to you in the interaction, in the here-and-now.  This is called phenomenological observation.  At its essence, it is the ability to constantly put your awareness on what is happening in your body while you are facilitating or while you are thinking about the group you are facilitating.  Continuous development of this kind of awareness, and regular exploration of your body as a sensor, is a core aspect of being able to work with organizational trauma.  You might want to try practicing this as you go through the coming days.

## 7.5  Creating a healing space

Once your ability to 'contain' difficult emotions starts to grow, this will be mirrored by a similar growth in your ability to give others the space to heal.  This is called (a) Holding Space and you begin by creating it for individuals and, as you progress, step by step, you'll be able to create this kind of healing space for larger and larger groups.

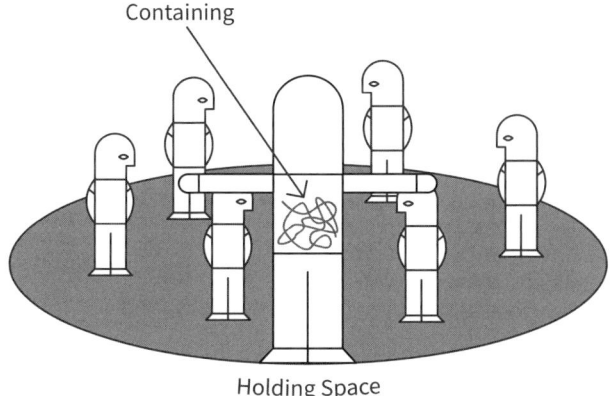

Containing

Holding Space

*Figure 54: Containing and holding space*

Bit by bit, it becomes clear that a fixer can be very active but at the same time very counterproductive, especially when dealing with the dynamics of groups and organizations. A healer, on the other hand, can also appear passive, while he or she is actually working extremely hard. The art is in knowing when you should do something and to what degree. Both fixer and healer can be appropriate depending on the context.

Earlier in the book, the Trauma Cube showed us that healing occurs on four layers: spiritual, mental, emotional and physical. So a good healing space must provide for all four layers. This stands in stark contrast to many organizations, where conversations are often confined to the mental, in the form of rational arguments. That usually has a counterproductive effect when working with organizational trauma, as those affected by it are usually looking for acknowledgment. So creating a space for healing, initially asks a lot from the facilitator, whose main responsibility is to keep the space intact and safe for everyone involved. When that happens, the self-regulating or self-healing power of a living system naturally arises. It is as if life begins to flow back through the damaged relational fabric. You can actually feel this happening and, almost immediately, 'see' the traces of healing as the warp and the weft of the relational fabric knit themselves back into wholeness. This is precisely the difference between healing and fixing, yet often we are far better trained and educated to do the latter.

As a facilitator of group processes – especially if organizational trauma is present – you will need to keep an eye on your tendency to want to fix.

One final comparison that fits within this framework is how a wound usually heals by itself if it is regularly disinfected and protected. The body does the rest of the work – as long as a number of conditions are met. When working with organizational trauma, the facilitator tries to create, monitor and maintain the conditions necessary for the self-healing ability, present in every living system, to do its work.

In addition to phenomenological observation/perception (i.e. deep listening, somatic awareness and being attentive to the relational fabric), there are a number of characteristics that are central to creating a safe healing space:

- Put your trust in emergence, a natural feature of living systems. Do not think about solutions, but give the living system – for example via one of the parties (or parts) involved – the chance to show you in which direction healing can start. This asks for surrender and letting go of control.

- Try to be alert, and present in the here and now. The more the people involved feel or notice this in you, the safer they will feel. The fact that you are visibly very alert increases everyone's sense of security. It ensures that you can intervene at precisely the right moment and it shows your involvement and attention.

- Open your heart, be transparent and authentic and allow yourself to be touched. Try to connect with all present. Some facilitators try to be objective by being distant, but that often leaves people feeling unrecognized. Try to empathize with everyone's perspectives without merging with them. Mediators call this a 'multi-party biased' attitude.

- Try to avoid judging, condemning, criticizing, disapproving or accusing. A judgment immediately splits the healing container in two; specifically into what is allowed to be said and what is not. This often blocks-off certain paths or possibilities and, rather than support greater connection, it causes further fragmentation, which you then have to spend valuable time and energy restoring.

- Be open to different opinions and ideas. Some ideas are really just participants testing your openness. Only when you deal with them respectfully, do people bring in what really concerns them. You can compare it to a brainstorming session. The first ten ideas might not be usable, but they bring a group closer both to each other and to a useful direction.

In essence, a facilitator is very consciously present. It is a question of being, rather than doing. People starting-out as facilitators, and learning to walk this path of being, often notice how quickly they want to solve the other's problems. However, by simply being present you will register all the relevant layers of communication: you hear what is being said, you sense the emotions, you feel the energy in the space, you register the patterns of interaction, you hear the cries of distress from the relational fabric, you notice when the (trauma) dynamic is re-activated or when a Trauma Capsule appears at the surface.

> *A consultant went to work with the operational team of a fruit processing company – that had been in the red for some time – and was struggling with the clear tension between the employees and the management. When the first session opened, there was absolutely no connection between the different participants. Communication was evasive and judgmental. After some time, one of the employees suggested that there could be more space for innovation. The consultant immediately felt the energy in the room change. Things felt brighter. A colleague responded to the suggestion and, suddenly, the atmosphere changed and people started talking to each other.*

> *When the consultant carefully described what he saw happening, one of the participants began to speak about the company's founder. He was the epitome of innovation and he always succeeded in launching new products and ideas in the organization. That always led to growth and profit. After the company was taken over, and a number of managers and directors had left, there was no longer any space for innovation. The totem (or soul component) of the organization was completely lost. According to those present, profits were funneled into bonuses for the management instead of being invested in the*

*future. That was completely at odds with the company's original ethos.*

*Once this familiar issue was out in the open, everyone started to talk about it together. The conversation was a bit rocky at first but after some time the atmosphere seemed to have completely shifted. It took a long time before the team was in the right condition to avoid falling back into old patterns. But, by following the path of emergence, as indicated by the living system, the organization gradually dragged itself out of the Trauma Trap.*

## 7.6 People as sensors

Horses – but also other species – increase their chances of survival through living in herds, because – when in the herd – they can feel everything that happens between and around them. A herd of horses registers much more – at all times and in all directions – than a single horse can. Horses are especially, and necessarily, sensitive to this intra-herd communication, because survival of the herd is contingent upon any sign of danger that is picked up by one horse, being immediately passed on to the rest of the herd. This ability is becoming particularly relevant to organizations operating in our rapidly changing, complex world. After all, in order to be mobile and flexible, organizations must be able to function as integrated units where all aspects of the organization are kept optimally connected. Classically-designed organizations are too static and compartmentalized in terms of structures, positions, procedures, scales, budgets and so on and, all too often, this is reinforced by the legislative framework within which organizations have to fit. So there is also work to do at the political and socio-legal levels.

When the design – especially the structures, the processes and the division of roles – of a well-functioning organization starts to become defective, people soon notice this. But, because the design is static, a subtle process of negation, denial and/or suppression starts. After all, it took a lot of time and effort to build it up. The theoretical or paper design of the organization and the informal or more effective design of the organization gradually grow apart.

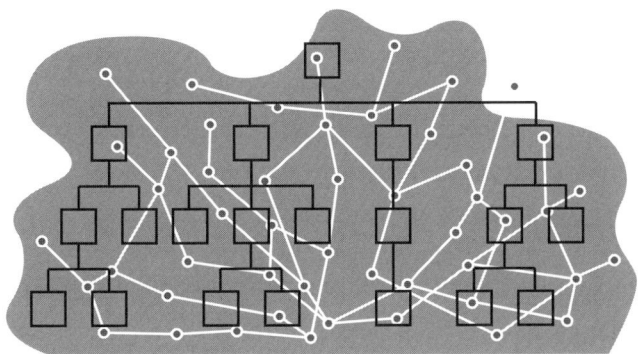

*Figure 55: Formal and informal organization*

And why would an employee risk flagging a need for change? Due to the static nature of the organization, this could make the employee feel exposed or vulnerable and open to ridicule. So the subtle stimuli, that could help the organization to keep evolving, quickly get stuck somewhere between the point of sensing and the point of reacting elsewhere in the organization. In short, the need for change is noticed and registered but never gets to the people who can do something about it. So these ideas, these opportunities, these stimuli endlessly circle round the minds of the employees. They are so busy with these thoughts and their inability to do anything with them, that they cease to be sensors. After all, nobody feels good when they can see tangible opportunities for progress and, at the same time, see no chance of progress. The best thing an employee can then do is to shut down his sensors and ignore these opportunities. In that way he only picks up what could be translated through the organization's structures – which is usually not that much – so the organization becomes even more rigid. It is strange too, almost funny in a way, to hear classic organizations complain that their people are so inflexible, oblivious to the fact that it is the organization's design, it's working structures that afford employees no space for flexibility, initiative or creativity. The organization sees the problem but is blissfully unaware that the problem is the organization. In the end, its people become insensitive, rigid and unmotivated, because their natural gift – to sense what is needed – is neither recognized nor valued.

*Client:* "I have a problem with the unit that you installed."
*Employee:* "Could you describe the problem a bit more accurately?"
*(Customer provides a detailed description of the problem.)*
*Employee:* "Sorry sir, but this issue is not registered as a problem that can occur with the unit we installed for you."

Can you imagine how you might feel, if your nervous system functioned like this? Because in essence, employees are sensory neurons feeding data back through the organization's nervous system. An organization functioning, as in the example above, alienates itself from the market and its management board from what is really going on in the company. This frustrates and demotivates teams and creates a fertile breeding ground for stress and toxins at all levels. An organization cannot function as an integrated whole if it does not learn how to integrate these stimuli in an effective and transparent way. And it is the design of the organization that is key to making this work. In recent years we have learned to see how the design of an organization can induce sinking into the Trauma Trap. This is one of the reasons this topic will be presented in this book's final chapter.

**A resilient system is able to respond appropriately
to both disturbances and opportunities.**

**Resilience**
**=**

**Quality of the Relational Fabric**
×
**Quality of the Sensors**

Classic or top-down managed organizations work in a totally different way compared to organizations that are ready for a rapidly-changing world. The latter approach their organization as a living system. A key asset in those companies is the relational fabric or wiring, through which their employees function as sensory neurons that continuously develop the living system based on sensing its internal and/or external needs. These organizations have learned that each employee has a feeling for a particular aspect of the organization's functioning. And they have also learned that it is impossible to process all that information centrally, so they ensure a certain degree of self-regulation is available to employees and teams. This is exactly what makes these organizations resilient.

Moreover, these organizations understand that toxins can contain valuable information: often they are the product of friction between what is and what could be. The process from friction to toxins has a number of steps. At first there is a vague feeling that something is not right. Then it becomes a permanent nagging feeling that endlessly points out a chance to improve or adjust something. If this is not processed, it will grow from irritation through anger, frustration, disbelief, sadness, … and in the end into apathy. A rigid system suppresses these stimuli until the system can no longer contain them and breaks down. A flexible, change-aware organization deals with this in a very different way:

- Employees who are very close to the market or the target group become external sensors (= exteroceptors). They feel the fit between the product/service and the target group and register changing needs or new opportunities during their daily activities. Their sensing is particularly important to the survival of the organization in its context.

- Then there are employees who are active in the production or value creation process; they are internal sensors (= interoceptors). They feel how smoothly, or not, processes run and where there is room, for example, for process improvements. Their sensing is particularly important to the smooth functioning of the organization's internal operations.

If the stimuli registered by employees can be processed without having to question the design of the organization, they will be dealt with within the current organizational structure. If, however, it turns out that the design of the organization is putting a brake on the integration of eventual solutions, they will identify and implement any necessary adjustments. This happens as low (hierarchically) as possible in the organization. It may involve shifting or adding responsibilities, creating new roles or adjusting a process, procedure or aspect of the structure. In short, the design of the organization follows the needs of the work, linked to the evolving needs of the target group or the market. This – design follows function – is an important condition to become an adaptable organization, a condition that is often overlooked.

By the way, the better the organization learns to process the impulses transmitted through these sensors and their wiring, the more accurate these sensors become and a virtuous circle is established, sustaining the organization as a living, integrated and adaptable system. Emergence automatically results from this.

> *A large, well-known producer of sporting goods designed a cutting-edge, high-tech logistics distribution center, installing everything needed to make it function as a living system. What they are doing is far-reaching: an integrated and integral system change. If employees on the production 'line' have a problem, they are expected to give a clear signal. All workspaces are arranged to make this easy. The goal is to get to work on the problem immediately – if that is possible – or to identify if the origin of the problem lies somewhere else and to start searching for it right away. This allows the organization to stay focused and to develop in an organic way, tuned-in to the unfolding future (emergence). This makes organizational development the interest and responsibility of everyone in the company.*

The major shift these kinds of companies are making, is learning to consciously and smartly use the natural process of toxin build-up, in order to keep the relational fabric healthy and to activate people in their capacity as sensors. Classical, top-down managed organizations do the opposite: unconsciously letting their toxins accumulate instead of translating them into useful adjustments. It requires a large shift for both staff and management to learn to work this way. It contradicts what they learned and requires a major change in everyone's mindset. In the past, we could hide behind the excuse that this was just not feasible. However, technological evolution over the last 10 years means that the only obstacle to it now, is lack of the will to implement it.

## 7.7 Daily mood-management

In Part II we saw that organizations perform better when they function far above the Trauma Trap. Creativity, empathy, joined-up communication, adaptability, internal or external customer orientation and problem-solving skills are abilities that thrive in that position, and are increasingly less available as an organization begins the slide down into the Trauma Trap. The success of organizations depends on the extent to which their structure supports these capacities to develop and be expressed. That is why taking care of the relational fabric of an organization is one of a leader's core tasks.

In groups or organizations that are sinking into the Trauma Trap, people tend to stimulate each other in negative ways and they (unconsciously) try to avoid disturbing any Trauma Capsules. This makes it pretty difficult to develop or adapt to new circumstances. It costs enough energy just to 'be'. Rigidity or chaos are both indicative of the start of this coping mechanism. And just like individuals, groups also need an ongoing practice that regulates their state of mind, their mood. This could be anything from team meditation, regular team check-ins or even a short break to play some ping pong or table soccer. This should not be a one-off, but a consciously initiated event, because the mood of a team directly determines its effectiveness. What daily hygiene is to our body, mood management is to the team's spirit; the term originated in Doc Children's book *From Chaos to Coherence* (Childre and Cryer, 1995, [7]) . Since groups – especially if the group has been recently formed – are not always able to regulate their 'communal' mood, making this a key responsibility of their manager is probably a good idea.

We all know the expression 'physician, heal thyself'. So, before the manager can help his team with mood management, he must be able to regulate his own moods. But so much can go wrong here. Many managers are so overwhelmed by their work that they hardly have time to take care of themselves, let alone their employees. Others have simply become laissez-faire (often under the guise of self-management). And others are simply not suited to working with people because they are much more focused on developing substantive and/or technical expertise. And all of this ensures that the relational fabric gets neither recognition nor attention.

In every situation, it is useful if the manager keeps in touch with the relational fabric for which he is responsible, whether that's the team, the department, the division, the entire organization, … so that even if damage to the fabric is not immediately repaired it is, at least, noticed.

For example:

- an employee who is suddenly confronted with a drastic problem in his family.
- an employee who cannot get to grips with the new software application.
- a conflict between two employees.
- an employee who appears to be heading for burn-out.
- unspoken tension associated with the manager himself.
- a lack of ongoing cooperation between teams, departments and/or disciplines.

The manager practising mood management prioritizes tensions in and between his staff, because he knows the negative impact those will have on the healthy functioning of the living system if they are not addressed. And whenever an organization or department undergoes a radical change, the need for mood management is essential.

> During a team coaching, the coach noticed that a particular issue had been occupying the team for years. When he polled the group about whether space was sometimes given to discussing functional problems, they replied that there was seldom ever time for this. During the debriefing, the coach discussed this with the team's manager. He responded: "I am not going to bother myself with all the hassle between them. I'm not their nanny". Step by step, it became clear that his posture was a kind of armor. Underneath the armor, the manager had no idea how to work with emotions and issues around relationships. Faced with his own vulnerability, he did not want to show his 'weakness' to his employees. So, unlike the previous case study, the relational fabric was a taboo subject.

If you, as a leader, are able to feel into what is going on between people, this is enough reason to call them together and clarify things, if and when that is needed. In organizations where mood management is common, a number of practices occur regularly:

- Teams – in some cases daily – take time out to talk about how things are going. Everyone gets a good overview of what's happening in the team and its relationships with the wider organization and the general mood of the team; 15 minutes is usually enough. And if something is 'wrong' the meeting can stretch to accommodate it.

- Meetings or gatherings start with a 'check-in' in which each participant briefly says how they are and what they need to say in order to be really present. Even this last practice can already be a big challenge in some organizations.

- There is a clear and agreed way of dealing with conflict, with various escalation levels. In the first phase, people are invited to solve it together, without support, in order to avoid support being needed for every situation, which would effectively diminish the self-regulating ability of people. If people cannot work it out together, they can call for help. Turning first to a colleague who has the trust of all involved, then to a manager and, ultimately, to the director of the department or organization.

*A large logistics organization opened a completely new distribution center. It was essential that the (new) working processes were implemented quickly as they should prepare the organization for expected, rapid growth in areas such as e-commerce. The new methods were very different to what the employees and the managers were used to. There had to be much faster role and task switching within and between teams and this asked for tremendous flexibility. A lot of time was invested in developing this new approach. Of course there were plenty of surprises during the implementation. That is why the management chose to hold a 'beer-crate session' every day, just before the lunch break. People gathered in a central location around an upside-down beer barrel and important information was exchanged. As a result, there was a great deal of commitment and involvement. This gave a kind of stability and meant is-*

*sues could be addressed almost immediately. Many thought it*
*a crazy idea when it was proposed, but it quickly became a cru-*
*cial component of the start-up phase.*

What has been described above – and illustrated in the example – is a combination of mutually-reinforcing tactics:

- A good balance of leadership and self-regulation.

- Attention – even priority – for tensions and the resulting toxins.

- Useful practices or small rituals throughout the working day.

- A collective belief regarding the added value of mood management to the overall functioning of the organization. It is universally accepted that the mood of an organization determines which capabilities will or will not manifest, just as with individuals.

The effect of all this is that toxins are detected and processed in a timely manner, which keeps the relational fabric resilient. For teams that see each other daily or regularly, this is fairly easy to organize. For teams that are geographically dispersed, there exist enough on-line tools to be able to work in a comparable way without having to come to the office. Many organizations now see such practices as crucial, rather than 'nice-to-do'.

## 7.8 Corporate Ceremonies & Rituals

Employees cannot be good sensors for the optimal functioning of the organization if toxins are not processed and released. To return to the metaphor of the fishtank: when the water gets dirty and toxins accumulate, the employees notice things too slowly or cannot report them. This is why the health of the relational fabric is so important. Arnold Mindell *Sitting in the Fire* (Mindell, 2014, [21]) uses the term 'third entity' (as already mentioned in Chapter 2). Thus he invites us to see the relational fabric as an entity, a crucial aspect of the living system that sits between everything and that needs much care and attention. Native people have built up a tremendous body of experience, over centuries, around keeping the relational fabric healthy. The survival of the tribe is directly linked to the quality of its relational fabric (remember the example of the horses). Those 'laws' – which they pass on from generation to generation – are called

LORE, as already mentioned earlier. Even more, for them LORE is equiva-lent to the man-made laws governing the 'civilized' world, that we know as our judicial or legal systems. In this book several examples are discussed where the application of civil LAW meant a negation of the LORE of one or more groups. Sometimes we get trapped in the illusion that a solution at the level of civil LAW also ensures fairness and recovery in the realm of LORE. But that is seldom the case. If, for example, the perpetrator of a crime is convicted, receiving a fine or a prison sentence (civil law), but does not acknowledge his guilt or give recognition to those to whom he caused pain (LORE), he blocks the victim's (and his own) healing process.

Ceremonies and rituals are practices that tribal peoples have devel-oped over centuries to keep the tribe's relational fabric healthy. A cere-mony is a formal occasion in which rituals, symbols, stories and so on are brought together to create a special moment, or memory, that is attuned to the purpose of the ceremony. This concept, of LORE – the wisdom ac-cumulated over lifetimes and handed down through rituals – has only re-cently been taken seriously by our Western civilization. In fact, during the age of colonialization, certain rituals were banned or made impossible to celebrate, causing serious disruption to the tribes in question.

Organizational leaders and managers, who can find inspiration in this 'ancient wisdom', can benefit immensely from it in their daily activities. Such organizations become much more attractive for employees and cus-tomers. They are the organizations that successfully crack the code that allows them to function as an integrated whole. In these organizations the third entity or relational fabric is cared for.

A way to recognize whether a manager is working with the relational fabric or not, is shown in the diagram below. On the left, all interaction goes through the manager, so very little happens that would build-up the relational fabric. On the right, the manager facilitates interaction in a way that is constantly developing the fabric. You might already have noticed how the diagram links to the four quadrants discussed at the beginning of this chapter: fixer – savior – healer of parts – healer of wholes.

There are two more aspects to bear in mind. First, the larger the group you work with, the larger the relational fabric. In this sense, a director of a large organization might shift his attention from the fabric between employees to the fabric between departments, disciplines, teams, hierarchical layers or even the fabric surrounding the organization: that which connects the company to certain partners, target groups or society. To do so, he must be able to feel into the quality of the relational fabric at different levels, which, in turn, requires the ability to zoom in and out. And it is also crucial that he is able (and willing) to work with the fabric when it is in good or bad shape. We often see product launches, birthdays or achieving targets being celebrated with formal rituals, but difficult events or episodes being mostly ignored. However, these too can be equally powerful connectors.

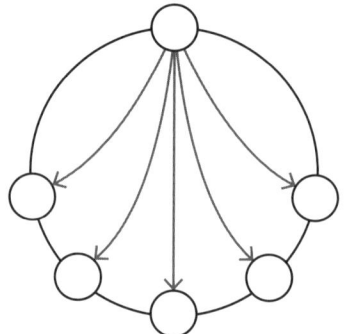          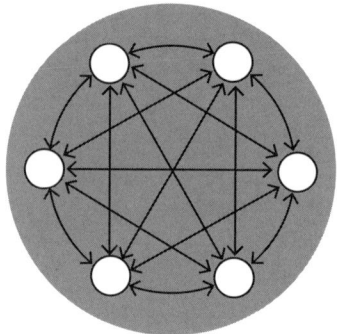

No development of               Development of the
relational fabric               relational fabric

Leaders and managers sometimes forget that their behavior has a kind of programming effect on the relational fabric and that this can occur through just one conversation with one employee. As soon as managers become aware of this, they understand that they affect the fabric more often than they might notice, and usually indirectly. Through this developing awareness they become guardians of the relational fabric in everything they do or radiate. We are talking here about moral power, a quality (and responsibility) embodied by people like Nelson Mandela. People with moral power inspire, compared to people with a more fear-based leadership style.

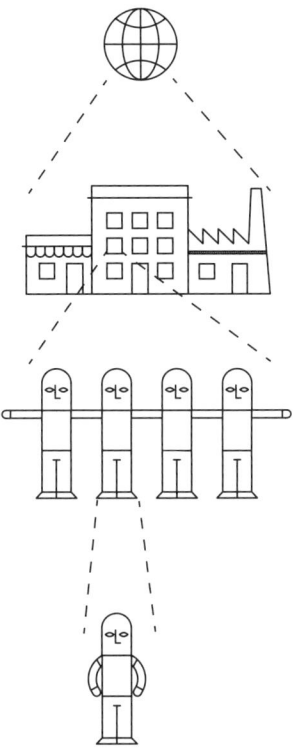

*Figure 56: Part – Whole visualization*

Ceremonies, rituals, stories and symbols – adapted to the zeitgeist and the individuality of an organization – seem logical methods to leaders that work with the relational fabric. All organizations are already full of formal and informal rituals. They are often an expression of the norms and values of the organization and a way of expressing the connection between individual, organization and society. If you want to get to know a new organization quickly, develop an eye for these rituals. They are an expression of the culture. Rituals are used in numerous circumstances:

- Transition rituals such as initiation, name changing or a new strategy.

- Farewell rituals: when employees leave, when the production of a certain machine ends, when the last of a particular model of car rolls off the production line or when a branch-office is shut-down.

- Reward rituals: promotions, closing new deals, anniversaries.

- Refresh rituals: to bring specific values back into regular use, to restore good habits that have been 'lost' or to revitalize the mission and vision.

- Rituals to process tensions and conflicts: in such a way that space is created for toxins and that these (potentially-toxic) tensions can be recognized and processed.

- Welcome rituals: to acknowledge membership, provide guidance during a takeover or to clarify the borders between members and non-members.

- Start rituals: such as inaugurations, openings, kick-offs, meeting check-in sessions and so on.

In short, rituals can strengthen and detoxify the relational fabric. They are mostly used to initiate and guide change or transformation but also to create stability.

What our experience shows is that it does not take much to bring the third entity of a group back to life. You really do not have to be a master of LORE. However, if LORE gets ignored, the flame can extinguish quickly. You have to feed a fire to keep it burning. That is why we – whether leader, manager or facilitator – must put more and more emphasis on what happens after our interventions. The frameworks and concepts provided in this book are intended to support this.

So we see that there are many possibilities for establishing nurturing and healing rituals. Keep in mind, however, that rituals require a particular kind of spirit and preparation, a certain attitude, especially from the people who play a leading or guiding role in facilitating them in the workplace. Without this stance, they easily can be experienced as sterile, soulless or hollow. Usually, facilitators do something specific to get themselves into the right energy. It is like a role they step mindfully into, just as a shaman puts on his ritual clothes before beginning the healing ritual.

Below are some examples of how toxins can be processed via cere-monies, or rituals, and how events – by handling them slightly differently – can be very nourishing. Lore in practice:

> *Some time ago a team leader received coaching on how to bet-ter organize his meetings. The coach started by observing a team meeting to get a baseline measurement. The team leader started by going through the agenda and told the team that a letter had been received from a customer to thank the team for the work they had done. At no time did the team leader make contact with his team. There was no emotion or spirit in his com-munication. He shared it as a robot might. There was no further response from the group and the meeting continued to wander aimlessly along. But two significant things had just happened: an opportunity had been missed to feed the relational fabric and the way it had been missed caused a build-up of toxins. Throwing away the letter and sharing the content with nobody would have done less harm. In that organization it seemed to be a part of the culture to pass up on opportunities to feed the relational fabric. The organization was slowly sinking in the Trauma Trap.*

Ceremonies are a way in which organizations can process the toxins built up during an overwhelming event, because space is given to express-ing and sharing emotions together. This can lead to communal cathar-sis, an emotional cleansing. Emotions arising in isolation, even when rec-ognized and accepted by an individual person like a therapist or coach, have a totally different effect than when they are allowed to arise and be shared in a group, especially when they are linked to a shared overwhelm-ing event.

> *Soon after the double bomb attack at Brussels Airport, when it had reopened and the first plane left, a ceremony was orga-nized. A symbolic choice, for the first flight, was made for the recently-unveiled Magritte aircraft from Brussels Airlines. "We will never give way to blind, barbaric terrorism. We will always come back stronger", said Marc Descheemaecker, Chairman of*

*the Board of Brussels Airport. "We are more than just 260 com-panies, more than just 20,000 employees: we are one close family", said Arnaud Feist, the airport's CEO, in a speech to the community. "Today, thanks to you, we can spread a message of hope. The reopening of passenger traffic is an important symbolic moment. We must show the world that we stand once more, stronger than ever."*

During ceremonies, stories are often used that combine symbols and rituals. It is important that everyone understands the symbols and rituals used. They form a kind of non-verbal language for a group, an expression of common values, ambitions and principles. Symbols can be visual like a logo, aural like a song, spatial like a certain historical place, or physical like a uniform or a badge of honor. All this works – after some time and if it is performed with the necessary spirit – as powerfully as triggers but in a positive, connecting way.

*A dynamic organization lost its initial focus through incredibly-rapid growth. Signals from the employees were ignored be-cause the numbers were fine. However, when it became clear that they were losing increasing numbers of old, loyal cus-tomers, it was accepted that something was wrong. The board of directors saw no option but to appoint a new director. The first thing she did was to start looking for the company's 'roots'. During her explorations, she repeatedly bumped up against symbols from the founding period that, unfortunately, had fallen out of the picture. Everyone was holding their breath waiting for the new director's first speech. But when she came into the room, carrying one of the original founding symbols, the energy went through the roof.*

It is true; this is anything but rational. But it shows us the difference between LAW and LORE. However, reading between the lines, we can see that people do not do what they think, they do what they feel. The era in which employees have to leave emotions at home is coming to an end. The truth is they never did, they just suppressed them, because that's what the company expected. That costs so much energy and stretches the relational fabric of the organization to breaking point. As described earlier, for a time, organizations were able to manage without caring for that fabric. But now that way of structuring and managing an organization is looking rather 'old'.

No need to give yourself a headache trying to put together a ceremony or a ritual. You are on the right track as long as you ensure you have a clear goal, a defined start, an intermediate phase – in which the ritual is performed – and a clear ending. As Jim Collins says in *Good to great* (Collins, 2011, [9]) get the right people on the bus and, before you know it, you will have more good ideas than you know what to do with. This knowledge is engraved in our collective unconscious and has been part of humanity for centuries.

> *Steve Jobs was a master in working with ceremonies, speeches, symbols and rituals. When Macintosh became too bureaucratic, he moved to a new location and set a pirate flag to flutter on the new building. When it was time to replace the operating system MAC OS 9, he did so very definitely, by using a black coffin and speaking a funeral eulogy as a symbol. He established an annual ritual to show Apple's latest innovations to the world. And when we think of him, he is always in Steve's 'suit': jeans and turtleneck sweater.*

## 7.9 Insights about Grief Processing

If toxins are not processed, they begin to cluster. This does not immediately lead to organizational trauma but it can push an organization nearer to the Trauma Trap. That is why working with toxins requires insight into the nature and course of the mourning process. A model, often seen in the context of change and transition training for managers, is the mourning curve developed by Elisabeth Kübler-Ross. The curve illustrates how the emotions that accompany change and crisis evolve through time. In recent years, this model has become increasingly disputed because it originated in the context of people in their dying process. Translating the model to transitions in organizations, however, requires some nuancing and, thanks to those people who are working with grief every day, a lot of new insights have been gained:

- Mourning and processing do not necessarily follow a series of successive, identifiable phases with standard characteristics, but are unique to each person.

- Mourning and processing are not just an intra-psychic private process, but also a relational, social and interactive process with which an organization can do something in a collective context, for example in the form of corporate ceremonies and rituals.

- Mourning and processing has been focused, too much, on 'getting over it', 'solving', 'rounding off', 'going back to how it used to be' or 'something that you have to get rid of'. People (and groups) are changed by an overwhelming event. They do not return to how it was before the event and the event can, from time to time, raise its head again. That does not have to be a problem if it can be dealt with in an acknowledging manner. Exactly here is a crucial difference between stress and trauma (as we already discussed with the Trauma Cube).

- Mourning and processing were often erroneously reduced to a confrontation with painful emotions, while they have the potential for so much more than that.

These insights are crucial, because sometimes people in organizations believe – often with the best of intentions – that people have to be guided through phases, as if they are a 'project'. However, this approach, so trusted by organizations, can be seriously damaging to individuals and groups. How, you might be wondering? Well, employees whose behavior does not match a particular phase of the model are often then judged to 'have a problem'. Showing positive emotions in a phase where, especially, negative emotions are expected, is often seen as resisting or repressing the grieving process. But for some employees their pain can appear much later. Men and women – simple as this generalization is – do turn out to have different ways of mourning. Confronting their emotions might well work for one person, but not for another. So every grieving process is unique.

*A far-reaching merger with many employee changes released a lot of emotions. A large meeting was organized, every four months, with all the employees, to discuss the current situation and to agree the next steps.  These meetings were intended to support the integration process.  Space was always and regularly given for reflection on the emotions that were still working through the organization.  While quite a number of employees needed this space for a prolonged period, after a while the majority felt ready to leave the merger behind and to move forward in the new organization.  When this became clear, it was decided that the 'grieving space' needed no longer to be a part of the large meetings.  Naturally, given the uniqueness of mourning, a number of people and teams found this difficult and so received individual support and monitoring, separate from the organization-wide approach.*

A much more-informed approach, which is certainly relevant in the context of organizational trauma, sees that mourning and processing do not go in phases. They are part of a fluctuating process that oscillates between two poles:

- Towards one pole the focus is more on the impact of the major event, through which contact is made with painful emotions, and feelings are expressed and shared, and the 'new' reality is accepted. Please bear in mind that our deep-seated assumptions about safety, security, trust, integrity, justice, solidarity, respect and connection can be abruptly damaged by a major event or prolonged, unhealthy working conditions.

- Towards the other pole the focus is that life and work just go on as usual. In this case, more attention will be paid to integrating learning for the future, adapting where necessary and/or possible, starting new initiatives and celebrating progress and new successes. Here, the tendency is to create distractions from the pain. Distraction differs from denial or repression because people remain aware of what happened to them.

Therefore, working in a balanced way with both poles and valuing and accepting what arises during the process, is crucial for processing toxins – whether or not there is a link to organizational trauma. Each situation is unique and requires a unique approach.

## 7.10 In conclusion

To complete this chapter, let's take another look at the Trauma Formula. Take this chance to look more closely at the different factors of the formula.

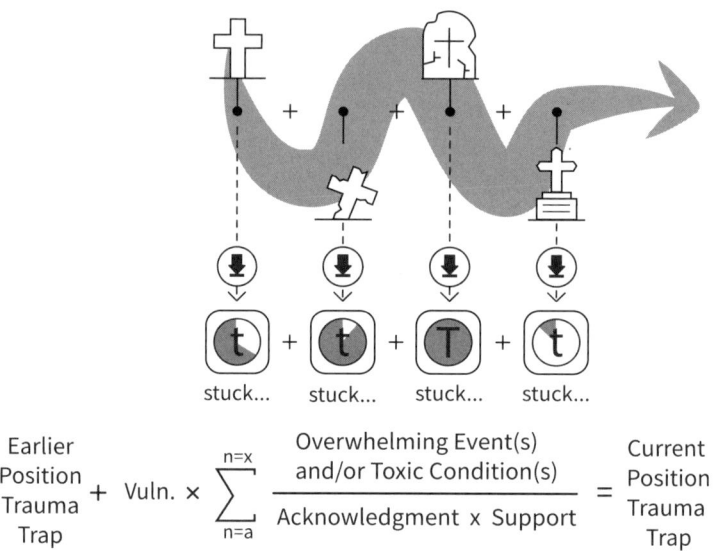

$$\begin{matrix} \text{Earlier} \\ \text{Position} \\ \text{Trauma} \\ \text{Trap} \end{matrix} + \text{Vuln.} \times \sum_{n=a}^{n=x} \frac{\begin{matrix}\text{Overwhelming Event(s)} \\ \text{and/or Toxic Condition(s)}\end{matrix}}{\text{Acknowledgment} \times \text{Support}} = \begin{matrix} \text{Current} \\ \text{Position} \\ \text{Trauma} \\ \text{Trap} \end{matrix}$$

*Figure 57: Trauma Formula 2.0*

When confronted with toxin build-up it could be interesting to examine the following questions:

- Where is the organization in the Trauma Trap?
- How many toxins are swirling around?
- Does the relational fabric feel healthy or fragile?

Maybe you start seeing that the current management has inherited unprocessed toxins from previous managers. In that case you'll know that you cannot ignore this. Toxins and trauma are not organized in a linear way (remember a tree's annual rings).

It is also worth identifying what is responsible for toxin build-up: is it via everyday work activities or the way the organization is managed. Try to understand how the work challenges people and/or groups or, perhaps, wears them out.

By doing so, you will also gain insight into any unhealed events and you will gradually understand why the organization is getting stuck in unhealthy dynamics.

This approach will also get you in touch with how – and how much – recognition and support was originally provided and also help you understand what kind of support and acknowledgment people and groups still need.

With these questions in the back of your mind you'll get a better feel for accumulated and unprocessed toxins, but also be better able to see those stressful situations, that you cannot alleviate, because they are just part of the work. Essential though, in the latter case, is that a way or practice is put in place to ensure these toxins are regularly and fully processed. If not they will weaken the relational fabric and undermine the resilience of the organization.

# Healing organizational trauma

8

Two faces of the Trauma Diamond were already discussed in the previous two chapters: emergency and crisis management are already fairly well established in most organizations, in line with legal requirements. This is especially so when it is a case of clearly identifiable incidents. The need for what the second face of the Trauma Diamond shows – namely the processing of toxins – is a lot less evident for most organizations. Lack of this processing might not immediately lead to organizational trauma, but it does ensure that the relational fabric of an organization becomes more fragile, making the organization more vulnerable. This is clearly undesirable in this rapidly changing and complex world that demands a lot of resilience. Here, especially, short-term thinking combined with an overly mechanistic way of working can take its toll. This brings us to the third face of the Trauma Diamond: working with organizational trauma that occurred when, for various reasons, shelter, healing and recognition were not yet possible: no time, no resources, denial, shock, uncertainty, lack of understanding or simply the hope that it would pass without interventions.

This third face of the Trauma Diamond is probably the least familiar. Progress in the field of individual trauma, which has accelerated in recent years, remains in its infancy with regard to organizational trauma. For that reason the goal of this book is to give this issue the attention it merits and invite you to build on what the book provides. Less denial or ignorance could be the first positive effect and, in many cases, would already be a big step forward. In the meantime, it is clear that working with trauma in organizations requires customization. There is no one-size-fits-all solution. So in this chapter you will not find a standard recipe but a set of tools and principles; building blocks to get you started.

**Organizational innovation is like ploughing. What is under the soil comes to the surface. The deeper you plow, the more surprises you turn up.**

Imagine a director or manager who inherits a team, department or organization with accumulated, embedded toxins or unrecognized organizational trauma. He wants to show, as quickly as possible, that he is the right person to take the group forward and set a new course. But, despite his enthusiasm, he notices step by step, that his teams are stuck in something he just cannot put his finger on. Even a trained (external) professional – coach, consultant, … – can get stuck in unhealed organizational trauma. After all, neither manager nor coach can know, in advance, an organization's complete story, even when told that it will not be a 'normal' assignment. Yet each quickly senses that something just doesn't feel right.

Throughout the years we've learned that organizational trauma rarely comes to the surface of its own accord – hence the reference to ploughing. Toxins embed in the deeper layers of an organization and people find ways to work around them (with a serious price). As long as they do not obviously impact the functioning of the organization and/or the wellbeing of the employees, there is usually no urgent need to change anything. However, the chance that unhealed trauma will surface, increases significantly when Trauma Capsules are triggered or when the capacities trapped in these Trauma Capsules – and therefore unavailable – have become crucial to a successful change process. As you might already have guessed, much that we learned earlier in the book will come together in this chapter.

In whatever capacity you work – employee, manager, director, consultant or coach – usually you do not know in advance that organizational trauma is the issue. And if you were to know – because you were invited in specifically to work on it – you still cannot know how deep or how broad its influence, whether the organization is ready for this kind of work, or whether it is really willing to take the steps needed to work on it. If you suspect that a particular change will not actually happen, because organizational trauma is present and the organization is too deep in the Trauma Trap, then it is important to work through the phases below. Mind you, do not consider these phases as linear time points, like milestones of a project plan. The phases flow into each other as in the drawing below:

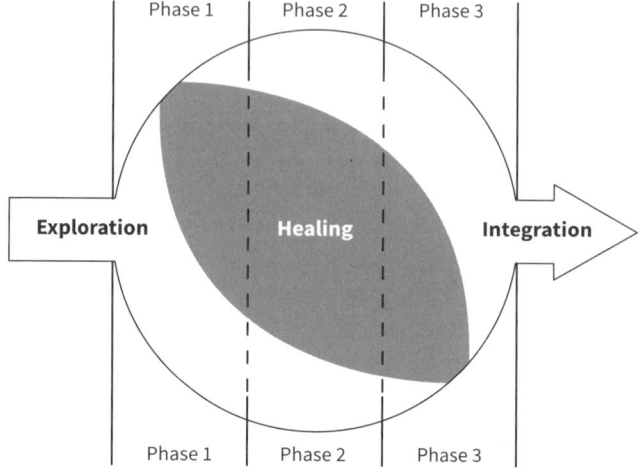

*Figure 58: Phases for dealing with organizational trauma*

### Phase 1: The exploration phase

This phase is particularly crucial. You try to gain insight into a number of factors that are critical when deciding whether or not to proceed to the next phase. Going too fast is a common mistake in this first phase and runs the risk of making things worse. Because only in one of the next phases will you be able to create space for the (unhealed) trauma to heal. You can compare this phase with preparing an operating room for a surgical procedure. This phase will be discussed – after this short introduction – in the first part of this chapter.

### Phase 2: The healing phase

In this phase you bring people and groups together to tackle that which is not healed. During this phase you'll be working on old toxins, making use of the toxin descriptions from previous chapters. This phase will be discussed in the second part of this chapter.

***Phase 3: The recovery and integration phase***

Already in phase 1, opportunities will arise to improve the situation. For example, a series of exploratory talks can already lead to a series of insights and, if possible, they can quickly be implemented (e.g. by adapting an aspect of the existing strategy). Such early integration has a good chance of benefitting the healing process, with the desirable side-effect of creating feelings of goodwill in everyone involved. However, and particularly when you are working with trauma, it will soon become clear what else is needed to ensure both recovery and prevention of relapse. The integration of these insights is at the core of the third phase that will be discussed in the next and final chapter. A series of insights will be shared on how you can care for the further development and progress of the organization (after being stuck in the Trauma Trap), a handy set of tools to keep the relational fabric resilient for the future.

## 8.1 Phase 1: providing safety, stability and resources

It may seem strange but, for a variety of reasons, much of this chapter will focus on the exploration phase. You'll see that good preparation opens the way for 'client' self-regulation, so that the healing process can, as it were, unfold in a natural way. You'll learn to feel when people have developed the particular kind of 'soft spot' that is needed for healing and you'll learn what helps make this happen. The exploration phase is particularly intensive and can take a lot more time and energy than you or your contractor might expect. Resisting eventual pressure will be crucial to protect the conditions needed for healing. However, we cannot state this too often: *"The exploration phase builds the foundations needed to work with accumulated toxins because, when working with organizational trauma, it is better to have strong foundations…"* As you'll move through this chapter, you'll start to see that this is the chapter that weaves many previously-discussed terms and ideas into a coherent story.

Preparation is crucial because once you move into the healing phase, you will invite people to lower their protective mechanisms – their proverbial armor and masks. This is necessary for healing but, at the same time, it makes these people and groups more vulnerable. Rushing (through the exploration phase) can happen for many different reasons. You will probably see a link here with the four-quadrant-model – fixer – savior – healer of parts – healer of wholes – that was discussed at the beginning of Chapter 7. For example, the situation may have been dragging on for so long that time is running out and the pressure on the organization to make a particular change escalates. Or you are new – or recently-hired – and you want to demonstrate your added value or expertise as quickly as possible (the pitfall of the fixer and the savior). Or problems – whether they are technical or psychological – pull you in to tackling them as soon as possible (the fixer). This is often linked to your (in)ability to 'contain' tension as mentioned in the previous chapter. Or the client sucks you into the role of savior without you realizing it.

As mentioned earlier, you can compare this phase with the preparing of an operating room for a surgical procedure. The following questions are a great help in this first phase:

- Is it really necessary to start with the unhealed organizational trauma? Is the healthy functioning of the organization and the employees so held back by it, that they can no longer work 'around' it?

- Is there a vision, a picture, of what this process is expected to achieve? Is there a clear and relevant goal for the organization and the employees?

- Do you feel – after the necessary exploration (see below) – that you have insight into what is going on, in such a way that you feel you know in advance what might come up? Is it about a clearly-defined major event or is it about a chain of events and circumstances? The more complex the cause, the greater the chance of a domino effect full of (usually unpleasant) surprises. Keep this in mind and there's less chance you'll be caught off-guard.

- Are there realistic expectations about the course and the possible duration of the healing process or are the decision makers pushing for a quick fix? Are people aware of the fact that the work will require a certain investment in time, resources and commitment?

- Do the people involved appear to be sufficiently capable of staying in balance, or are some of them too vulnerable to start such an intensive process? Are there sufficient resources to fall back on or to support people to just hang in there if it becomes very stressful? Should some training be provided first; such as non-violent communication, managing emotions and/or managing conflict. Or do people need some advance learning about trauma, so they have a framework that facilitates understanding? And is there sufficient support available within the organization (colleagues, managers, HR and so on)? Because, as an external facilitator, you are unlikely to be present often enough to offer support exactly when it is needed.

- Do you feel that people are willing to open up, to forgive, to apologize or to grow? Or are people still stuck in their silos? Sometimes there are external factors that make the above qualities very difficult to apply, specifically, for example, if there is an ongoing judicial investigation.

- Do you think that, as a facilitator – if necessary supported by an experienced colleague – you will be able to create a healing container (aka holding space) that makes authentic contact possible, even when (as it surely will) it becomes emotional, conflicting or painful?

- Is there a willingness to question and adjust aspects of the organization's operation (e.g. procedures, decision-making, hierarchies, structures and so on). If there is not, it could be difficult to integrate some of the insights gained, and that would cause more damage, rather than reduce it.

As you can see, preparation is crucial. Combined with your experience and intuition, the answers to these questions will help you – in consultation with those involved – to draw up a roadmap for recovery. The chance of unhelpful surprises, of not being careful enough, and of taking the wrong direction remain great. Do not step into the healing and processing phase if you cannot answer the previous questions adequately. When you can't, keep working on the conditions for healing until it feels right to move on.

Trauma-informed working also means that you try to get a feel for the individuality of the organization, its personality so to speak. In this way you tailor your interventions to the character and the condition of the organization. Try to take into account the Trauma Trap, any other elements that already have been provided in earlier chapters and trust your gut feel. After all, we all are capable of sensing into the dynamics of living systems and aligning ourselves with them. It is a capacity that every child develops in the womb and it largely determines the character of a child. Insight into your own roots and how they formed – and formed you – is an important resource that can increase the efficacy of how you work.

> *She was the oldest daughter and grew up in a family where the parents were often absent.  She did part of the housework and she learned to take care of her younger brothers and sisters and, occasionally, her mother, when things were difficult.  Without being aware of it, she was sucked into a caring role: caring for others became internalized and automatic.  A person or group only needs to emit the vaguest of cries for help and she'll be there, as fast as she can.  So she is hypersensitive to any questions about care, even if they are not explicitly expressed.  Since she is aware of that pattern, thanks to coaching and personal development, she quickly feels if a group evokes that in her.  She now uses her developed sense of the pattern to get information about groups, with which she now works professionally, and makes a conscious choice to be, or not to be, the carer.*

Anthropology is a great source of inspiration about many elements crucial to exploring an organization. Anthropologists use participative observation to gain intimate knowledge of the culture of a particular tribe or population group.  This means that they do not observe from a distance, but actively participate in the life and customs of the tribe.  After all, understanding depends on far more than what we can perceive with our eyes and ears. Your physical sensations are, perhaps, the most important tools at your disposal when exploring the dynamics of an organization. Howard F. Stein *Listening Deeply* (Stein, 1994, [29]) , a renowned anthropologist, talks about 'deep listening' as a tool crucial to learning how to observe what is happening in the deeper layers of an organization.  This deep listening – a holistic collaboration of body, mind and spirit – enables you to quickly feel if something isn't right. Experience and self-insight can, therefore, lead to a very refined sense of feeling, one that is essential to working effectively with organizational trauma. What anthropology teaches us, is that you must be willing to immerse yourself in a living system. Only in this way can you feel both the existing tension, and the present, but blocked, potential. This asks for respect and empathy.

This might seem strange to hear, but it is important to accept that you cannot change or restore anything yourself. You can only bring into the light the painful, unprocessed emotions and events and help people acknowledge them. That is precisely what opens the room for recovery and self-regulation. After all, what is not allowed into the light continues to work in the darkness.

Usually the process goes as follows. Intuitively you begin to feel that something is wrong. Your collaboration or guidance costs more energy than you are used to. You realize you've begun walking on eggs, you start to pick up tensions and emotions, or you feel yourself being sucked into a particular dynamic. You notice a number of trauma symptoms. This could be an indication you have bumped into a Trauma Capsule. In short, something will appear on your trauma radar. If your suspicions are correct, it is better not to mention this immediately, because you won't yet know if your clients are ready and willing to begin this part of the work. After all, this phase is about exploration. As mentioned earlier, it is best not to cut into an infected wound until you are in a sterile room with the right tools and the necessary training and experience, otherwise you might make things worse than they already are.

> *During a meeting with the management of a medium-sized organization, an encounter with a Trauma Capsule made it clear that a department was probably suffering from organizational trauma. The consultant inquired into the history of the department: it was a heavy story. Many people had left and there had been a burn-out problem for some time. When a number of the historical events were brought into the open, the CEO became very restless and insecure. Possibly because he feared that he would be blamed for certain things. What he showed, was that he was not yet ready to start with this issue. In cases like this, you need to work one-to-one with the (in this case) CEO until he is ready to take the next step.*

This example is not, in any way, pointing a finger at the CEO: his reaction is understandable. Nevertheless, this incident contains an invitation to – with his agreement – work towards establishing the necessary conditions. Now, with this example in mind, let's take a look at a number of ways in which you can train 'deep listening'. The picture below gives you an overview of what's involved:

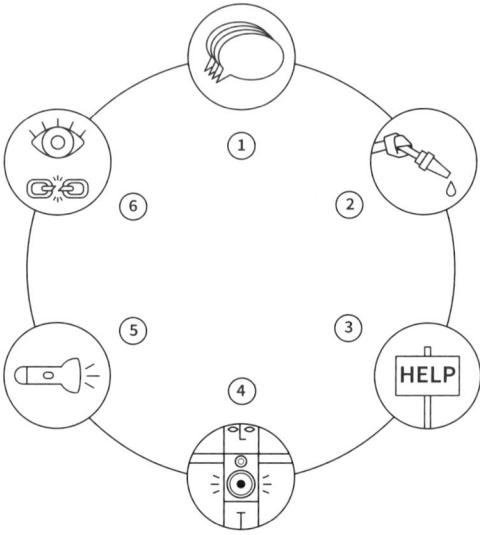

*Figure 59: Building blocks for Deep Listening*

**Exploring requires an eye for layers**

Listening is a very underestimated skill. It goes far beyond hearing the words of the other. The way you listen, and exactly what you listen to, during your exploration, is critical to gathering relevant and useful data. Do you listen in a sterile way, like someone who values pure facts, or do you listen to and between the layers when you are in a dialogue with someone? In the latter case you will much sooner get a feel for what is going on in an organization. Here are a few of the layers you can look out for, based on a well-known communications model from Friedemann Schulz von Thun *Störungen und Klärungen: Allgemeine Psychologie der Kommunikation* (Thun, 2010, [33]) .

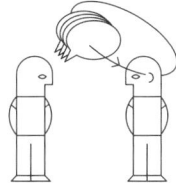

*Figure 60: Building block 1: Having an ear for the layers in communication*

### The layer of factual information

A group of people can share a number of stories about the ins and outs of the organization. These stories will sound like facts you can use in a report. Pure content, then, is speech without emotions.

### The layer of self-revelation

There is a lot of information between the words. It is found in the emotions and non-verbal signals. While stories are being shared, you might notice that group members start to shine, that they become dejected or that they get angry. Paying attention to this layer is a rapid way to reveal accumulated toxins, unsolved conflicts or even Trauma Capsules. However, this layer also shows you the path to the resources you'll need, as the process continues, to create an emotionally-safe environment. Paying attention to this layer ensures that you can connect quickly to what's really going on in other people's lives.

### The relationship layer

This layer is about how people relate to each other and provides insight into the state of the relational fabric in, around and between groups. You might notice that opinions are very appreciative or equally judgmental about the organization, the manager, another department, a certain colleague, a certain stakeholder of the organization etc. This layer points you to where the relational fabric is frayed or torn.

After all, how someone relates to another person, and the world around him, will influence, to a large extent, how that person behaves.

How we are connected determines, as it were, the extent to which we open up or close ourselves to someone. Listening in this layer can provide much useful information.

This layer also shows you – in real-time – how people relate to you, and this is really important. Do people feel safe with you as 'their' facilitator – or not. It is, again, crucial that you really listen to this layer in order to create the healing container, the essential holding space.

### The appeal layer

This layer talks to us about people's needs and expectations and is often the most subtle or implicit of the layers. If you want to get this on the table faster, ask explicitly what people expect from you. Otherwise there is a good chance that you will fill this in, guaranteeing yourself unwanted hassle with your clients.

It is important to be aware of the fact that we use our communications – verbal and non-verbal – to influence others. This might involve gaining something tangible (e.g. better service or a company car) to something less tangible (recognition, appreciation, respect, attention, an apology).

When you are more familiar with this layer, you soon notice when people are trying to seduce you onto their side. This can make you biased; no longer seen as impartial or safe for other parties involved. In that case, it will be much more difficult for you to create the safe setting needed, in the next phase, to bring everyone together.

Although this theory was formulated in the 1980s, it is still difficult for many people to listen through these layers. But it remains a convenient way to get directly to the heart of the matter. Some people consciously choose not to listen through the layers, out of complacency or to avoid dealing with what is not explicitly expressed. Of course, this makes acknowledgement impossible, and is catastrophic to the chances of a successful outcome when working with organizational trauma.

Listening through these layers is something you need to keep on doing. It is how you feel when things are shifting between and among people. By paying attention to these layers, you'll notice when there is sufficient safety and support to move to the next phase, and when it is right to bring specific people together. With this information you can map out what is needed for healing – for example an apology or some kind of compensation – and you can also check whether this is possible or desirable for the people who would have to give it. In short, by listening to and through the layers, a path unfolds towards healing. This will help you to sense if you're getting closer to the 'soft spot' for healing, already mentioned at the beginning of this chapter.

Finally, it is good to tell people about layers. This will help them to listen to each other in a more focused way when you bring them together. Only when people are able and willing to take layers into account are they ready for the next phase. Otherwise there is a good chance that emotionally-charged stories will take precedence, fixing the group in the content layer. Healing work, however, usually happens on many layers. If nobody is looking out for the relational fabric, the chance of it tearing further is particularly great.

**Exploring demands systemic wisdom**

Earlier we made reference to the distinction between LAW and LORE. While LAW helps us to regulate the tangible world, LORE works to keep the relational fabric of groups healthy. In the Western world most of us have lost touch with LORE.

*Figure 61: Building block 2: Systemic wisdom*

During the last 25 years, a number of Western movements have focused on recovering LORE. Those movements took their inspiration from the centuries-long accumulated traditions of indigenous people. One of those important movements – which gave birth, among others, to Deep Democracy – has its origins in the work of Amy and Arnold Mindell *The Deep Democracy of Open Forums* (Mindell, 2002, [22]) . Another important movement – known via family and organizational constellations – was developed  by people including Bert Hellinger, Gunthard Weber, Hunter Beaumont, Albrecht Mähr, Bertold Ulsamer, Jacob Schneider, Stephan Hausner and Jan Jacob Stam. The work of these pioneers has yielded important insights into what is needed to make families, groups, organizations and even entire communities flourish. Their way of working is called systemic phenomenological.  Systemic because of the focus on the interplay or the relationship between the parts of a living system and its wider context (zooming out).  Phenomenological because great importance is attached to feeling into what is happening in the present moment.  This has proven to be a particularly effective way to bypass the lens of our familiar thinking patterns, unconscious assumptions and to see things as they really are. An organization, for example, can appear clear and healthy on the outside, while deep listening tells you that something is not right. By exploring hundreds of thousands of cases involving families, organizations and communities – all of which are different forms of living systems – a number of patterns slowly became clear. The patterns revealed a number of principles that are essential for the flow of life energy. If these principles – consciously or not – are crushed or ignored, life energy becomes stuck and the relational tissue becomes more fragile.  Developing an understanding of these principles, and an ability to sense into them, is a necessary skill for keeping an organization healthy.  That is why this is also known as systemic wisdom.

A little warning.  Once we are given 'principles', we often, and too easily, stop investigating, lose our curiosity and use them as if they are laws. However, it is fundamental that you continue to work with a systemic phenomenological approach; otherwise all you will ever see is confirmation of these principles. What follows, therefore, are guidelines, not laws written in stone.

The best way to activate your systemic wisdom during the exploration phase is to ask questions about the history of the team, the department, the organization, whatever part you are working on. The questions that follow are divided into a number of categories, and each has a brief explanation.

Living systems thrive when:

- they can be whole (inclusion)
- there is healthy internal and external exchange (balance)
- there is logical, functional organization (order)
- they can evolve to their destiny (purpose)

### Systemic principle: inclusion (able to be complete)

Key questions for this principle are:

- Who (by exclusion) or what (by shadow) has no place or is not in-cluded?
- Who or what was not let go and now takes a wrongful place?

Later we'll see an example of what can happen when a group of employees, who have been made redundant, cannot be fully let go by the 'colleagues' who remain. This attaching and letting-go turns out to be about more than just people; it also happens with products, projects, values or working methods (referred to earlier). When you are exploring the history of an organization, first ask about people who have left and assess how well (or not) this was done, and how it was processed by those who left and those who remained. Pay extra attention to founders. If a founder leaves, the impact on an organization can be extreme, especially if the leaving was difficult. There are a number of other concepts related to the principle of inclusion, that you can investigate via the following questions:

- Which departments, products, functions, branches and customers still belong? Which are in shadow? How did this happen?
- Which departments, teams or (target) groups are easily forgotten in this organization?
- How are temporary employees, trainees, flex-workers, freelancers, part-timers, long-term sick and seconded-staff treated?
- Who has or has not been involved in rituals?
- Who does not actually belong (anymore), but still takes a place?

- What functions or people do not really belong anywhere? Have no place or are wrongly excluded?

- What happens to people that the organization would like to get rid of, but cannot for financial or legal reasons?

- What events are silenced, and so are excluded from the company's history?

Joining and leaving are – as you can deduce from these questions – crucial to the healthy functioning of a living system. They ensure a clear distinction between whether or not someone is a member of the system. Often there are rituals associated with gaining or losing membership of a group or community. There are good reasons why these rituals have been passed down through the centuries.

As we noted in a previous section of the book, sinking into the Trauma Trap starts when overwhelming circumstances, among other things, surge in from the outside world. In the case of organizational trauma, you often can see that the border with the outside world has been seriously damaged, as if a knife has sliced through the psychological membrane. An overwhelming event can either destroy the border completely or elicit a kind of counter reaction that forms a concrete wall between the system and the environment, severely disrupting comings and goings – which sit at the heart of this principle. In the long term this is detrimental because a living system survives only when it can keep in touch with its environment and at the same time, the distinction between inside and outside stays clear. Imagine this psychological membrane as a kind of skin, which defines what is in the living system and also protects it against the outside world, while allowing exchange to occur and the possibility to 'sweat out' toxins. You will quickly feel if something is wrong with the membrane of a team, department or organization. So see this as an important signal while you are in the exploration phase; which brings us to the next principle.

### Systemic principle: balance (healthy internal and external exchange)

Key questions for this principle are:

- Was the balance between giving and taking ever seriously disrupted in relation to the outside world?

- Was the balance between giving and taking ever seriously disrupted in the inner world of the organization?

- Has it been restored?

Have you, as an employee or manager, ever been in a situation where you felt that you were the only one who was really willing to invest and contribute? Have you ever experienced that a favor was refused despite all the energy you had invested in the organization? We maintain a kind of 'unconscious' balance-sheet for giving and taking in every relationship. It does not always have to be perfect but should never tip too far or for too long to one side or the other. As you will see later in Chapter 9, healthy organizations know how to do this well. They use resources, raw materials and space from the community, but also find ways to return them to the community. In recent years, many organizations have had a somewhat greedy, almost parasitic way of being, which is beginning to be costly in many different areas. The balance between giving and taking can, therefore, be disrupted on a very large scale or on a very small scale. This principle is about this balance, and we look at it via the following questions:

- Where (or with whom) has giving and taking stagnated within the organization?

- Is there an equal investment in the training and development of employees and, if there are differences, are the differences appropriate?

- Is there a lot of illness, staff turnover or burn-out? Is there a pattern in that? Why do people stay? For the money? The colleagues? Because the work is fun and educative? Because they get development opportunities and freedom? Because it allows them to make a positive contribution? Out of fear? Because the organization gives them a certain social status?

- How do salaries compare to the market rate? Does this affect the relationship between the employees and the organization? How is overtime reimbursed? Are volunteers rewarded and how?

- How does one deal with trust, working from home, time management, telephone use, company cars and so on?

- Is the organization sucking energy: taking without giving? How does the organization relate to society? Does it express values of sustainability, ecology and social involvement? Are these values real or just window dressing?

It is almost impossible to consider all these questions during a single meeting or discussion. That is why it is so important that you use your body as a sensor. And, once you start to get an eye and a feel for this, you will be surprised sometimes that other people do not notice what has become so clear to you.

Finally, do not forget that you will definitely experience the principle of giving and taking in your cooperation with an organization, whether you are a contractor or an employee. This manner, of consciously sensing in the moment, will often help you to feel whether something is going on in the field of this, or any of these, principles.

### Systemic principle: order (logical, functional organization)

Key questions for this principle are:
- Is there a healthy, functional hierarchy?

- How is seniority handled?

- Is there appropriate ordering between the various functions (purchasing, HR, production, IT and so on) within the organization?

- Are the values and/or guiding principles of the organization well and clearly ordered?

Recent years have seen a growing interest in 'horizontal' organizations. This can (and often does), however, lead to the misunderstanding that there is no longer a need for any hierarchy. Yet even the flattest of organizations have a founder or owner who makes choices for the whole, and so ensures consistency of values and guiding principles. He or she might well engage in dialogue and conversation, but ultimately that person(s) still determines much about the organization, especially the choice to work with a flatter, more participatory, structure.  Hierarchy can also bring peace, clarity and order.  Organizations pioneering this approach do not have a rigid, positional structure. They enjoy and benefit from dynamic ordering and use hierarchy differently to the norm, in ways such as these.

- It is more democratic.  Leaders are elected and can lose their mandate on the basis of agreed, predetermined criteria.

- Leaders receive their formal mandate only after they have (informally) shown leadership qualities.

- Leadership evolves according to the needs of the organization and is carried out in a more project-based manner.

- The management does not have an authoritarian or all-knowing position but rather a serving, anticipatory role that makes it a kind of catalyst for the future that wants to unfold through the organization. We will come back to this later on.

As long as this is a fluid movement of following and leading, the way a flock of birds flies, then there is flow. When the 'followers' no longer want to follow the chosen 'leader' – or vice versa – a team or an organization tends to lose this flow, and can become stuck, suffering disturbance and pain.  If such a situation goes on for too long, it can weaken and even destroy the relational fabric.  Hence the following questions to explore the principle of 'order':

- Who bears the most responsibility for the whole?

- Who is the longest in the company (or in a specific department) and do they feel recognized in that sense?

- How is the ordering between the various functions in the organization?

- What about the pecking order between internal and external employees? Who gets heard, who does not?

- In the case of a family business, is the place of the family members above the rest of the people of the company, even when the family members are lower in the hierarchy of the organization? If so, what does that do to the employees?

- What gives status: position, seniority, age, expertise, place of residence, education, experience, relationships, member of the family? Has that changed at a certain point in the past? And how do people feel about this?

- Does gender, religion, cultural background, place/country of origin or sexual preference influence a person's position and is there a link with the origin of the organization and/or the founders? If the roots of an organization are Catholic, for example, but most current employees have North-African roots, which rituals are given space and which are not?

### Systemic principle: purpose (to evolve to its destiny)

Key questions for this principle are:
- What is the raison d'être and/or the destiny of the organization?
- Has it changed over the years and how did that happen?
- Who are the most important target audiences, clients or customers of the organization?
- Is the destiny still relevant?
- What is the soul of the organization?

A destiny, a goal and a mission are all parts of an organization's creation, and reasons for its existence. When a course is set, the living system moves in that direction. An organization can forget that course, drastically change it, or hold it tightly in spite of changes in the market or society. When an organization chooses a course that takes it away from its destiny, organizational trauma can arise, especially if such strategic decisions are made without appropriate care. A (perhaps unhelpful) change of strategy and its consequences, can be triggered by mergers and acquisitions. We have already discussed some examples of this. In the book, *De Corporate Tribe. Organisatielessen uit de antropologie* (Braun and Kramer, 2015, [5]) the authors speak of the totem pole of an organization and how this totem pole can get broken, lost or forgotten. When this happens, the core or the soul of a company can be wounded.  Life-giving forces, that drive emergence, will become stuck, opening the way to the Trauma Trap. Everyone will feel it, even if they cannot name it. Healing will be needed.

In a number of different ways, I have gained an intimate knowledge of these principles. First and foremost by working with companies for almost 20 years, but also by participating and facilitating many organizational constellations (more on constellations later in this chapter). My exploration of systemic work, with some of the leaders in this field, has given me a deep understanding and feeling for those life-supporting principles (= development of (my) systemic wisdom).

By using your systemic wisdom in the exploration phase, it will become clear where there are unhealed wounds in the organization and when and how they might have originated.  Moreover, the questions above reveal where in the operation or design of the organization things are malfunctioning, often outside of people's consciousness. This points you to where healing is needed, but also uncovers issues or processes that – if they are not adapted into the operation of the organization – will continue to cause toxins.  As previously mentioned, lack of respect (again usually unconscious)  for those systemic principles, makes the relational fabric more fragile, causing an organization to sink into the Trauma Trap and, in extremis, can lead to organizational trauma.  In short, systemic wisdom is essential when you start mapping what is needed to support an organization that is in the grip of organizational trauma.

### Listening via symptoms and messengers

Earlier in this book you were invited to see symptoms as cries-for-help from living systems.  In addition, it is important to recognize that living systems cannot communicate as an entity might, and certainly not in the ways that people communicate with each other.  If you suspect organizational trauma or start feeling that certain capabilities seem to have become unavailable, then it is good to keep the following questions in mind:

- Where and in what way do I see cries-for-help?
- What are they trying to make visible?

- For what might certain symptoms actually be solutions?  If the innate emerging capabilities of a living system are blocked, second-
best solutions are found.  Often these show up as symptoms.  Remember the example; if you do not drink enough, the body creates
hunger feelings in order to get water from food.

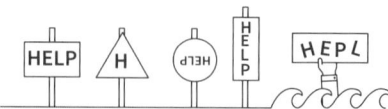

*Figure 62: Building block 3: Seeing symptoms as cries for help*

This brings us to the third stage of our exploration. Here you learn to listen via messengers and symptoms. You try to get in touch with the source
from which someone (or a group of people) talk. The following examples
will clarify what we mean by this.

Someone (or a group) can talk for themselves:  from being in contact
with their own needs, motivations, desires and ambitions.  Think back to
the appeal layer discussed at the beginning of this chapter.  What drives
people in such cases is the fact that they want to achieve things, be given
the opportunity to make something real.  They will talk of concrete plans
and ambitions that usually correspond with what is common and desirable in the organization.  The communication is rooted in the person and
is delivered clearly, energetically and consciously.  People that communicate from this place, do so with the intention of being good, exemplary
members of the group of which they want to be part.

*Figure 63: Acting or speaking as a member of a living system*

By now you will probably have realized that people can simultaneously
be part of several systems: immediate and extended families, profession,

nationality, religion, sports club, etc.  If someone is communicating very clearly, but is still struggling with the direction of the company, you could ask a question such as:  *"From which membership is that person actually speaking?"*  Or *"Which membership is he or she trying to protect".*

> *In this way, someone from a certain professional group, e.g. IT, might feel more connected to the IT profession than to the company that employs him.  If his employer wants to implement an IT system that is neither respected nor valued by his professional group, then that could 'pull' him away from his membership of the professional group. Any criticism from that employee might then appear to be at odds with the direction of the organization and yet still be very powerful and clear.  However, for him, one membership is more valuable than the other.  That is why the phrase "... of which they want to be part" is particularly important in the text above. This is very recognizable in the following examples: doctors and specialists in hospitals, trade unionists in organizations, bakers and butchers who work for supermarkets, and so on.*

Anyhow, a person speaks for himself but also from a particular membership.  The latter can confuse you if you forget that everyone is part of multiple systems.  So it is worthwhile to identify, as early as possible, if someone is responding from themselves or a group, and what group.

Someone (or a group) can also – consciously or not – communicate or act for or from the whole of the living system.  As mentioned earlier, a living system manifests what it needs to be able to continue functioning well.  It does so by sucking someone into a certain role, often a role that has not been formally filled or has been excluded (as mentioned in the systemic principles).  Imagine an eldest daughter who – as an adult – is quickly sucked into a caring role because she also unconsciously did so in her family of origin. This pattern brings her, time and time again, into a caring role when there is lack of care from the management.

*Figure 64: Acting or speaking for the whole of the living system*

Knowing that the cries-for-help, coming from the living system, can show in this way, is very helpful to finding your way when working with organizational trauma. Concealed within these cries are signposts pointing to issues for further exploration, or that it is time to move on to the next phase. As you become sensitive to the different stories contained in the cries-for-help, you are likely to notice a number of themes, events or situations that you could use when moving to the phase for the healing of organizational trauma.

Someone who communicates from the needs of the system often speaks slower and lower, more emotionally, more from feelings than thoughts. There is less decisiveness. Nothing is black or white. The talking is more about feeling and intuiting. If you are someone who likes action and clarity, then chances are that you'll get irritated by this. The person communicating from here is acting – most of the time in an unconscious way – for the well-being of the living system, which makes him do things that might be unexpected from a person in his role. The people that are sensitive for the needs of the whole, are often the ones who take the biggest risks at the expense of their own well-being. Even more, sometimes they'll risk losing their membership in order to care for the whole. If these people are not provided with a safe space, which you must create and guard, they won't feel safe to speak-up although their message greatly help moving to the healing phase. Groups are capable of ejecting someone if the group cannot face something difficult that such a person has unveiled. Think back to the concepts, containing and holding, that were discussed in the previous chapter.

Persons or groups can also be connected to what wants to unfold, or the potential of a team, department or organization. In both cases there is often no rational explanation for this pre-sensing and yet, to the person 'affected' it seems very clear. Visionary people often have a feeling for what wants to unfold. Talent-spotters of young athletes, artists or new (music) bands often are able to get in touch with what others can't yet see. Someone who is communicating from this 'pre' place might have difficulty finding the right words to explain what they feel while, for them, it is crystal clear. Emergence – of that which wants to unfold – often shows itself through such people but, unfortunately, they often go unheard in the heat of conversation. Often, these are the people who can show us new paths or, in the case of organizational trauma, the path to healing. In addition to providing safety and space for emotions, it is also important, when working with organizational trauma, to have an attractive perspective on the future. Most of the time, we put in the effort needed to climb a high mountain because we hope to be rewarded by a stunning view from the top. This 'attractive future' often arises through these visionaries, as if they are tuned to the frequency of tomorrow.

*Figure 65: Acting or speaking from the emerging future*

Leadership in socio- or holocratic organizations is organized in such a way that everyone can be a sensor for the future. After all, being in his or her right place in the organization, each person has a kind of sensitivity for what might be next in the area of his work. And the founder or director of such an organization tends to be the person who is in touch with what wants to unfold through the entire organization. In that way he is the sensor for the future of the whole.

Learning to listen via the messenger is a particularly effective way to connect with the deeper layers of living systems, bringing you into contact with themes that will need addressing in the next phase. You will also see how people respond to difficult themes and, with some luck, you might even pick up the scent of a more-attractive future. So while you are exploring, you are simultaneously walking the following four paths inspired by the work of Dr. Sandra L. Bloom *Restoring Sanctuary* (Bloom and Farragher, 2013, [4]) :

- You monitor the safety of everyone. The path of holding space.

- You create room for toxins and emotions. The path of emotions and toxins.

- You try to get in touch with what needs to be released, what people cannot let go. You try to get in touch with what people have lost, without them re-experiencing the impact. The path of loss and mourning.

- You create space for emergence. Allowing a mobilizing future perspective to unfold. The path of the future.

*Figure 66: Threads for healing: safety, emotions, loss and future*

Working with organizational trauma means we are continuously walking these four paths, as shown in the drawing above.  Why are these four paths so important?  Because it is along these four paths that organizational trauma develops:

- People and groups no longer feel safe and secure.

- People and groups are no longer able to regulate their emotions.

- People and groups have been overwhelmed by experiences of loss. Their ability to detach, and later to reattach, is damaged.

- A kind of paralysis has arisen so that people can no longer imagine another, more positive future for themselves, the team, the organization.

**Exploring by listening phenomenologically**

Listening has a somatic component.  This was already mentioned when we introduced the concepts of 'deep' and 'phenomenological' listening. Listening with your body is a capability you'll need when working with organizational trauma.  Even more, your body can help you find the path that leads to healing organizational trauma.  Just as tuning forks resonate with each other or start to vibrate together at the same frequency, so do our bodies pick up resonation.  With the right kind of development, your body becomes an accurate sound box, through which you learn to what your body is sensitive and in what way.  My background, which I outlined in the beginning of this book, has made me particularly sensitive to complex mourning and trauma situations.  My body knows this intimately.  In mourning, the words spoken out carry a charge.  You can feel sadness or anger in someone's words.  This is an important part of the self-revelation (communication) layer, discussed earlier in this chapter.

*A while ago a colleague and I were doing an intake.  Based on our intuition, we started with the director of a large department.  During the conversation we heard a lot of words; some were explanations about the context, some were anecdotes and many were about events in the department's history.  At a certain moment the director began to tell us about an incident with an employee.  Immediately, the conversation took on a different*

*energy.  My colleague and I looked at each other and saw that*
*we had both picked up on the same thing.  That is why we often*
*work as a pair.*

Listening somatically is done by consciously feeling the way someone's
words touch you.  It means registering the impulses that arise within you
when someone is talking.  You let yourself be touched by the words of a
person or group and you consciously use that information.

**When exploring a traumatized organization,**
**your body is your compass**

You can evolve this ability to a very refined level.  For example by considering the following questions:

- To what are you sensitive?

- What do you intuit quickly?

- What are you inclined to suppress?

- What tendencies do you have around anger, sadness, fear and so
  on?

- Which of your emotions are you easily pulled away from?  For example, children have a precise feel for the emotions that are best to
  convince mum and dad or for the emotions mum and/or dad are not
  able to contain.

- What feels very familiar to you?

- What signals do you pick up in your body when the tension in
  a group rises?  Or when you're in the vicinity of a Trauma Capsule?

- What unhealed pain and injuries, and particular sensitivities, do you
  have, that make you vulnerable when something rubs up against
  them?

- How do you feel that healing has started?  It really is possible to feel
  that difference.

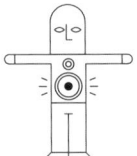

*Figure 67: Building block 4: Phenomenologic listening*

This ability, to feel the difference between healing or not, is recognized by many people via this example.  If you have a splinter in your finger, you feel a certain type of pain.  Pain your body uses to communicate that something is wrong.  If you take that splinter out of your finger and, as so often happens, a little bit is left behind, the pain doesn't really go away.  When the last piece of the splinter is finally out of your finger, then the pain changes.  It is as if the wounded place sighs with relief.  In a similar way you can feel with your body whether healing is starting or not.  So your own development is about refining your somatic sensing.  And when people notice that you listen more broadly or deeply than other people, they often spontaneously come to you.  It seems as if they can feel, from a distance, that, at last, here is someone who wants to hear about the stuckness in the organization.  This is a great help in creating a 'holding space'.  Finally, you also learn how to distinguish between 'professional' complainers and those who are genuinely concerned about the well-being of the organization.

**Exploring via de shadow-parts**

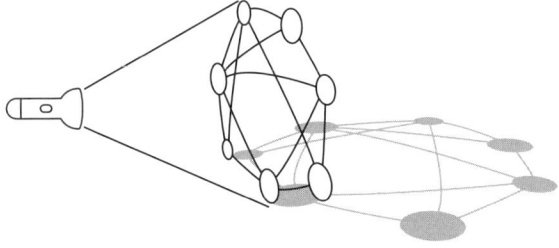

*Figure 68: Building block 5: Looking for shadow parts*

If you work with groups as a facilitator, you'll quickly bump into the shadow-parts of an organization. Every organization has taboos, sensitive areas or subjects, which may not see the light of day, which must not be mentioned. Issues and aspects that, so to speak, are not part of the everyday ins and outs of the organization, and often are at odds with the current culture or the stated values and norms.

> *In teams that work in a 'high performing' culture, there is often no room for even a little small talk or just hanging out. If this pressure becomes relentless, it literally means that something is being suppressed. Often this will then pop up in a different context, for example during a training session or team building activity. As an external facilitator you might then notice just the opposite; that there seems to be a kind of a container without any pressure. It feels almost impossible to get the team into action and they don't respect any aspect of the agenda or plans you have made for the day. In one way or another, their energy has no place in the normal operation of the organization, and is looking for an outlet, anywhere. This is one of the ways you can identify important patterns in an organization.*

> *In some organizations criticism is not permitted. You cannot mention a problem unless you also offer a solution. In reality, this means that many important issues are never discussed. When a group, from such an organization, is taken out of their familiar setting, they can suddenly behave as if nothing in the organization is right. As if that suppressed energy wants to take all the space, and you, as it were, have ended up in the whingers room.*

There are, of course, many more factors that play a role in understanding groups and organizations than what we see from these short examples. Yet it is important to be aware that, as a facilitator, you will often come into contact with the shadow, the unwanted, what has been divested or split-off from an organization. Anyway, what is not, or no longer, given a legitimate place in an organization will always find a way in through a back door.

So, in that case, you might ask: *"For what is there no room or space (anymore)? Since when, and how, did this happen?"* To understand a group and its boundaries, it helps to find out how that specific group differs from other groups. This gives you more insight into the underlying patterns and helps you understand more quickly why things in that group go the way they go. The same patterns can repeat and repeat – just like fractals.

> *A group of technicians complained, during a workshop, that the management never listened to their input. A little later the head of the maintenance team said that his people had put forward a proposal for a better way of utilizing a number of machines. One of the technicians immediately laughed that solution away, supported by his colleagues. At that exact moment, something dawned on one of the facilitators running the workshop: "Influence comes from above. They are the ones with the 'brains'". And, indeed, this pattern ran throughout the organization. The same people who complained about this pattern, applied it to people who were lower than them in the hierarchy. As a result, the know-how and knowledge potential of the employees was never fully realized and so the organization struggled to build on the potential of its people.*

Learning to recognize such patterns is very useful. When you are comfortable with zooming out, you'll start recognizing, much faster, the everyday choreography; how the different parts (teams, departments, disciplines, etc.)  of an organization interact with each other.  This unconscious choreography largely determines what an organization can handle and what it cannot. Often a new strategy or change process fails because people are unable to grow out of their familiar – but no longer useful – patterns.  And failing to develop a new choreography is often linked to the quality of the relational wiring.  All too frequently, new procedures, structures and practices are introduced without taking into account the deeper patterns and/or the ingrained choreographies of an organization. This happens because people (especially when in their organizational roles) are often unable to see their own patterns. As the well-known saying goes, "*If you do what you've always done, you'll get what you've always got*". This statement applies equally to organizations.

And when an organization collapses into the Trauma Trap, certain patterns will have become so rigid that the familiar choreography remains the same even when the music changes substantially. If certain patterns turn out to be particularly rigid, if there is a lot of resistance or certain individual or collective abilities are found to be stuck, this can be a symptom of organizational trauma. Then you can start with questions like these:

- When, where and why has time stopped?
- What is not or no longer allowed here and how did this happen?
- What capabilities are likely to be stuck in Trauma Capsules?

Organizations which make a point of being proud that they have no hierarchy, are simply making hierarchy taboo. It is almost certain that hierarchy exists but is playing-out in very subtle ways. The employee who feels she is at the bottom of the – so-called but not existing – ladder and is suffering this illusion of a 'horizontal' organization, might feel she has no right to speak, because what she is talking about is taboo. If this organization wants to stay healthy, it has to face its shadows. Unfortunately, this is a pitfall for many organizations that are now willing, whatever the cost, to embrace the hype of self-regulation, without really knowing what they are getting themselves into. Raising the issue of hierarchy could well expose an interesting dynamic. Doing so will soon reveal how open or rigid the company is in this context.

> *An organization that claims the banner of harmony, just pushes all the natural tensions and conflicts into the shadow. The capability to deal with these, as they arise, has less and less chance to develop. Slowly but surely, rigidity and fear of chaos arise when faced with tensions or conflict. Avoiding these is fine, but not if there is never any space for it. Then it becomes a shadow that impacts the healthy functioning of the organization. Where does that fear of conflict come from? Here again an invitation to open up for conflict – in small doses.*

> *Organizations that preach excellence, could have difficulties in making space for experimentation and failure. How much space, if any, is there to develop or learn? And what failures have not been processed, making the company cramped and stuck? What happens in and with a team where something they have done turns out to be wrong?*

Whenever an organization frenetically pursues a particular goal, the opposite gets suppressed or excluded. This creates rigidity and certain abilities can no longer develop.  This can be pretty annoying, especially when a new 'dance' or new patterns are needed.  Often there is a proverbial fence around these, suddenly necessary, capabilities, or they could be stuck in a Trauma Capsule.  That is why we need to learn to identify the shadow of a living system and ask questions about its history, so the origin of that shadow can be revealed.

> *An organization that lacks entrepreneurship among its employees, must be willing to see that they might have stifled it for years, perhaps even punished it. Here, healing will be needed to set that entrepreneurial capacity free again. This issue is at the root of why many challenging, yet promising, strategic plans end up half-baked.*

> *Organizations with an unhealthy pattern of 'busy-ness' often find themselves, unknowingly, acting without learning, with the result that certain structural problems persist. Delay, reflection and analysis are then needed to get out of this pattern. If these three complementary powers do not appear to be available, then one should investigate why, and where, these powers might have been trapped. Perhaps, long ago, a team was 'optimised' because the added value of some team members was hard to put a finger on, or was visible only indirectly through others. In such a situation, busy-ness – rather than doing business – is one way to protect your membership. Think back to the question: "For what is this pattern a solution?"*

**Awareness for the relational fabric**

In her PhD thesis *"Connecting the dots.  A social network perspective on social-organizational processes in secondary schools"* (Meredith, 2017, [20]) Chloé Meredith demonstrates how the relational fabric of a school has an impact not only on the well-being of teachers, but equally on the academic performance of the pupils.   What is particularly impressive about her research is the way she makes social networks tangible via visual representations of the relationships. You could call this a 'photo' depicting how rich or poor the relational wiring is. This is a particularly good tool for making systemic perception physical, tangible. It makes this 'invisible' reality more usable, and this will be very useful when you want to bring organizational trauma to the table. Mind you, a photo is always just a moment in time, a static snapshot, while the relational fabric is a dynamic living entity. Your systemic antennae therefore remains crucial to learning to see where the relational fabric has become very fragile or is beginning to show signs of wear.

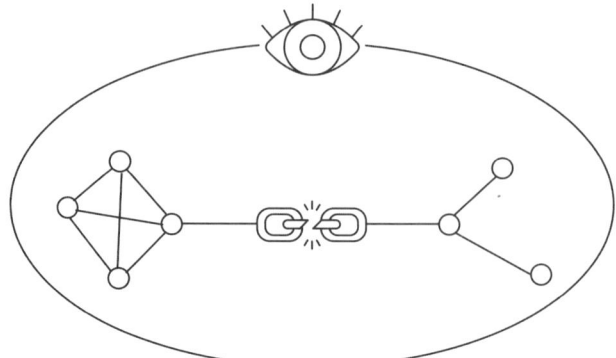

*Figure 69: Building block 6: Having an eye for the relational wiring*

Getting in touch with the relational fabric is a crucial aspect from the start. You'll be using this information to fashion the interventions needed to start working with the unhealed traumas. A number of questions can help with this:

- Which connections are robust?
- Which are non-existent or still untapped?
- Which are wearing thin and which are already torn or broken?
- Are there certain themes that place the relational fabric under more or less tension?

Some themes could be used to restore fragile connections. These could be used as resourcing themes. Other themes could be linked to organizational trauma and thus show where healing is still needed.

On the impact and intensity axis of the Trauma Cube, we talk first about post-traumatic injuries and only then about Post-Traumatic Stress Disorder or Syndrome (PTSD or PTSS). In both cases – but with a difference in intensity and vulnerability – the relational fabric can switch from looking quite healthy at one moment to very fragile in the next. Usually, this indicates you are getting close to a Trauma Capsule with unhealed issues. Those sudden changes are your compass in the exploration phase; they point you to the most needed path at that moment. As a result, you learn how to find out which theme might be playing out. It also will show you to what degree the organization is stuck in the Trauma Trap. For example, you'll notice that there are topics that support connection and topics that put the relational fabric under stress. This information is particularly important to a subsequent phase.

In our work we have learned that mapping the (state of the) relational fabric – as early as possible – is particularly important. Even more, we have learned to use the weakest or most-damaged connections as our trusted signposts. Compare this with an athlete who starts training after a muscle tear: he adapts his training routines to the muscle that needs to recover.

> *An organization had been stuck in the Trauma Trap for some time. It had had a number of difficult issues in its recent history. Fueled by cost-cutting measures, middle management had been abolished, leaving a number of autonomous departments that had to report to the same – newly appointed – director. This jeopardized the autonomy of the departments, which had already been triggered by a major, imminent merger. None of these emotions and uncertainties were given space for processing and so most were projected onto the newly-appointed director. She couldn't bear this increased stress, which caused more and more relational damage within the organization. People split into camps, leading to an unhealthy atmosphere.*
>
> *Various analyses – with accompanying reports – failed to build bridges between those camps; they had the opposite effect because the people doing those analyses were not aware they were dealing with organizational trauma. This pushed the organization even deeper into the Trauma Trap.*
>
> *During the exploration phase it became very clear that the fabric around the director had become extremely fragile, but not based on her (in)competence as some of the people in the com-*

*pany wanted us to believe. She was unconsciously scapegoated for all the problems and unprocessed toxins of previous years based on decisions she had not taken (e.g. abolishing middle management and merging departments). Because of the heavy burden she carried it was almost impossible for her to survive in that role. Our first interventions were aimed at supporting her to find a new balance in her position. With this new equilibrium, she could start functioning more effectively without being dragged down by the burden projected onto her.*

*When she started to gain strength and could feel her capacities returning, we opted for interventions geared to develop a support network around her. From the start, we knew quite quickly which conversations would be challenging – but feasible – and we knew, just as well, which conversations would not be possible  at the start of our exploration. This helped us to build bridges where needed. After each intervention we reassessed the relational tissue, as we lifted it, step by step, out of the Trauma Trap.*

While conducting exploratory talks we simultaneously map the relational tissue. What we want to be particularly sensitive to is the degree to which the so-called drama triangle manifests between people, teams, departments, disciplines or hierarchical layers. The triangle will always be present when an organization starts sinking into the Trauma Trap.  How do you recognize the drama triangle?

Certain people or groups identify completely with the position of 'victim'. Because of this they put other people or groups wholly in the position of 'perpetrator' This usually sucks a number of other people or groups into the third position of 'savior'. The 'savior' and the 'victim' then form a bond against the 'perpetrator' who then, increasingly, will end up paralyzed (walking on eggs).

The drama triangle can develop very quickly and can damage or separate the relational fabric and trigger a very unhealthy dynamic. Here are some examples.

*A manager gives a team member a poor evaluation. The employee then sinks into self-pity and the victim role, immediately attracting a number of people around him who confirm his victim status. This pushes the manager into the perpetrator role and from then on he'll start feeling that nothing he does or says can affect this, as they see him through the lens of perpetrator. Sometimes this victim position is justified, but in time it can also become a means to regain some sense of power. This makes some people – consciously or not – hold on to their victimhood for that feeling of control. It is not always easy to see when victimhood is leaning towards this dysfunctional form of power. Whether or not these kinds of drama triangles form on larger or smaller scales, the organization will be completely trapped by them.*

We can see this play out on a very large scale, when political decisions are put off, or put aside, because a politician or political party wants to avoid being seen as the perpetrator. They know the electorate could punish this in the next elections. And it is the nature of politics that other parties and interest groups know exactly how to activate a drama triangle. Watching the news through these lenses is a great way to start recognizing these dynamics.

Over the years we have learned that organizational trauma that has its origin (the proverbial perpetrator) outside the organization (see Chapter 3) is often less persistent than organizational trauma whose origin lies within the organization. An external enemy ensures that people connect with each other. They bond as victims and/or saviors.

When the origin lies within the organization, the drama triangles that form inside the company will endure unless and until the trauma is healed. Gaining insight into where drama triangles are at play, helps you to map the relational tissue. In the near future, we would like to better map-out these differences, accounting for, among other things, the following factors.

- The origin or perpetrator can be Nature or man.
- The perpetrator or origin can be outside the walls of the organization or anywhere inside those walls.

- Victims can be in the organization or outside the organization and have been put into this difficult situation by actions of the organization (e.g. pollution, contamination, etc.)

- The organization can take on the role of 'savior', or another external party can fulfill that role while the organization looks on. An organization can also get stuck 'in shock'.

- 'Perpetrator', 'victim' and 'savior' can all exist, at the same time, in the same organization.

- The trauma-causing event can be a total surprise that no one could have prepared for, but it can also be something for which they should have planned. Then the authorities, for example government or management who appear to have been negligent, also are placed in a (passive) perpetrator position.

- The trauma has been around for so long that the wound is almost impossible to heal. Bridges can be burned in such a way that healing can take years or even generations.

The extent to which people or groups fully identify themselves, and therefore others, with certain positions (of the drama triangle), gives you an idea of how stuck the knot might be. If people or groups are still fully identified with a certain position, chances are that, for them, any conversation will simply confirm their beliefs. Only when people can see that they are in more than one position, is there a chance of movement. This is one of the indicators of the 'soft spot' that guides us from Phase 1 to Phase 2.

There is an important difference between a 'savior' and a 'healer of systems' (see the Four Quadrants in Chapter 7). A 'savior' will further tighten the knot, or the identification with a certain position, further confirming the dynamics of the drama triangle. When people are, or keep each other, stuck in a certain position, the approach is to try and weaken that identification. We do this by giving recognition, showing empathy, explaining certain contextual factors, providing insight into the background of their own behavior or that of others, giving feedback, providing insight into the effect of certain choices or behaviors, giving space for emotions and listening and inquiring in an appreciative, non-judgmental way. These are skills that you develop as a coach, mediator and/or therapist.

## 8.2 Phase 2:  When a door opens and the work on organizational trauma can begin

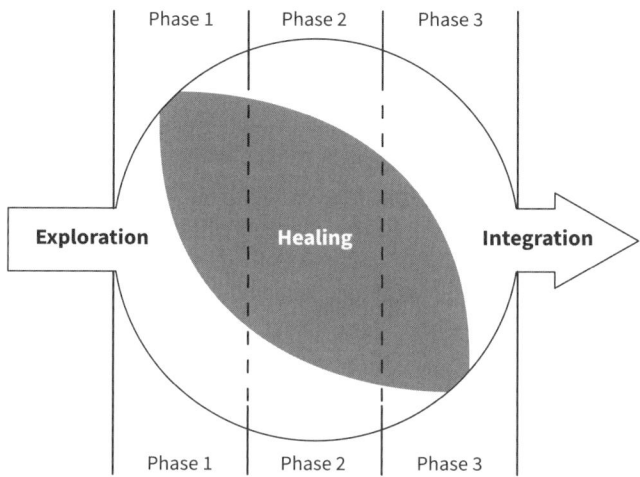

*Figure 70: Phases for dealing with organizational trauma*

During the exploration phase, healing paths and unexpected resources will appear:

- You begin to see where, how and (possibly) when the relational tissue became fragile or torn.  This points you to where mourning and processing are an issue and might already give you some idea of the kind of rituals needed.

- You start to recognize the positions different people and/or groups have 'taken' and how rigid or stuck they are in their corner of the drama triangle.  You start seeing who has formed coalitions.  This points you to those connections where healing will be necessary.

- You realize the extent to which the organization has been affected or how deeply certain groups have fallen into the Trauma Trap.

- You also gain insight into the presence or absence of resources in people and groups (skills such as resilience, emotion regulation, relevant information, listening skills, connectedness and so on). But also in the organization (support, time and space, resources, involvement, patience, openness and understanding, flexibility and so on).

From the very start you are preparing people, groups and the organization to move – when possible – into the healing phase. Often, and this will be familiar territory for mediators, you will start with people, or rather, groups of homogeneous people. So you first start working with 'parts' and only then with the 'whole'. We usually choose first to support healing at a homogeneous level before we move towards groups composed more-heterogeneously (on the level of perpetrator, victim or savior). However, this is only one of many equally-correct approaches.

Earlier in this chapter we referred to a kind of 'soft spot' that you start to feel when certain people or groups are ready to engage in pre-healing conversations. We usually recognize this 'soft spot' because people or groups start leaving their rigid identification with a certain position (e.g. victim) or no longer perceive others as occupying a certain position (e.g. perpetrator).

In *I Carry Your Heart in My Heart: Family Constellations in Prison* (Cohen, 2009, [8]) , Dan Booth Cohen describes how he works with prisoners convicted of violent crimes. He succeeds because he dares to meet them person to person, creating a space where they are, temporarily, no longer a perpetrator. In this way he comes to where they are hurt, their own 'victimhood'. Only then are they able to face the real impact of their crimes. And only when someone gets to that point can he take responsibility for his behavior or actions. Only then can someone really apologize to victims, survivors or next of kin, who are then able to sense when someone is apologizing from the place of completely accepting their guilt. Without this 'perpetrator's recognition', a prison sentence or a compensation rarely leads to peace in either life. Without this recognition, perpetrator and victim can remain stuck for years. Here, again, we see the difference between 'LAW' and 'LORE'. In this context, we have already referred to 'Restorative Justice', a form of justice that attempts to combine 'LAW' and 'LORE' and has been developing in its modern form since the mid-20th century.

And this brings us to the method referred to earlier, and fundamental to our work, which we call (organizational) constellations.

## Working with constellations

Constellations are a very powerful way of gaining insight into underlying dynamics. As you facilitate a constellation it guides you in learning how to map the relational wiring of an organization. If, for example, you notice during a conversation the way that someone talks about another person, another department, society, whatever, then you are also noticing something about how that person relates to that element or concept. And so, step by step you gather information about the quality of the relational wiring. Constellations can make this very visible. One of the simplest set-ups is a 'table-top' constellation: you arrange the system and relevant players on the table using stones, blocks, … you can use pretty much anything that comes to hand. Place, separation, proximity, direction they face, … are all elements that suddenly carry significant meaning. This is an excellent tool for looking systemically at a specific issue, either with a colleague, the client or even those involved.

Constellations are a very strong intervention for the client to become aware of how a certain dynamic, identification or problem is maintained. This awareness will help us – as facilitators – in co-creation with the client, to make the right healing interventions at the right stage. Whichever form we use, constellations are a superbly effective way to help people see much more than they could from their 'old', fixed perspectives.

**Not everything that is faced can be changed, but nothing can be changed until it is faced.**

James Baldwin

As you will see below, constellations can be used in the exploration phase to map the problem space. However, they can also be used to support healing for individual group or team members, for example to give them more insight into a particular situation or to help them towards a more-flexible perspective. Constellations can also be used to better understand the origins of organizational trauma and can even point to possible healing interventions. In short, they have a place in every phase of the healing work.

Systemic-phenomenological work and constellations often go hand in hand.

In recent years, this field has evolved profoundly and I have been helped and inspired by the practitioners whose books you'll find in the bibliography of this book and my website. In addition, there are training courses, from year-long to weekend, where you can learn more about this way of working. We recommend combining reading with practical learning if you intend to work with organizational trauma.

We distinguish three concrete ways to start working with constellations, which we'll discuss in turn:

- Constellations with Representatives

- Constellations with Floor Anchors

- Table-Top constellations (see above)

As just mentioned, you can use constellations to map the origins of organizational trauma. After all, it can be that there is no one left who actually witnessed the event(s) that led to the trauma. This is often the case in organizations, because of their frequent staff turnover. The relational wiring of an organization might, at some past date, have become damaged and still be showing symptoms, without there being any witnesses left to consult or listen to. Or it might also be that you are unable to bring the origin of an irrational dynamic to the surface. Some events need several generations before they can surface. Constellations – guided by someone with the necessary experience – can be a powerful method to explore the hidden layers of a living system in a way that enables new and powerful decisions. Constellations have been in use (in the developed world) for more than 20 years and we owe them a debt for much of the insights described above.

A constellation with representatives is still a strange approach for many people, especially in organizations. Fortunately, there has been increasing interest from the academic world over the past few years, which means that more research is being done into this methodology. This evolution not only aids acceptance, but also helps to further refine and substantiate the method. Roughly speaking, a constellation with representatives goes like this:

- We usually start with a facilitator and a group of at least 12 people, preferably from different organizations (if you are holding an 'open workshop'). Later it will become clear why this is important. Usually, during a half-day workshop, two to three cases can be constellated. The work needs a number of the participants to bring in issues specific to their organizations.

- The person presenting a case/issue (aka the client or issue holder) is first questioned by the facilitator (aka the constellator). The facilitator briefly explores the case with the client and uses all the elements of listening and exploration that we discussed earlier. Through the client's story the constellator dives, so to speak, into the living system where the client's problem is playing out. This conversation determines, to a large extent, how the initial constellation will be set up.

- The client is then invited to choose representatives for the elements of the constellation (the elements are usually decided by the client), from the group of people present. Representatives are sometimes compared to actors in a film or play. But this can cause confusion because, although they do represent someone or something from the client's case, they do not play a role. This is the main reason why it is better that they know nothing about the case. This ensures that they represent, rather than try to act a part. This allows a person to represent an individual, a team, a part of the organization, a product or service, a value, a mission, a belief: an element can be almost anything in fact. Indeed, as mentioned earlier, we define ourselves not only by our relationships to other people but also to concepts, groups, values, products, and much more. All of these can be placed into a constellation via representatives.

- Next, the client is asked to set up the representatives in the space (this can be something as simple as a circle of chairs) and time and time again we have seen that – from that moment on – the representatives sink, as it were, into the relational fabric of the original situation. The dynamics of the case unfold, there and then, in the space. The constellation reveals, step by step, what is not healed or where there is still tension. In an indirect manner, you get direct insight into the health of the relational tissue.

*Figure 71: Constellation with representatives*

- The constellator then starts making interventions based on the healing paths that are revealing themselves. These are inspired by a mix of experience, feeling, intuition and systemic wisdom. With these interventions the constellator is looking for what is needed to restore balance and/or order, to include what was lost or suppressed, or to face what needs healing. Interventions are movements or sentences or combinations of both. The constellator sees, almost immediately in the constellation, the effect of his interventions on the elements and so on the relational fabric. By doing so, it becomes clear – step by step – what kind of healing will be most effective. At the same time, we see how the relational fabric became wounded. This shows where acknowledgement will be crucial to healing. Healing, which, if it does not occur, will leave the living system stuck in the Trauma Trap.

*After years of rigidity and stuckness in a young business unit, the director of the parent organization (HQ) went for an organizational constellation. The representatives, chosen for members of the business unit, all seemed to be staring at an empty space in the middle of the room, and the representatives for some managers of the same business unit, also seemed drawn to that space. It felt as if these people were being sucked into a hole in the ground.*

*The facilitator started with this question:* "Who was important to your business unit and left in a painful way, irrespective of whether or not it was their choice?"

*This revealed that the founder had been forced out, and that this had not been handled in a correct and respectful way. Why? During the last few years of his tenure, the founder of the business unit became very frustrated because, in a way, he was too entrepreneurial for the management of the parent organization. He often overstepped the boundaries set by the directors, preventing him from realizing his own strategies. This led to an ever-increasing conflict with them, which was never openly discussed. Mainly because the company was not prepared to pay him off, due to his many years of service, and because his business unit was making a great deal of money for the company, the founder was eventually forced out. But the way this was done caused a lasting wound. A deep mistrust had grown towards the directors.*

*After he left, 'his' business unit sank into a series of dysfunctional dynamics, despite its earlier success. Hence the representatives' initial reaction in the constellation. The business unit had fallen into the Trauma Trap due to the 'departure' of the founder (excluded vs. included). The effect of his being forced out had only gradually become clear in the dynamics of the business unit. It took seven years for it to show in the numbers. Only then was the director of the parent organization prepared to really look at the situation. In this case with a constellation.*

The constellation showed that employees and managers who had worked with the founder were still connected to him. The 'hole' in the floor, the sucking force in the constellation, showed that those people wanted to follow the founder, and were loyal to him instead of to their new director.

Because it was the founder's entrepreneurship that led to this situation, being entrepreneurial became – in an unconscious way – something that could endanger your membership.  Entrepreneurship had become trapped in a Trauma Capsule. The position of the founder's successor eventually became untenable because she had played a role, in consultation with the directors, in forcing-out the founder.  The people still connected with the founder could not be loyal to her and so didn't support her in her new role as his successor.

When it became clear for her that leading the department out of the Trauma Trap, without support from the employees, would be impossible, she decided to leave.  This (re)created space for the entrepreneurship of the early years. However, it took some time before trust was restored between the business unit and the parent organization.

In this example, a constellation was used because it was not yet clear why the business unit had, bit by bit, slid into the Trauma Trap. Take care – because, although there are already many coaches trained in working with constellations – a constellation like this one may only take place in consultation with the director of the business unit or the management of the parent organization (in this case).  They are the only ones with a mandate to start working on this. Subsequently, it is important to use a constellation, in this situation, as an instrument for gaining insight and possibly testing a number of hypotheses. The insights that come up in this way should be checked – as far as is possible.

In recent years, more and more managers and board members have opened up to the constellations approach, as it allows a safe way of looking at the hidden dynamics in their organizations.  After a constellation, managers or executives can still choose to do nothing. If they do choose to act on the insights gained from the constellation, they do so with a much better feel for what might or might not work.

However, sometimes there just will not be enough people available with whom you can do a constellation with representatives. It might also be that the issue is too confidential or too fragile to be aired in public. These are situations where you can opt for a constellation with floor anchors. Here, the different elements are not represented by people, but by placing floor anchors (often a simple sheet of A4 paper – a place card) into the held space and inviting the issue holder to stand, one anchor at a time, in the different element positions.

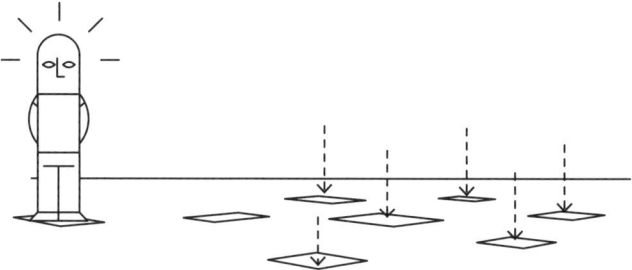

*Figure 72: Constellation with floor anchors*

This approach is often a very good way to literally stand in another person's shoes. At its best, it ensures people experience not just an empathy for the 'other', in whose shoes they stand, but they actually feel exactly what that person is feeling and/or why.  While exploring those different positions, the facilitator and issue holder get a feel for the relational fabric of the living system. This way of experiencing other, relevant perspectives, makes it possible for the issue holder to open up to a painful situation he wasn't able to face or acknowledge until then. We have learned that a constellation with floor anchors can be very effective in helping people step out of their identification with a certain position (e.g. perpetrator, victim, rescuer). Once again, an example will help.

> *A director noticed that his staff had lost all interest in their work after a number of people had been fired. He did, however, make every effort to please them.  During a constellation with floor anchors, he was asked to take a moment and try to get in touch with what he felt and to put place cards on the floor for every element that he saw as relevant to the situation.  He chose – in consultation with the facilitator – these elements:*
>
> - *himself (as director);*
> - *the employees who remained;*
> - *the employees who were dismissed;*
> - *the clients of the organization.*

*Then the facilitator invited him to stand, one by one, on each place card. He started with the employees who had been fired, and noticed that his (their) attention was drawn to the employees who had stayed. When he stood on his own anchor, he was pulled in the direction of the clients. When he stood on the floor anchor of the 'remaining' employees, he noticed that his (their) attention was entirely on the employees who were fired and that he had no interest in the clients. It became clear to him that there was still an intense bond between the two sets of employees and that something had to be done before the 'remainers' could, again, fully focus on the clients.*

*Standing on the place card of the employees who remained, the director became very emotional, although he was not really an emotional type. This felt very strange to him at first. By standing in that place, he felt that the employees who had remained were unable to let go of their ex-colleagues. The 'remainers' were still in mourning. It looked like survivor guilt, the phenomenon of feeling guilty that one is allowed to stay. The director suddenly realized exactly why his earlier, enthusiastic, attempts to motivate the people who were allowed to stay had had an opposite effect. It was a total denial of the letting-go process that they still had to go through. Hesitantly, he admitted that he was not so sure how to deal with these emotions. Together with the facilitator he worked out a way to approach this with the employees who had remained.*

*The constellation allowed the director to better understand what was really going on and also made him more receptive to how his employees felt, ensuring that he did not continue with his previous, but well-intentioned efforts, which had only made things worse.*

Sometimes, working with floor anchors can be a step too far, or too fast, for certain people. In that case, you can map the living system and the various relevant elements via a table-top constellation.

*Figure 73: Table-top constellation*

This method is usually used in one-on-one sessions or with small groups. By putting the living system on the table, you can look in different ways at what is going on. You can look through the eyes of each party involved, but you can also see the relationships between the different parties and/or the dynamics of the whole. This method is ideal for teaching people how to zoom out and how to switch perspectives. It also has quite a low threshold – in comparison with the previous approaches. We often use it during the exploration phase. Almost every time we use this method, people immediately get a sense of what we mean when we talk about choreography, dynamics, patterns and relational fabric.

As you can see, constellations can help us to understand and see the hidden dynamics of organizations. There is no need for organizational trauma to be involved in order to use this way of working. Constellations show what is needed to heal or support the relational tissue – wherever it might be in the Trauma Trap – and bring to the surface that which is making the tissue fragile or is damaging it. You could call it a functional MRI-scan (fMRI) of a living system.

**Pendulation and titration**

I came to know this concept, which is central to trauma work, through the work of Peter Levine, Babette Rothschild and Anngwyn St. Just. Let's take a first look at it through the analogy we used earlier, of rehabilitation after a muscle injury. Stressing the muscles – e.g. through strength training – causes minute fissures in the muscle tissue. The body's healing process ensures that these fissures heal, but it does more: it makes the muscle tissue a little thicker; able to handle a greater stress next time. This is how muscle-mass develops. Recovery does not occur only through rest, but also through step-by-step, precisely-measured exercise.

If we translate this into working with trauma in organizations, we first have to look back at how a human being tries to deal with an overwhelming event. It is clear that he becomes overwhelmed because he fails to process all the components of that event (emotions, sensations, smell, noise, images and so on). When these are not fully and correctly processed, the event stays present in his body and mind but fragmented, scattered and incoherent throughout his system. The consequences of this failure-to-process are: loss of integration, feeling disconnected and/or overstimulation. Toxins keep accumulating in Trauma Capsules. The person or system 'carrying' these Trauma Capsules is now constantly at risk of them being triggered, which would reactivate the sense of being overwhelmed, and would activate all kinds of defense, coping or protection mechanisms. That is why irrational or avoidance dynamics develop or certain capabilities – which are stuck in these Trauma Capsules – seem inaccessible. As a result, a human being, but also a team, a department or an organization (any form of living systems) can get stuck in the Trauma Trap, and its existing potential cannot fully unfold. If confronted, anew, by an excess of stress, the chances are that the living system will sink, deeper and deeper, into the Trauma Trap.

And so we come to the concept of 'titration'. In concrete terms, this means that drop-by-drop, hence the word titrate, you bring the traumatized living system back into contact with situations that could cause reactivation and overwhelming, especially if you make the mistake of administering too high a dose. Compare it to lightly-loading a recovering muscle. This low-dose activates the release of the toxic contents sequestered in the Trauma Capsules, but in a controlled way. The dosing should prevent the person/system feeling overwhelmed again.  In addition to releasing accumulated emotions, the capabilities that were stuck in the capsules can start flowing again.  The clock can start ticking again for all that was stuck in time.

*Figure 74: Titration (and pendulation)*

This approach is a form of desensitization, applied with a high degree of attunement, containment, compassion, protection, guidance, trust and non-judgement, qualities that often unfold in a natural way if intentions are correct.  Because the accumulated energy is channeled in a manageable way, peace and stability can be restored and the ability to channel accumulated tensions and emotions can grow.  As a result, the defense mechanisms, such as rigidity or extreme avoidance behavior, can relax, albeit little by little.  This is how dysfunctional dynamics or patterns get worked out of a living system.

Take care, though, to titrate only when a sanctuary has been created: a place that feels safe and familiar, that people can (re)turn to when it becomes too stressful. Because, at this stage, the risk of being overwhelmed again is ever present. As the facilitator, you lead the group to re-experience what is exciting, stimulating or potentially re-activating. And you prepare the parties involved – possibly separately – by developing and/or providing resources.  Hence the crucial nature of the first phase.  For example, developing resources can be done by first training people around a number of themes, by providing sufficient safety, by giving guidance around trauma and by developing certain skills (non-violent communication, breathing techniques, body-scanning and so on).

If, after working with a group, you notice they are again in danger of being overwhelmed – for example by an accusation, or by the public naming of something that went wrong – then you retreat with them to the sanctuary or you remind the group of the resources you have provided and that they have developed. Here we are revisiting the concept of 'container' and 'holding space' from the previous chapter. And over the years we've learned that this kind of facilitation is best done as a pair; able to strengthen and support each other. And, even as a trained facilitator, you'll find this work can still touch you deeply.

This movement back and forth, between sanctuary and titrated re-activation, is called 'pendulation'. It is the process by which, for example, a traumatized group learns to move back and forth between safety and 'danger' in a controlled way. It is precisely that the group knows and feels they have a sanctuary to return to, that gives them the confidence to open up to the parts and emotions that have been split-off. In addition, the group feels supported, as they can see that someone is taking care of the process. This dampens the fear of getting overwhelmed (again) or getting completely stuck (being overwhelmed forever). Either of these events could cause re-traumatization, pushing the group or organization even deeper into the Trauma Trap.

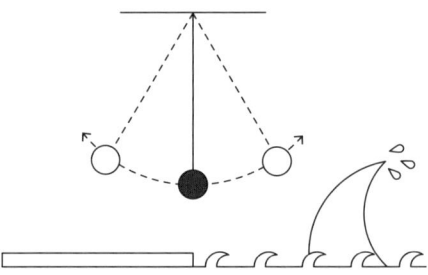

*Figure 75: Pendulation (and titration)*

A previously-mentioned concept, from the work of Daniel Siegel *Mindsight The New Science of Personal Transformation* (Siegel, 2010, [25]) , provides an extra framework for pendulation and titration. Siegel talks about the 'river of integration' which flows between two banks: chaos and rigidity. When a living system is flowing in the river bed (the part between the banks), there is a sense of peace, safety and integration. This is the place where you take the group when it gets too overwhelming; after all, straying too far from the middle could lead to being traumatized again. Pendulation means consciously, but carefully, seeking out the banks of rigidity and chaos in order to widen the river bed, while staying in touch with the safety of being in mid-stream. How narrow or wide the river is, can be seen as an expression of the resilience of the living system. Titration is carefully-controlled contact with both banks. The ultimate goal is to continually widen the middle by pushing apart the banks of chaos and rigidity. Giving increasing room for the system to flow, while replacing rigidity and inhibition with flexibility and resilience. Fluency and control arise where once there was fear of chaos or of losing control completely. This drags the living system, step by step, back up out of the Trauma Trap.

Leaders and managers confronted by a team that is stuck in the Trauma Trap can – if they are aware of this way of working – restore and sustain resilience in that team.

> *Due to frequent changes and being overloaded for too long, a team had become completely stuck. There was hardly any work-related consultation, or even conversation, between the employees. Who did what was decided by the manager alone. As long as there was only small talk, there was no problem in the team. But when it came to the redistribution of work, everyone went immediately into a kind of cramp. The manager became the savior, the ogre and the bottleneck all at the same time. Any tension between team members was completely attributed to her.*
>
> *Getting the employees to decide, together, who did what would be a big step forward, but the willingness did not exist, and switching to more self-regulation, all at once, would be devastating in this case. Unfortunately, self-regulation is often introduced in cases like this, with all its negative consequences: the tap is opened fully and there is no longer titration, there is drowning.*

Careful titration and pendulation – tuned to the rhythm of the team – might look like this:

1. Regularly organizing a planning meeting in which the team is facilitated very actively, so there is only room for constructive exchange. In this case, making difficult decisions remains entirely with the facilitator. At that moment the facilitator embodies the safe place for the team.

2. In a next phase, we might conduct a team discussion about the criteria for redistributing the work when needed. Because the criteria are still relatively abstract, the probability of difficult situations is still small (= titrating small doses of stress).

3. The team members, with less-active guidance, can – when they seem to be ready – create a simple plan based on previously-established criteria. If it becomes too stressful, a facilitator can still intervene (pendulation).

4. …

In this example a combination of titration and pendulation is used. A trained facilitator could support this process, but we believe that managers and team leaders could easily be trained to guide this kind of process once they become more trauma-informed. We even believe that this knowledge is crucial when guiding teams towards self-regulation, especially if it is their first encounter with this approach.

In order to find a good way to do this, the manager must (with or without the support of a facilitator) understand what are the group's triggers and must divide the desensitization process into small, subtle steps. That way he or she can begin with pendulation and titration. He can do this by consciously building up the agenda of team meetings based on this approach. As a facilitator, it is worth training the manager in the approach, as we want to wean him off his dependence on your (external) support. You can also explain pendulation and titration to the team members (= psycho-education) at the right time, and in such a way that they can gradually take the growth process into their own hands. 'Pendulation' and 'titration', supplemented by the concept of the 'river of integration', are crucial concepts in the processing of trauma in and by organizations.

**Repairing connections**

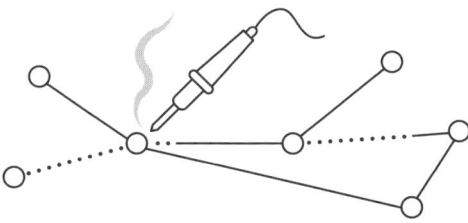

*Figure 76: Repairing connections*

In our Western society, most of the trauma work to date has been done in an individual setting. But you will soon see, once you begin working with organizational trauma, that this only addresses part of the issue. Sooner or later you have to work with the relational fabric. In concrete terms, this means that you'll bring people or groups together, whose shared relational wiring has become extremely fragile or has even been torn apart. At the beginning of the exploration phase, these are often the parties that were stuck in polarized positions (see the drama triangle). Whoever you bring together – and at what time – depends on the issue with which you wish to start. It can be an existing team, people from different teams, people from the same or different hierarchical layers. There might be language differences and/or cultural differences. Choose a group composition that is manageable, and where you feel a fair amount of willingness and stability. This is 'just' a feeling, and it can feel rather exciting, but here are a number of possible criteria for where to begin:

- You start to feel the proverbial 'soft spot', partly because people identify themselves, and/or others, less and less with one of the positions in the drama triangle.

- During the exploration phase and the initial coaching, albeit with homogeneously composed groups, you begin to see that more resources are available to them: self-reflection, understanding of the context and others, emotional regulation, communication skills, support, etc.

- As a facilitator you have sufficient insight into what is going on that you know, more or less, what might be the real issue(s).

- You feel a shared wish or an explicit choice, among those involved, to heal the situation. After all, healing cannot be forced. It's a choice!

- You feel that you still have the trust and respect of those involved.

Furthermore, the complexity, intensity and/or size of the group determines whether several facilitators are needed. We usually opt to do this type of work with at least two. Because when you are working on the relational fabric between people and/or groups, it is all too easy to get sucked into individual stories and emotions, with the result that you are seen as biased in some way.

Also, be aware of the fact that people – especially at the beginning of such an encounter – can hide behind a kind of façade. They pretend that nothing is amiss, but only for as long as the toxic theme is not mentioned. Or they arrived, already feeling unsafe. That's why each encounter must start with the creation of a safe container for healing.

We use a number of approaches, or ways in, to bring people into proper contact with each other, in order to start working on organizational trauma.

In Chapter 7 we discussed rituals and ceremonies. Earlier in this chapter we discussed three types of constellations. Within the scope of this chapter, we will discuss a number of extra working methods that we often use to support healing in and between groups, in particular:

- Working with a timeline;

- Working with 'healing circles';

- Apologizing.

In Chapter 9 we will explore a number of concepts that are part of the recovery and integration phase, in particular:

- Mapping how the day-to-day work causes over-stimulation, creating 'compassion fatigue', 'vicarious trauma' or 'burn-out'. Also, if this initially affects 'only' individual employees it will, in time, lead to a weakening of the relational fabric in and between teams and, eventually, the whole organization

- Standing still and reflecting on the operation of the organization in all its facets: culture, structure, processes, work pressure, leadership, etc., in such a way that what constantly over-stresses the relational tissue can be identified and tackled.  Here we think of issues such as too many drastic changes, an accumulation of losses of various kinds, inconsistencies in the organization's operation, lack of clarity, etc.

- During the exploration phase, much has usually happened that makes people and/or groups seem ready to reach out across the cracks in the relational fabric; the only way the fabric can heal.

Naturally, this remains an exciting, possibly stressful, step for everyone involved, even though the work in the exploration phase should have ensured the right conditions and preparation for all involved. Before you bring people and groups together, you need to prepare yourself. You have to be emotionally available to guide such a meeting. You have an 'advantage', however, in that the exploration phase should have ensured that you know – more or less – what to expect.

### Working with a timeline

How you introduce the work is very important.  You outline the purpose of the meeting in a clear, concise way and you make a number of 'agreements', or rules, with those present.  You'll need a number of them, that you can fit to whatever is unfolding at any moment.  What follows looks like a check-list but that is not the way to introduce this important preparatory stage. Here are some typical agreements:

- Everyone chooses, for themselves, what they are comfortable sharing.

- Everything shared during this meeting is confidential.  You might find that you are asked to make yourself a lot more vulnerable than you are used to.

- You are invited to speak in your own name and support others to do the same. You don't help others by speaking for them.

- Everyone's opinions and feelings count.

- Each of you is invited to make an active contribution, so that we can move forward together.

- We show respect for each other, and each other's differences and experiences.

- Emotions are welcome, and they do not have to be resolved. It is fine for them to just be there.

- We share responsibility for how this meeting goes.

- Let us know, in a timely manner, if you need something.

- Let us know if we are missing or overlooking something.

Precisely because it can be exciting to meet each other in this context, it is useful to have a working structure. This provides guidance and a framework through which you can engage with the work, step by step. It makes pendulation and titration a lot easier. An approach that we often use in our work is to build and reveal the shared history via a timeline. This approach is inspired, among other things, by the Spanish Descansos Ritual that I learned with Anngwyn St. Just. A 'descanso' is a cross placed on a spot where someone lost their life in a violent or unexpected way. Everywhere in the world you'll see these crosses by the side of the road where someone lost their life.

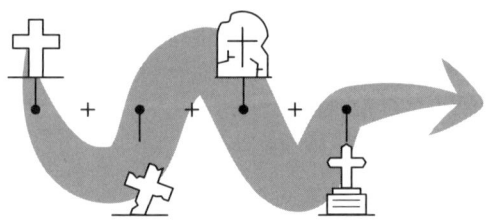

*Figure 77: Working with a timeline*

Building a timeline means going through the history of the organization (or the entity with which you are working) and, together, mapping their descansos along that timeline. This joint exploration usually makes a number of things clear:

- Was that event given a place, or was it swept under the carpet?

- Is there still need for recognition or healing?

- Is there something or someone still attached to that event or has it been carefully processed?

Choose – after you have explained the timeline method – a long, clear wall to work on, or free up the floor. It helps to make the timeline visible with a long strip of tape. Then give clear instructions so that people feel solid and supported. Some questions that can help, follow. Use the questions that best suit the situation. The following questions are an extract of questions linked to the systemic principles mentioned earlier in this chapter:

- Were there significant events, reorganizations, relocations, mergers, etc.? Are they still having an effect?

- How has the organization changed or evolved over the years? Did everyone grow and develop together or did some people get stuck?

- What or who have you lost on the way? What or who is still missing today?

- Have any people, goals, products, departments, functions or values been let go, or did any join? What effect did either 'movement' have?

- Do they still have their first customers? Did the target group change? Was that a conscious decision? How did that happen?

- Were there products, services or activities that were harmful and, possibly, caused accidents?

- Where in the past was there any crime or injustice?

- Who or what was insufficiently acknowledged, honored, rewarded or compensated?

Then let people form pairs – a safe intermediate step – and share what they have found to be impressive or overwhelming during their time in the organization. Use large post-it notes, colored A4 paper or (if you have been able to prepare them) photos or images that represent the moments and events in question. Then place all the different moments on the timeline. Start at the beginning and work forward to the present moment.

People will bring in what they feel ready for or feel safe with. Maybe not everything will come up. This is not something you can force. Based on their reactions – recognition or denial – people unconsciously measure the strength (the safety) of the healing container and how well the facilitators are watching over it.

If it all begins to feel a little negative, you can add some balance by asking about events in the organization's history that people are proud of. This is also a way of pendulating and titrating. Take care though, that you do not use this to gloss over or nuance the unhealed history. Sometimes people must face up to the stark reality of a situation in order to fully take in its impact. It helps if you consciously limit the opportunity for nuance.

As you become more able to observe, in real time, the systemic phenomenology (which we explored at the beginning of this chapter), you will be able to judge, moment by moment, the quality of the relational wiring – in the context of what is being shared. You will notice when a certain moment (from the past) is still alive or at what stage of healing it is.

> *An organization had radically adjusted its strategy in response to changes in the market. The roots of the organization were in technical, expertise-related knowledge, but the change had made its commercial people more central to the organization. The long-serving, expertise oriented, staff felt suddenly and deeply undervalued.*
> *When new people joined, the 'older' staff immediately tested their expertise, which often created a hostile setting, resulting in a high turnover of young, new hires. Because the company continued on the new course, it became increasingly difficult for the 'older' staff and, eventually, one by one, they left the company.*
> *At the time of the change of direction, nobody knew that something in the soul of the organization had been touched. The older staff were keeping the old values alive, while the new people were recruited around new values. That created a deep fissure and polarization.*
>
> *Through looking back together, the effect and results became visible. All those involved were able to get a clearer perspective. The feelings that were discussed were recognized and, above*

*all, seen as normal.  What initially seemed incomprehensible, was given a place – for most of those involved.  Ultimately, this session resulted in a solution for honoring both technical and commercial work in the right way, so that the us or them situation could grow towards us and them.*

When, and because, it is possible to reflect on painful times or events that have not yet healed, in an investigative, acknowledging way, different perspectives can be explored and space can be made for expressing locked-up, hardened emotions. In this way everything can be given meaning by the collective, and a coherent, unfragmented story of reality develops. This is what a group of people needs to feel connected again, and is what is lost when an organization falls into the Trauma Trap.

As are probably noticing, working with a timeline is the Trauma Formula at work. By walking along a timeline the people in the room will start seeing how the organization (or the entity with which you are working) became stuck in the Trauma Trap.  And, as we already stated, only what is faced, can be healed.  So, most of the time this work opens the door for (mutual) acknowledgment and understanding.
Often there are moments of ritual, during such a meeting or workshop, where you notice that people spontaneously complete something previously unfinished. It is part of your role to help the group do this.

*When employees of a large organization built a timeline together with the management, it became clear that the merger of the original, small, independent organizations had, for many employees, not yet been processed.  One by one the names of the original, small organizations were written down and people stood back in their places in their original organization.  Issues were shared and tears were shed.  This made it possible to respectfully let-go of the 'old' organizations, which released the energy needed to embrace the new structure.  This issue was at the root of a lot of the problems the company had been trying to solve for some time without really making any progress.*

Not everything can be revealed or healed by making a timeline.  Although you often see which issues and paths need further work, things sometimes go wrong in organizations because, after such a session, the focus understandably falls back onto day to day operations.  Often there is not enough time, or the organization lacks the experience to take the next step. In that case, further support is indicated and the facilitator needs to have made this clear well in advance. So you do not agree a contract for a number of interventions or meetings, but for a certain result or effect. After all, nothing is more painful than seeing a way forward and being unable to take it. This could easily re-activate the trauma.

### Healing Circles

Healing circles are another method you could use, but offer less structure. They are inspired by 'dadirri'. This is a way of being present or listening to each other. Aborigines use dadirri to keep their community healthy and use it to create a safe container for people's stories and emotions. Those of the tribe not speaking, sit in a circle and offer deep, authentic recognition, in particular through their way of listening and being present. This spontaneously results in a feeling of solidarity and acknowledgment, which can have a particularly healing effect on the relational fabric of the tribe. My colleagues and I usually use this method with smaller groups. In practice, we have learned that stories or testimonies follow each other in a natural way. One story makes room for the next story. The big difference between a timeline and a healing circle is that the latter follows a more organic flow. The order of the stories is like a natural way of pendulation and titration. The deep wisdom of groups at work.

Also during healing circles, small rituals arise or it becomes clear where further steps are needed. This brings us to the closing subject of this chapter: apologizing.

### Apologizing

To avoid ambiguity, we'll use the terms perpetrator and victim. In the context of organizational trauma, each of these positions can be taken by an individual, a group (e.g. the Board), a role etc. Often it is not so clear. A person or a group is seldom completely on one side or the other. Part of the healing process involves untangling these knots. Just as a group of employees can become the victim of a choice of the organization (e.g. a closure), a complete organization can just as well be the victim of the behavior or the choices of a group of employees (e.g. sabotage).

In any case, perpetrators and victims are inextricably linked to each other by the sharing of an overwhelming event. That connection – especially if it is not yet healed – is usually colored by crude, raw emotions resulting from the damage caused and the loss or suffering. Sometimes we see that victims continue to hold onto their pain until the perpetrators are punished, acknowledge their actions and/or apologize.  This allows victims to choose a kind of dominant or power position in an attempt to restore the balance. However, victims who continue to nourish resentment can, in a certain way, block the perpetrators so they will never be able or willing to face what they have done.  In that case, the victims remain trapped by the action that the perpetrator cannot take because they are 'blocked' by the victim's position. A snake biting its own tail. This makes it even more difficult to find peace or allow the relationship between perpetrators and victims to grow into a milder, softer form.  In any case, an important key to healing is linked with apologies, knowing that this is perhaps one of the most complex systemic knots to disentangle.

An authentic apology, from the right people or authorities, is a deep recognition of the damage caused or the suffering endured, and very often an essential healing step.  The absence of an apology can begin to weigh more heavily than the initial damage.  Yet often there is no apology. Because it could be seen as a concession or confession that opens up the way to claims for damage and compensation: LAW getting in the way of LORE. Of course, the ego of the perpetrator can also stand in the way. We see, more often in organizations, that the gap between managers and employees cannot be bridged, because of egos and also because there is insufficient courage to take this step.

Because the healing power of an apology can be substantial and because, at the same time, it is an extremely complex exchange, within which there is a real chance of re-traumatization, it is essential that you have well-developed systemic wisdom and bodily consciousness.  This will be decisive in feeling, before it is spoken, whether an apology will have the needed healing effect or not. Working towards this 'apology moment' has something of a ritual character and, as facilitator, you can play an important role here too.

Apologizing requires a lot of courage: you make yourself very vulnerable. It goes hand in hand with taking responsibility, in the right proportion and by the right people or groups. A person can take too little responsibility, but also too much – for example, to get someone else out of a difficult place. With organizational trauma, responsibility is often divided across different parties, as in the following example.

> *A team had been sitting on the edge of the Trauma Trap for a long time. Some team members were already burned out. The dynamics were fueled by an old and profound conflict between two employees. After an intense guidance process, the conflict seemed to be settled. Yet something continued to be wrong. It felt like a wound that could not heal completely. When another person left with burn-out, the situation was explored via an organizational constellation. Quite quickly, it was clear that the manager of the team also carried some responsibility for the injuries that had built up over the years, in particular by not intervening. It was not until the manager apologized and accepted his responsibility that peace returned.*

An apology is only appropriate for those things over which a person or role had control or were responsible for from a particular role. One can be responsible for a certain act, choice or decision, but not for how others deal with it. You cannot apologize for how the other person responded to your actions, because that would release the other of his responsibility. If the organization decides to close a department and the people in that department decide to sabotage the machine rooms, causing a staff member to be seriously injured, then the organization can only apologize for the decision and the way it was taken, but not for the reaction of the employees.

Apologies do not work if – and often this is done in a subtle or underhand way – you also place some of the responsibility on the other party. For example: *"We did not communicate or guide this closure properly. Thus you felt humiliated and treated without respect, despite your many years of loyalty to our company. We apologize for this because we would have liked it to have gone differently, but you also failed to be sufficiently flexible in response to the changing expectations of our customers".* Apologies interlaced with ifs and buts are often a precursor to even more problems.

Effective apologies come from the heart and are best when as short as possible. Too many words blur the effect and weaken the transmission.

An apology is not a magic trick, wiping the slate clean and making everything immediately forgotten or forgiven. Healing will not happen just because everyone wants to forget a particular event. On the contrary, healing often only starts when a terrible event gets a place in the history of an organization. Apologies initially create the foundation to restore the relational wiring, which could, eventually, lead to healing.

An apology without action, such as ensuring the trauma has no more power in the future, misses its purpose and is a complete waste of energy. For example, an organization or agency can apologize once for being unprepared for a particular overwhelming event. But if nothing is done to avoid that in the future, that apology was, in effect, nothing more than a trick.

If a number of employees are killed by safety negligence, the organization can apologize to colleagues and family members. However, that apology will only be of real value if the organization does whatever is possible to prevent such accidents happening again (= Phase 3: Integration, which will be discussed in the next chapter).

**The sincerity test of an apology**
**is in the follow-up.**

Harriet Lerner

The power of healing circles lies in the fact that they facilitate deep listening to the experiences of victims. Only then is their pain and their suffering faced and can there be acknowledgement. Apologies work if perpetrators are also willing to listen to the victims' stories of the effect of their negligence, their wrong decisions, their disruptive measures. Involving the perpetrator – rather than letting him listen remotely – is crucial. In a certain way, the perpetrator has to be willing to stand in the wave of emotions expressed by the victim. This only happens if the perpetrator is willing to drop his armor. Repeating what he has heard, felt, seen and thanking them for their honesty and openness will help.

Once victims have been heard and feel acknowledged, the possibility arises that they might understand the rationale for a particular choice, decision, or apparent negligence. Not to gloss over things, but to make clear that you – for example as a director – can end up in situations where you have to make choices, without having an overview of all the possible consequences.

In the untangling, of the knot of responsibility, too often the focus is on perpetrators and victims. This allows a number of parties to get out of jail free, in particular the passive witnesses and the saviors (see the drama triangle). Passive witnesses are people who, due to their silence, are just as responsible for certain abuse. Organizations that consciously choose to care for the health of the relational fabric understand this well (see below). Saviors, because of their behavior, can get in the way of healing or can make the wounds even bigger. When the knot starts to come loose, we often see that these people also apologize for actions and roles that were not theirs, but where they could have acted but did not. This often indicates a healing process that is going well.

Healing then is a shared choice. But there are also some 'rules' for victims. Their attitude can also prevent healing: after all, to be labeled as a perpetrator – even when justified – is one of the most difficult positions to be in. It leads to shame and can shatter a person's self-worth. So it takes a lot for someone to stand in that position and embrace that truth. The attitude of the victims can make this so difficult that the perpetrator eventually becomes totally stuck and cannot utter a single word of what is needed to release the shared knot.

It makes apologizing extremely difficult if victims link a perpetrator to someone (or an organization) who is actually really terrible (= fully identifying someone with the perpetrator role). In that case it becomes particularly difficult for the perpetrator (e.g. the management) to apologize. It is only human to try to protect yourself by pulling up a shield or raising your armor if you or the organization are attacked by disdainful and contemptuous judgments, criticism, accusations and so on. If there are too many, albeit understandable, emotions among the victims – which you as facilitator might, by now, be sensing – then it is still too early to work towards an apology.

Victims can also demand apologies too early or too emphatically. Perpetrators must be allowed to grow towards that point of vulnerability (or 'soft spot'). Only in the most extreme cases is it ever a conscious choice to cause human suffering. This means that the proverbial perpetrator (manager, director, etc.), in the case of an organization, also needs their own process to arrive at the place of an apology. Forcing the process only leads to a cosmetic apology from behind their armor, rather than a true apology from the heart.

Victims must also have the courage to show their vulnerability to the perpetrators. If victims stay behind an armor of anger and accusations, chances are that the necessary contact will not occur. The time might not yet be ripe and you might be better off taking a rest break (= pendulation and titration). Often, however, we notice that something happens to the perpetrator when a victim breaks unexpectedly. At that moment people touch each other person to person, beyond perpetrator or victim. You cannot stage or direct this. As a facilitator you can only create conditions that make this possible, knowing that it can be a long road to get to that point.

Once sincere apologies have been expressed, each should thank the other. The more often a person apologizes, the more he will realize how high the mountain someone must climb to be able to apologize sincerely. Receiving the apology opens the space to heal torn relationships.

As the facilitator you can play another particularly important role during the session itself (see holding space). It might be early in the engagement and the space for authentic exchange might still be very fragile. All those involved, on both sides, are particularly vulnerable and often not able to keep that healing container safe. So here again pendulation and titration are appropriate. For example, if the victims become too accusatory, too angry or too critical, because they do not feel heard or acknowledged, the people who are expected to apologize, will close up again and make it a painful experience once again. As the facilitator, you must constantly monitor the quality of the fragile, healing connection. You must protect everyone involved. If you are unable to do so, you cannot facilitate such a meeting.

An inspiring example in the context of organizational and social trauma is the speech by Julia Gillard as Prime Minister of Australia (PM Gillard delivers apology to victims of forced adoption on Youtube). From her mandate she apologized publicly to the many victims of forced adoptions. The government took newly-born babies away from unmarried mothers for many years, because it did not consider them capable of raising their children. This dreadful practice had been used for decades by the government and caused a great deal of suffering. Only an apology from someone who holds the highest mandate – in this case the prime minister – had sufficient 'weight' to truly and effectively apologize to the victims. Knowing who is the right person to apologize requires a certain kind of sensitivity from you as a facilitator. If there is one decision that a manager or director cannot delegate, it is this one.

To complete this chapter, a reminder of the Trauma Formula:

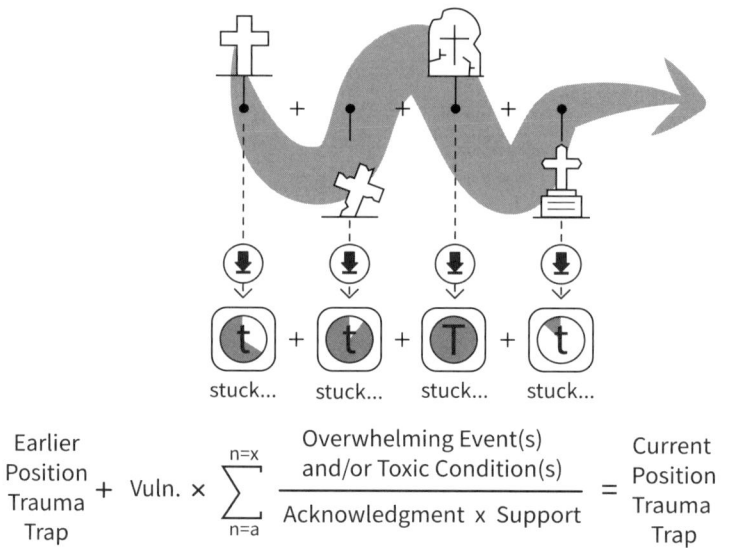

$$\text{Earlier Position Trauma Trap} + \text{Vuln.} \times \sum_{n=a}^{n=x} \frac{\text{Overwhelming Event(s) and/or Toxic Condition(s)}}{\text{Acknowledgment} \times \text{Support}} = \text{Current Position Trauma Trap}$$

*Figure 78: Trauma Formula 2.0*

If an organization, or parts of an organization, seem to be stuck in the Trauma Trap – which you will find out during the exploration or first phase – the healing or second phase only starts when someone decides to take real responsibility for starting a healing process. Too often, we see that unhealed, organizational trauma continues to drag on much too long, unnecessarily tightening the knots and widening the wounds in the relational fabric. Often then, when we are invited into an organization, we find a living system that is completely stuck.

- The organization has become hostage to all kinds of dysfunctional dynamics.

- Complaints are submitted by people from the organization through the trade unions, confidential advisers or safety and security advisers.

- Because the energy for a reorganization, critical to the business surviving, such as a serious change of strategy, is completely stuck somewhere in the Trauma Trap.

- If this is the case, looking back is the only way to move forward. At the beginning of this chapter, the focus was on careful, step by step work. In the first phase, you mainly explore the organization to get a clear picture of what is going on. Working with a timeline starts to give you an idea of how, where and how many times the relational fabric has been wounded.

Based on these insights, you start building up resources and start checking if the organization is ready and willing to make a real go of it. Only then, you can start with the (unhealed) trauma. It's very important to check whether a space opens for the acknowledgment and the support that was previously not offered. At the beginning of the exploration phase, you are totally in the dark about what caused the organization to sink into the Trauma Trap, in particular the impact of specific events or toxic conditions. You are unlikely to find a list of overwhelming events. Every organization – just like every person – has its particular sensitivities and peculiarities. This means that this work asks for a more instinctive, intuitive approach rather than a rigidly-planned one. You will need to earn the space, trust and confidence of the organization, before you can dive into the deeper layers of an organization. Only through this will it become clear where healing is still needed, who should be brought together, which rituals could help, who could apologize to whom and especially how the organization could learn from it. The following questions bring us on to the recovery and integration process (= Phase 3), which will be discussed in the next chapter:

- How, in the future, can we take better care of the relational fabric, while considering what makes the organization, and its employees, vulnerable, and the fact that the organization will still be challenged by a number of risks, challenges and changing conditions, only some of which will be predictable?

- How can the organization be structured so that it continues to support the resilience and flexibility of people and groups, knowing that the world around the organization is unlikely to get any easier?

# Salutogenic Organizational Design

**9**

In the previous chapter you became acquainted with the first two of the three phases, relevant to working with organizational trauma. The third phase blends with the last facet of the Trauma Diamond and will be explored in this last chapter. If you suspect there is organizational trauma, then you begin with an exploration phase. You investigate if, where, and to what extent, trauma exists and you create the conditions needed to start the work. When the people involved are properly prepared and the right conditions are established, you can begin, step by step, to engage with the trauma. These first and second phases will lead to insights about how further recovery can be supported. Using these 'new' insights puts you immediately into the final phase of recovery and integration.

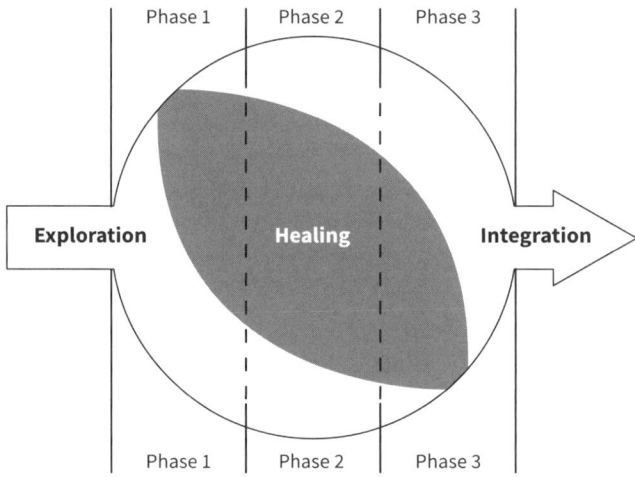

*Figure 79: Phases for dealing with organizational trauma*

You will remember that it is particularly important, during the exploration phase, to ascertain the levels of willingness and ability in the organization to actually start working with the insights that have arisen. Only then is the chance of healing and post-traumatic growth possible. After all, if nothing is done with the insights that are revealed by the process, it is likely you will push those involved back into the old pain. In this ninth chapter we will offer a number of tools for the third, and final, phase.

At the same time, this chapter also discusses the fourth and last facet of the Trauma Diamond: Salutogenic Organizational Design. Salutogenesis is a term created by the Jewish-American professor Aaron Antonovsky, see: *Health, Stress and Coping* (Antonovsky, 1979, [1]) . Instead of looking for what leads to illness and decay (pathogenesis), he began by looking for what leads to, and sustains well-being and recovery. He took into account the fact that people and groups are constantly being challenged, sometimes because of particularly drastic or overwhelming events. His research was stimulated by noticing that some people who had survived concentration camps had a particularly high degree of well-being. His curiosity led him to developing his Salutogenic Model, which we can apply to groups and organizations. We have learned that organizations can induce or maintain trauma through the way they function. But organizations can also provide growth, development and healing, internally and externally, as shown in the diagram below.

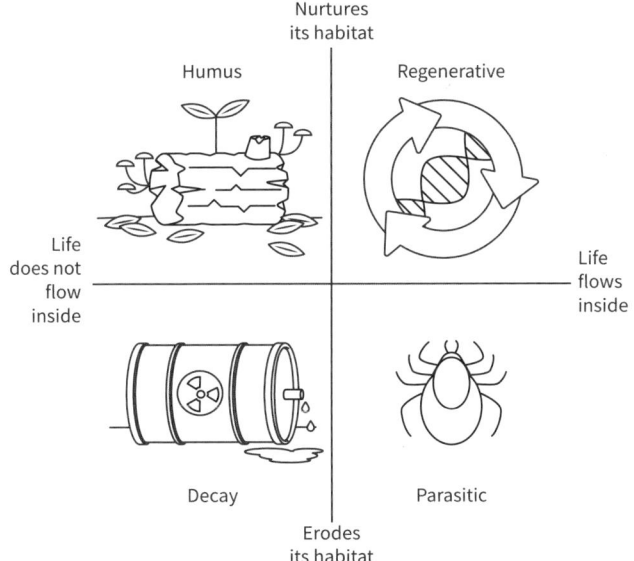

*Figure 80: Regenerative or not?*

This book discusses guidelines to 'recovery after organizational trauma', and so it is logical that we also talk about 'organizational health'. How an organization works with the insights from this chapter, determines whether it becomes more agile, resilient and/or healthier. Those last few words remind us that working with organizational trauma requires a systemic approach. This is the only way you will develop the sensitivity needed to 'see' how – and how much – life flows through a living system (whether it be team, department or organization) and learn to see the way that a particular living system interfaces with its immediate environment. This is how we arrive at a coordinate system with the following axes:

- X axis: to what extent does life flow in the living system?

- Y axis: to what extent does the living system feed or erode its context or habitat?

When using this diagram, first determine the living system you are working with: a team, a department, an organization, … Only then you'll be able to see the difference between parts and whole or living system and context. What brings us to four quadrants that are particularly important to this last chapter and its context of recovery and integration.

## Decay

This quadrant is marked not only by degeneration within the living system, but also how the system causes degeneration in its surrounding environment, its habitat. A sick, dying, traumatized system, that drags the rest into decay. For example, a management team that is completely stuck and is dragging the rest of the organization into 'their' trap.

## Parasitic

A living system that finds itself here is doing well. But life only flows at the expense of its environment. So there comes a point – if this goes on for too long – when the environment is exhausted and no longer able to nourish the living system that resides there. Often the living system moves to a nourishing new habitat. There are numerous examples of organizations that deplete a certain region of, for example, raw materials, and then relocate once the reserves are used up. This is life at the expense of other life: harvesting the fruit without caring for the roots. This kind of living systems creates trauma more often than they fall victim to it.

## Humus

A living system located here is nourishing for its environment, but not for itself. Here, the degeneration of the living system leads to development or growth for the environment. System as humus, so to speak. For example, an organization that closes down, but whose knowledge and experience moves on into new, different organizations.

## Regenerative

This living system is in good health and also nourishes its immediate surroundings. There is healthy interaction and mutual growth or interdependence. Organizations in this quadrant are doing well and at the same time creating conditions for others to also prosper; often they are called Forces for Good.

Over the years we have developed a keen eye for organizations that reside in the last quadrant. We gained increasing insight into the principles underlying the design of such organizations. In addition, we noticed that organizations which do not respect these principles become more sensitive to organizational trauma, or even induce (organizational) trauma, both internally and externally. These organizations are pathogenic, sometimes even destructive. More and more we started to notice that these principles became important guidelines during the recovery and integration phase. And, so, we consider them to be salutogenic: healing or supporting recovery from trauma which leads, by definition, to post-traumatic growth.

**What doesn't kill you,
makes you stronger.**

Organizations also gain maturity when they heal from organizational trauma. So, post-traumatic growth is possible for organizations. But that requires a few things:

- In the first instance, the willingness to see symptoms and irrational dynamics as disguised cries for help, knowing that these can be heard even when the business figures are still good.

- The willingness to listen, in an authentic way, to employees who paint a different picture to the polished image of reality within which much management imprisons itself. Not listening allows crippling incoherencies and inconsistencies to impact the business.

- The willingness to be open to the less tangible aspects of living systems. In particular: soul, energy, relational wiring, culture, dynamics and patterns.

- The willingness to free up time for contemporary ceremonies and rituals that support the connectedness – rather than fragmentation – of the organization.

- The willingness to build organizations that are regenerative for the community and the people who work in or for them.

- Finally, and this requires the ego to step back a little in favor of the soul, making organizations Forces for Good. Organizational trauma only heals when the soul is allowed back on board.

So the recovery and integration phase is not about dissolving, but about transforming. Therefore you must be clear as a facilitator, from the start, that healing could be linked to several aspects of the organization's design, especially if the origin of organizational trauma is internal. The following story has been drawn from a number of practical experiences and the insights it offers were the motivation to write this chapter.

After an overwhelming event, especially if it is due to external factors, we see, again and again, that peoples' hearts are opened, no matter where they sit in the organization. You experience authentic connectedness. The relational wiring blossoms, as it were. However, we also noticed that this often does not last. Daily life takes over and people fall back into their familiar routines. What does this look like in organizations?

Shortly after an overwhelming event, the formal organization retreats – just for a short while – and the informal organization takes the lead bringing more room for spontaneity, self-regulation and emergence. After a while, the formal organization moves back to the front and the space for all those 'soft' qualities disappears although these are qualities that make organizations very attractive and are very nourishing for the relational wiring. This limited window for transformation often goes unnoticed, hindering post-traumatic growth and ensuring only partial recovery.

It is important to bear in mind that trauma leads to a splitting-off, which results in some of an organization's capabilities becoming stuck in time. In addition, a whole series of survival strategies unfolds in an attempt to forever banish the overwhelming feelings of trauma. However, these always remain – split off into Trauma Capsules – in the hidden layers of the organization. Due to this it cannot function at full power, as part of its potential remains stuck. And because the survival strategies are actually a kind of detour and protection, they will in every case lead to new problems and stressors. If the willingness for healing and transformation is not present, then the only option is stabilizing the organization via survival strategies. In that case, you – as a facilitator – will not get beyond the first phase. If there is a willingness to go further, a space can open up for new potential, around which the organization can be built, a choice often not made due to ignorance, impatience or uncertainty. After all, it asks for a dive into the unknown. Thus, post-traumatic growth often occurs only if that opportunity for transformation is grabbed with both hands. This can then translate, in relation to the outside world (e.g. with new services or new ways of interacting with customers and stakeholders) or to the inside of the organization (changes in procedures, internal communication, leadership). As a result, an organization shifts to the regenerative quadrant of the model that this chapter introduced. This reconnects us with the beginning of the book, where we looked at how organizations can form a healing link between individuals and society, and so become a Force for Good. And then you will see development in the following areas:

- The relational fabric – internal and external – will become healthier and more finely-woven.

- Influence will circulate much more freely rather than just in one direction, as in top-down organizations.

- The number of parasitic relationships on the inside and outside of the organization will decrease.

- The organization will gain in maturity but also in resilience.

Meaning appears to be a very crucial factor for post-traumatic growth. It is a crucial building block for healing. It is, as it were, a source from which energy can be used to carry on, even when things get really tough. Viktor Frankl brought this to the attention in his bestseller *Man's Search for Meaning* (Frankl, 1959, [12]) decades ago. Frankl wrote that meaning (in a person's life) ensures that a person opens up more to the surrounding world, becomes more sympathetic and therefore less egocentric. The latter qualities are, in any case, prerequisites for getting into the regenerative quadrant. It works the same in organizations. For example, if an organization is sued for malicious practices (internal and/or external) that lead to individual or collective trauma, then recovery can only occur if that organization chooses for transformation.

Organizational redesign – after organizational trauma has been acknowledged – inspired by the 'Salutogenic Model', starts from a number of healing principles that are crucial to ensure the healing of the damaged relational fabric and becoming resilient again. These regenerative principles help an organization to function as an integrated and resilient whole. One of the most progressive and integral models for organizations, which often arises in this context, is B Corps. The B Corp Certification offers organizations a whole series of tools to develop into a Force for Good. Growth and success within this model are also defined in a completely new way. 'Old' growth – at the expense of something or someone else – is not seen as growth in this model. Much of what we call success today is still in the parasitic quadrant.

B Corp wants to stimulate organizations to develop success in the regenerative quadrant. An increasingly transparent world and a growing awareness that our planet is finite, will pressure more and more people to equate success with regeneration, although we should not expect great changes in the near future.
Within the scope of this chapter, B Corp offers a set of principles to carry with you during the recovery and integration phase. They form guiding principles that can help to redesign an organization in a way that restores the health and resilience of the relational tissue, hence Salutogenic Orga-

nizational Design.  Below is an overview of B Corp's five guidelines and a scheme that you can use to map it to organizations.

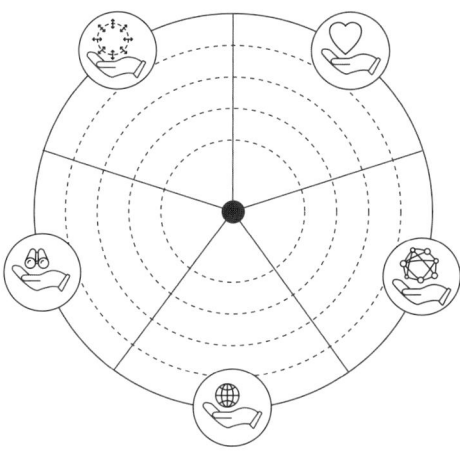

*Figure 81: Five guidelines for Salutogenic Organizational Design*

## 9.1 Guideline 1: Good for the inner relational fabric

*Figure 82: Guideline 1: Good for the inner relational fabric*

The quality of the inner relational fabric of an organization largely determines the organization's resilience. Flexibility, adaptability, coherence, energy, stability and emergence are abilities that thrive in those circumstances. These characteristics are an expression of the extent to which an organization functions as an integrated whole. They are indispensable for survival in a rapidly changing, complex or VUCA world and this points us to an important aspect of the Trauma Trap. For example, the nested systems (teams, departments etc.) of a larger living system can be connected to each other in the following ways:

- In a dependent (child/parent) and/or counter-dependent (adolescent/parent) way.  Here the chances are very high that unhealthy dynamics will develop within the framework of an organization especially when it comes under pressure.

- In a rather independent manner where only very limited account is taken of each other. In this case, people sometimes talk about silo formation.  In this case, the development of collective intelligence between the various silos is very limited, while this is just what organizations are looking for.

- Finally, there might be interdependent relationships.  In this case, both solidarity and individuality are taken into account.  This is the quality of connection that is needed to develop and express collective intelligence.  In this case, influencing becomes a mutual process.  One part can influence the other and vice versa.  In this way, influence and information flows in both directions according to the needs of the moment.

While this concerns the quality of the relationship between the parts of a living system, you can also apply this to the relationship between part and (e.g. the next higher) whole.  You can use this way of thinking at different levels depending on the entity with which you are working (as a facilitator):

| Part | Whole |
|---|---|
| Team member | Team |
| Team | Business Unit |
| Business Unit | Division |
| Division | Company |

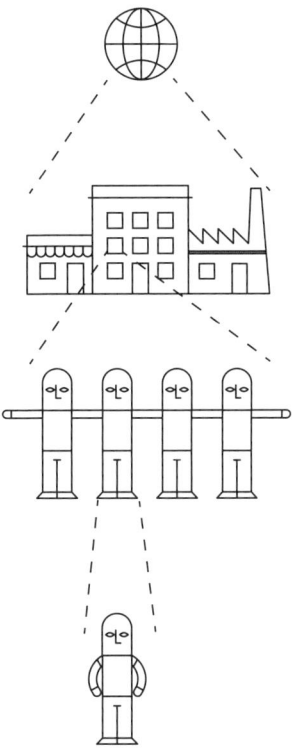

*Figure 83: Part – Whole visualization*

After all, in order to build an integrated whole, the quality of the relationship between parts and whole are very important.  Why should a part take care of the whole if the care is not mutual?  An important effect of the quality of the relationship is that it can lead to improved self-esteem, which we know is essential to effective, interdependent working together. Even worse, people and groups, who are not given the chance to develop self-esteem, become destructive and turn against the system that deprives them (organization, society etc.). This is precisely why this issue is crucial in debates about, amongst others, the integration of refugees, and radicalization. Self-esteem is key to lifting people out of destructive behavior. Work can be a great lever to achieve this if it's organized in a way that ensures self-esteem and development – in both the short and long term (= employability).

As the quality of the relational wiring improves, resilience grows. And it applies very broadly, to the many organizations that work with vulnerable target groups: schools, hospitals, psychiatric institutions, NGOs, prisons, homeless shelters and so on. It is becoming increasingly clear that the quality of service provided by such organizations is determined by the health of the relational fabric as in the following examples:

Children in the classroom are often a mirror for the mood of the teacher. If the teacher feels comfortable, the class will follow him and vice versa. What happens to teachers when the school dynamic is one of continual tension? Indeed, a bullying problem between pupils can be a symptom of an unresolved or hidden conflict between the teachers and the management of the school.

How much energy do nurses have left for their patients if there is constant tension between the nursing staff and the management?

If prison staff feel unfairly treated by certain government measures (e.g. too few resources, unsafe working conditions, etc.), do they retain the capability to support reintegration of prisoners?

If the operation of the organization constantly makes you feel insecure, this will be stressing, even triggering (touching on your own emotional history) while your job is to supervise traumatized children who come from complex, often broken, family situations. You can be sure that these children will regularly challenge you (= re-enactment). Chances are they will challenge you, albeit unconsciously, to do what they 'learned' at home. When this happens, the child falls back into the patterns that originally made it necessary to remove him or her from the family situation. In this way, a child can end up in a so called healing context that feels as unsafe as the home context.

In short, in such organizations the quality of the relational fabric is the foundation for correct service or care. Even more so, if the relational wiring is poor, it is almost impossible to realize the mission of the organization. Organizations in these categories are ideal candidates for trauma-informed interventions. Consider the following questions and themes as inspiration to work with the guidelines for a salutogenic organizational design. Remember that these questions are central to facilitating the recovery and integration phase:

- Are people who work for the organization appropriately compensated?

- How do salary packages compare to the rest of the market or sector?

- What is the ratio between the highest and the lowest salaries?

- What kind of differences are structurally installed between men and women (= gender mainstreaming)?

- How much difference is there in the benefits offered to employees at each level in the organization? And how are particular benefits (bonuses, flexible working hours, … awarded)?

- Is profit sharing offered to any/all employees and if not, what criteria are applied to do so or not?

Remuneration sits very close to the systemic principle of a (correct) balance between giving and taking that was discussed earlier. The relational fabric can easily wear thin if there is structural imbalance in this area. Excessive wage differences undermine cooperation, create space for aggressive self-interest and rarely lead to shared responsibility, but rather to passing the buck. The drama triangle is also activated more quickly in a context where imbalances in this area are too large. Other questions to work along this first guideline are:

- To what extent does the organization invest in the professional and career development of its employees?

- Does the organization ensure that people remain attractive to prospective (future) employers (= employability)?

- Is support provided for employees whose contract is terminated by the organization (e.g. outplacement)?

- Does this take into account those who remain in the company, by supporting their feelings of resentment, loss, injustice, … as mentioned in one of the earlier examples in Chapter 8?

At some point in time the term human resources became accepted in the corporate world. Unfortunately, when people are seen as 'resources', this does, to some extent, define how they relate to the organization and vice-versa. The likelihood of counter-dependency arising is, therefore, particularly high. During the last 30 years or so, many organizations have failed to perform well in this area.

- Is there a program for the physical health and safety of employees, and also for their overall well-being?

- Is there a department tasked with monitoring the health, safety and well-being of employees, which can provide advice and support where necessary?

- Is there a clear process for following-up such advice?

- In addition to professional development, does the organization also give attention to personal development. Is there room, alongside intellectual development, for physical, emotional and spiritual development? These questions fit seamlessly into the theme of prevention, covered in Chapter 6 about crisis and emergency management.

- Is there a manual for employees describing the ins and outs of the organization and giving them access to their rights and obligations?

- Are flexible work contracts available (part-time, temporary, home-based, etc.) to support a good balance between work and family life?

- Is job satisfaction and employee involvement regularly assessed?

- Do employees get access to metrics regarding satisfaction, retention, absence, diversity? These contain a whole series of indicators that tell us much about the health of the relational fabric.

- Is anything actually done with these metrics?

The previous questions are directed more at the situation and experience of the individual. Now, let's look at some questions about the working of the whole:

- How are decisions made? In a co-creative participatory way? Or top down? You often hear people say: *"An organization is not a democ-*

*racy*". At the same time, we know that top-down decisions seldom lead to involvement and connection. The way in which decisions are made always has a deep effect on the health of the relational wiring.

- How is change handled? Is it seen as only a rational, mechanistic process? Or is attention paid to the emotions associated with change? During the change process (the tangible side) is guidance also given to what is triggered by the change (emotions and relational issues)?

- What forms of communication do you see between people, teams and departments? Do you see a tendency for connecting and non-violent communication? Or do you see communication that leads to exclusion and avoidance? Are dialogues and exchanges assertive? Or do you see aggressive or sub-assertive forms of communication?

- If something goes wrong, how is it handled? Is the time taken to look at the issue in such a way that everyone learns from it together? Or is the choice to look for the guilty party? The first leads to transparency and collective learning through which the organization can develop. The second leads to masquerades, illusions of efficiency or effectiveness and a scapegoat culture: just the right mix to tie the relational wiring in knots.

- What and how does communication flow through the organization? In a rapidly changing world, this 'what' and 'how' are crucial factors in enabling a certain degree of self-regulation. At the same time, this requires a higher level of trust in all directions. Effective communication goes hand in hand with the relational wiring of an organization. You can compare it to the body's nervous system. Where nerves are damaged, the rest of the body lacks the input necessary for fast and appropriate responses. In a rapidly changing world this can be particularly dangerous to both organizations and humans.

This first guideline is particularly important in the context of this book. Healthy relational fabric is virtually impossible if there is no attention within the organization around the above themes. Interventions in this area are, almost always, needed to restore a damaged organization. We cannot state this too often! If there is no willingness to continuously rebuild the relational fabric, especially during the recovery and integration phase, it is almost guaranteed that, although some measure of stabilization and coping will be achieved, there will be zero post-traumatic growth. Also be aware that the health of an organization is determined by all five guidelines and that there is a multiplication sign in between the five guidelines. You know what will happen to the end product if one factor scores very low. So we come to the following guideline, one that we already discussed in the quadrant at the start of this chapter: *"How does the organization relate to its environment?"*

## 9.2 Guideline 2: Beneficial for the surroundings

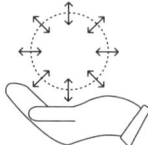

*Figure 84: Guideline 2: Beneficial to the surroundings*

An organization can score particularly well on the first guideline and still show little care for its surrounding community. In this situation, an organization is operating from the parasite quadrant. That is why any organization wanting to become a Force for Good, needs to take some positive steps towards its environment. For example, if an organization is doing well in a poor and run-down society, then its leadership can decide to try to improve the environment. This reduces the gap between rich and poor and eliminates much of the need for 'protection' for the rich. So it is clear that how an organization relates to its environment is also important to staying healthy. This guideline has also a number of themes:

- Does the company create jobs for vulnerable target groups (ex-prisoners, people with disabilities, people below the poverty line, young people from risk groups, refugees, …)

- Does the organization create opportunities for diversity (gender, religion, color, …) and does this diversity translate into the higher layers of the organization in the way decisions are made or even in the composition of the management of the organization?

In this way an organization becomes part of the environment instead of an island or enclave. Involvement with the local community ensures that more account is taken of the impact of the organization on the local community: issues like smells, noise, pollution, housing prices, etc. Moreover, organizations can become a place where certain imbalances, such as oppression or discrimination, are healed, as a conscious choice rather than being forced via legislation.  This is just one way in which an organization can contribute to social healing.

- Are employees encouraged to contribute to the development of the local community through volunteer work, for example?

- Does the organization contribute to charities that are supported, set up or chosen by their employees?

- Is the surrounding community formally supported by aspects of the organization's operation?

- Does the organization have partnerships with organizations that support the local community?

- Does the organization use goods and/or services from local institutions that work with, for example, vulnerable target groups?

Previously, we made reference to the impact of these types of initiatives on organizational health.  Many inspirational organizations (in this area) are particularly involved with society or contribute to one or more good causes.  But we also saw the salutogenic effect of these kinds of projects when working with organizations that have dropped a little deeper into the Trauma Trap.  During the weeks of such a project, we always see a growing level of solidarity and enthusiasm. At such a moment more energy flows through the relational fabric, energy that brings with it regeneration and rejuvenation.  Looking at the opposite situation, when an organization takes little or no account of its surroundings, you can be certain that particular people or groups in the organization will identify with community members who are exploited, excluded or disadvantaged. This easily becomes food for the drama triangle.  You'll hear statements like: "*I no longer want to work for such an organization*", "*I'm actually not proud of the practices of our organization*" or even "*I feel shame when people connect me with the organization*".

Surroundings are more than just local.  The influx of raw materials, goods, parts or services also falls within this framework. Increasingly, organizations are striving for a healthy chain (clean chain) from producer to buyer (What the food industry calls from field to fork).  This is in stark contrast to organizations that sell products made under miserable conditions (e.g. in sweatshops). Increasingly-transparent production chains encourage well-known brands and retail chains to address this serious social problem.  Social pressure, growing transparency and increasingly-aware consumers are forcing this issue into the scope of many organizations.

As you can see, this second guideline contains much potential to work on the overall health of an organization. Obviously, this trickles down into the internal health of the organization. It provides resilience, pride, meaning, solidarity and often makes an organization more innovative.  Choosing to develop this aspect of its business and to build balanced, nurturing relationships with its chains – so they become partners – compels an organization to tap into the creativity of its people. This always benefits the organization, also in its bottom line.

## 9.3  Guideline 3: Good for the Earth

*Figure 85: Guideline 3: Good for the Earth*

Trauma has an important relational dimension. This brings us to a significant difference between ownership and relationship, and to one of the least-worthwhile features of the industrial era: Earth, nature, seas, forests, animals, and so on, are seen as possessions, as owner.  Forces for Good have a relationship with the Earth in all its facets. They reap the harvest but care diligently for the roots.  Something you are unlikely to do when you have reduced something or someone to an object. Caring for the environment and one's surrounding is about changing how we relate to the

Earth. That relationship programs, as it were, all other relationships; becoming a kind of blueprint or DNA of an organization.

And here again, building on sustainability is a source for innovation and creativity. This can support the relationship with suppliers, especially if you involve them in the search for sustainable solutions. Such a partnership often leads to development and innovation on both sides. Sustainability can also strengthen the bond with the consumer, customer or user. It offers the chance for people to be proud of the company they work for. If not, the relationship with the organization grows into a subject-object relationship. A totally different potential unfolds in organizations where possession makes room for relationships. The relationship with the Earth – however abstract this may sound – is an excellent indicator of the freedom given for regenerative or salutogenic forces to flow through the organization. Some questions that help assess this perspective:

- Is the use or consumption of energy, water and waste efficiently monitored?

- Does this happen from a purely economic perspective or is it a true externalization of commitment to the health of the planet?

- Are emissions and pollution measured and controlled by the organization?

- Does the organization make all the above transparent to the outside world?

- Are energy-efficient applications used for lighting, ventilation, heating etc.?

- Is renewable energy (solar, wind, tidal, geothermal, biomass) used?

- Are employees encouraged to use alternative means of transport (bicycle, train, car-pooling)?

- Are efforts being made to improve the life cycle of products and goods in order to create as little waste as possible?

- Can used goods be recycled and is recycling made easy?

- Does the organization make efforts to work towards a closed cycle (e.g. cradle to cradle)?

- Are suppliers encouraged to make similar efforts? If that is not the case, then an organization can outsource polluting practices, which means that, in reality, they are only image building.

Reconnecting with nature is proving to be a particularly effective way of healing trauma and features in many highly-effective therapies. Reconnecting with nature stimulates reconnecting with the essence of being human. It provides inner peace, wonder and gratitude and places us as a part of the whole picture instead of putting ourselves above it. This is just as valid for organizations.

## 9.4 Guideline 4: Good for the long term

*Figure 86: Guideline 4: Good for the long term*

Organizations that transform into Forces for Good do not see the Earth as inherited from our parents, but as something precious that we are borrowing from future generations. The fourth guideline is about those next generations: the long term. These 'two futures' are very often elbowed aside in the blind rush to present good quarterly results, that leads, in the long term, to degeneration. This 'results now' ethos ensures, for example, that much-needed adjustments – that might establish a healthily-functioning organization – are postponed. There is no investment in the relational wiring or time to process toxins which, logically, makes a living system more fragile. And this approach creates unhealthy, unbearable pressure on employees and executives with increased stress and burnout, especially in the Western world. The following questions can help you map out this perspective:

- Are long-term values and commitments integrated into the mission of the organization?

- Are these commitments specifically monitored, so that they are more than window-dressing?

- Are mission and values translated to the workplace in such a way that they are tangible and recognizable to employees?

- Are essential financial figures shared with the employees, in ways that give them insight into how the organization plans for the short and long term?

- Is there an annual report that details the organization's long term planning?

- Does the organization try to encourage other players in its sector to follow the same path?

- Have the values, the mission and the associated practices been defined in such a way that these commitments cannot simply be ignored by a change of management or a takeover?

A living system needs a degree of 'slack' in order to be resilient. 'Slack' can be, for example, financial reserves put aside for possible future problems (saving for a rainy day) but also can apply to time (do-nothing time). A living system without slack will degenerate. Another practice that we often see in businesses is skimming the profits – knowing that profits are a necessary prerequisite to building slack – of particular branch offices by the HQ of, for example, a multinational, to the degree that the local organizations become vulnerable. When 'slack' starts to decrease, an organization becomes more rigid, risk averse and loses innovative capacity and resilience. We have seen this become such a vicious circle that it ended in organizational trauma with businesses closing down as a result.

Organizations that remain faithful to their values or guiding principles (their totem pole), while responding to changes in the market, appear to be more successful in the long term. Value coherence is, at the same time, a condition for, and a consequence of, resilience. It feeds the regenerative capacity of an organization.

**Values are a moral compass that
keeps an organization on course
through the waves of the future.**

## 9.5 Guideline 5: Good to the core

*Figure 87: Guideline 5: Good to the core*

Healing trauma can lead to post-traumatic growth. People start relating to the world in a different way: more connected with themselves and the world around them (from ownership to relationship). Meaning and spirituality frequently arise or are strengthened via this kind of transformation. The soul component, of being truly human, often breaks through the hard shell of the ego after an overwhelming event.

**There is a crack in everything.
That's where the light comes in.**

Leonard Cohen

***Doing good, heals***

An important factor in healing trauma is developing an attractive future perspective, a vision of how things can be. That perspective activates regenerative energy. During the exploration phase it is important to identify if this particular organization, in its current state, can develop such a perspective. In past engagements with organizations, where we did not get very far in working with organizational trauma, there was usually little or no material to build an attractive perspective of the future.  Such a perspective must meet a number of conditions if it is to be a regenerative force:

- There must be a positive challenge that is worth pursuing together;

- This positive future must free up energy to step out of the drama triangle or let go of rigid identifications with one of the positions of the drama triangle;

- This perspective has to move people to take responsibility for their own and the joint healing process;

- This future perspective must be worth pursuing and give people hope for a better individual and collective situation.

Most business goals are ultimately, and sadly, only about growth and profit: they lack soul and are often empty of the power of regeneration. If an organization chooses, increasingly, to make an essential contribution to the world, from its core activity, then completely different capabilities unfold. Capabilities such as resilience, creativity and agility develop more easily from such a choice. Fréderic Laloux, author of *Reinventing Organisations* (Laloux, 2014, [18]) , points to this path.  He encountered a whole bunch of special organizations around the world that had something in common: a Living Purpose, the deep desire to make a positive contribution to this world from their business activities. The organizations he mentions in his book, called 'TEAL', are often organizations that are developing these five guidelines. We have learned that organizations have to heal to become TEAL and we believe there are no shortcuts to getting out of the Trauma Trap.

   Organizations starting on this fifth guideline are organizations whose core activities already embrace the Global Goals for Sustainable Development that we met in Part I, and many organizations are on this path. For them, investing in these guidelines has simply become a part of their DNA, a part of who they are. Such organizations are healing; for the people who work there, their immediate environments, the earth and future generations.  They reflect the essence of salutogenic organization design.  The next series of questions will help you to look at the core activities of such an organization;

- Does the organization provide products or services that contribute to health, well-being, education, cultural development, integration and social development?

- Does the organization contribute to solutions that fit the framework of the United Nations' Global Goals for Sustainable Development?

- Is at least 40% of the organization owned by the employees?  For example, a cooperative of wine producers which also co-owns the production, logistics and commercial functions?

- Are all relevant partners or stakeholders actively involved in the development of the organization through participative and co-creative forms of cooperation?

- Does the organization use its production chain in such a way that all stakeholder organizations involved can also develop a healthy level of operation?

- Are these Force for Good principles taken into account when selecting partners?  For example, an organization can collaborate with a start-up offering vulnerable young people a particular service, making this a transformational cooperation instead of a purely transactional one.

- Does the organization financially support non-profit organizations? Or does it cooperate positively in a different way by, for example, providing some or all of locations, materials training and advice?

Working along these guidelines creates a salutogenic 'cocoon' that helps an organization pull itself up out of the Trauma Trap or feed its resilience in a rapidly changing, complex world. Additionally, it leads to integration and coherence, necessary conditions for regenerative energy, ensouling and spirit. This could be an important part of the recipe for Organizational Soul Retrieval. It will come as no surprise that once again, at the end of this chapter, we revisit the Trauma Formula:

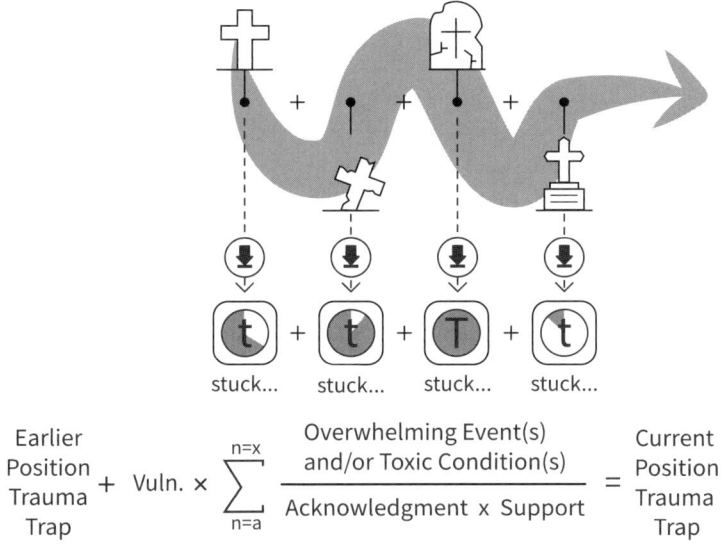

$$\underset{\substack{\text{Earlier} \\ \text{Position} \\ \text{Trauma} \\ \text{Trap}}}{} + \text{Vuln.} \times \sum_{n=a}^{n=x} \frac{\substack{\text{Overwhelming Event(s)} \\ \text{and/or Toxic Condition(s)}}}{\text{Acknowledgment} \times \text{Support}} = \underset{\substack{\text{Current} \\ \text{Position} \\ \text{Trauma} \\ \text{Trap}}}{}$$

*Figure 88: Trauma Formula 2.0*

Working with the five guidelines is a powerful way to activate regenerative forces. It provides healing, increases resilience and reduces vulnerability.

Searching for inconsistencies in the organization's design (such as praising teamwork but awarding individual bonuses only to the top management) and working step by step through this book's guidelines will ensure that unnecessary toxin sources, large and small, are eliminated. Erasing such inconsistencies has a particularly healing effect on an organization. And do not worry, the people from the organization know the most pressing issues: they are your most important sensors. This has a bi-directional effect: where inconsistencies are removed, people act more consistently.

Then find where meaning seems to have been lost and look for ways to restore it. This is the most powerful way to bring back the soul. The ego is focused on the self, often at the expense of others; the soul's focus is on connecting with the greater whole. Working with this relationship between meaning and soul can reveal many opportunities to make the work more fulfilling and always strengthens the relational fabric.

Finally, seek out the parasitic relationships. Relationships with a broken balance between giving and taking disrupt a living system. Expose these relationships. Look for relationships at different levels: between individuals, between disciplines, between departments, between hierarchical levels, between organization and environment, between organization and suppliers. Leave no stone unturned.

Unfortunately, there is no quick-fix to escape from the Trauma Trap. However, as soon as regenerative forces begin to flow again, progress can very swift. We notice, time and time again, that if action taken is sincere, intention is clear and good, you can be almost certain that healing will follow. In essence, living systems crave for healing and for a healthy exchange with the environment. Particular organizational approaches – top-down, controlling, power-plays, silos, short-term thinking and so on – just get in the way of healing. Organizations designed on those practices and principles have a degenerative effect on the relational fabric, its people and its environment. Hence this last chapter.

# Closure

I've always been an explorer. I guess it is part of a coping mechanism I developed as a child. It helped me to make sense of the 'strange' world around me. Luckily coping mechanisms can become strengths when healing takes place. In a way, that's logic because that part of my wiring has been trained for more than 10.000 hours. At least one important aspect of what it takes to develop a very specific and unique talent referring to the book *Talent is overrated* (Colvin, 2008, [10]) by Geoff Colvin.

Only years later, I bumped onto the work of Gregory Bateson and learned about the modeling of capabilities in individuals and systems. His question: *"What is the difference that makes the difference?"* has since been like a companion in my work. It brought me to the writing of my first book on Organizational Design that was first published in 2013. Inspired by that question, I started recognizing some patterns in the way healthy, energetic organizations were build and lead.

Once being more conscious about these patterns, I became even more sensitive for the neglecting of them. And knowing it can be different makes it even more difficult to understand why a lot of businesses keep acting against those principles (that are pretty close to common sense). There again, I started seeing patterns, but now leading to getting stuck. This kind of organizational stuckness was isomorphic to what I saw when an organization had been overwhelmed by an acute, external event without having provided proper healing.

Organizational trauma was on my radar but not in a way that I planned to use this label as the new core of my work. No, I just kept on doing my work but in a trauma-informed way which anyhow transformed my way of working. I started feeling a kind of inner resistance when I wanted to use some of the approaches I had learned along the years. A deeper dimension opened. The different disciplines that inspired – and keep inspiring – me started meeting each other. My inner world moved from silos to a coherent system where art, sports, health, therapy, coaching, spiritual practice, leadership, organizational architecture and common sense all came together.

Exactly that made me write the first, Dutch, edition of 'Trauma in Organizations'. I was not certain about how the book would be welcomed but it was awarded as OD-book of the year 2016. Tons of feedback on the Dutch edition led me to dive in the manuscript for a so-called second time. The translation and re-writing of the book took me more time and energy than the writing of the original book, but I feel that I had to do this. I had no choice. I had to go through this to bring this another step closer to organizations. Maybe it's the gift or the harvest of my personal healing journey? Anyhow, it makes me happy to see that more and more people start embracing the concepts of the book in the way they build, lead or manage their organization, department or team.

I'll keep building on this work. I hope to meet like-minded experts and colleagues, so we can push this emerging field to next levels. No, we won't be able to avoid (organizational) trauma but maybe we could become more competent in dealing with it. This would balance our current way of neglecting and/or trying to avoid the negative, the difficult, the dark, …

This book would not be there without the inspiration, help and support of a lot of people. It takes a village to write a book. That's why I'd like to thank a lot of people, standing in concentric circles (like the annual rings of a tree) around me and my work. Let's start with the first circle:

My tower of strength is my wife, Mieke and together with our two kids, Marthe and Simon, they form my sanctuary. It's not always a pleasure to have a writing husband or dad at home, so I'm very grateful for their presence, patience and support. In this same first circle is my family of origin and some close friends and colleagues.

In a second circle are the people that put their shoulders, together with me, under the creation of this book:

- James Campbell was my guide in the translation of the book. His eye for detail pushed the book to a higher level.

- Hans Hoegaerts joined me in the creation of the visuals throughout the book. His vivid work brings the concepts of the book to a level, much easier to grasp.

- Bas Dekker helped the book to come alive by his incisive work on designing the text.

- Siets Bakker from Systemic Books knows how to embrace and guide a systemic author. Her entrepreneurship felt like a tailwind along the process.

- Erik de Soir took the time to give me tons of feedback on the first edition of the book and connected me with interesting academics in the field of organizational trauma. He has played a central role in the upgrading of the book.

- Jan Jacob Stam was already an important source of inspiration for the first edition of the book. His feedback pushed me to go another step further.

- Catherine Carton feels like a buddy in the development of this work, in a way that suits the corporate world. Her supportive and healing presence made a difference in the development of this work.

In a third circle are the people and companies that opened up for my ideosyncratic way of working. Receiving the trust to work with wounded or shadow parts of organizations feels like an expression of deep trust. And yes, the proof of the pudding is in the eating, whatever the depth of the concepts that are discussed in books and seminars. Without those companies I would never have been able to write this book.

In the fourth circle are my sources of inspiration. As already mentioned, I'm an explorer, which means that the number of books I have been reading and the numbers of trainings I have been following the last 20 years is enormous. A list of those sources would not encourage you to start exploring. That's why I limit myself to the different fields and authors that inspired me in this work. On my website www.traumainorganizations.com you can find more specific information to start your journey in the field of organizational trauma.

**People to follow in the field of individual trauma:**

Peter Levine, Babette Rotschild, David Bercelli, Daniel Siegel, Ingeborg Bosch, Thomas Moore, Bessel van der Kolk, Stephen Porges, Viktor Frankl, David Grove, Stephen Gilligan, Anné Linden, Hal & Sidra Stone, …

**People to follow in the field of shamanism:**

Daan Van Kampenhout, Martin Brune, Michael Harner, Sandra Ingerman, Alberto Villoldo, …

**People to follow in the field of system and/or organizational trauma:**

Arnold Mindell, Jeffrey Alexander, Anngwyn St. Just, Sandra Bloom, Heather Plett, Wilfred Bion, Yiannis Gabriel, Erik de Soir, Earl Hopper, Howard Stein, Mark Steinkamp, Patricia Vivian and Shana Hormann, Judy Atkinson, Jacques-Antoine Malarewicz, …

**People to follow in the field of systemic work:**

Bert Hellinger, Jan Jacob Stam, Gunthard Weber, Franz Ruppert, Dan Booth Cohen, Wibe Veenbaas, Stephan Hausner, Ursula Franke, Indra Torsten Preiss, Leanne Steeghs, Siets Bakker, …

*"It takes a village to write a book, thanks a lot."*

Philippe Bailleur
Sint-Katelijne-Waver, 2 mei 2018

## Some words about the author

After my training at the Royal Military School, I worked for a number of years on an airforce base on the other side of Brussels Airport. I just started working as an HR-partner – in 1996 – when one of our well-known C-130 transport aircrafts crashed in Eindhoven, in the Netherlands. The Belgian crew members and all the Dutch passengers died in the accident. 41 families were directly affected and many more friends and colleagues. As a result, I was invited to be trained within the field of emergency and crisis management. That caused a turning point in my career.

From then on, I started working with groups on various topics: communication, leadership, teamwork, group dynamics, creativity, self-management, coaching, … Since then, a process of personal development started through coaching, therapy and healing work. Each client – organization, team or individual – challenged me to dive deeper via training and hours of self-study. That gave me – after almost 20 years – a very broad and eclectic foundation that is helping me to work on the link between people, organizations and society. My work consists of:

- Keynote speaking on organizational renewal, leadership, organizational trauma, coaching, collective intelligence, management innovation, systemic work,…

- Facilitation of organizational development and organizational healing

- Training, mentoring and coaching of systemic organizational coaches and leaders

- Facilitating organizational constellations

- Research and writing

You can learn more about me via Social Media – Facebook, Twitter, Instagram or Linkedin – or via the website build around the book:

www.traumainorganizations.com
Feel free to connect with me via mail:
pbailleur@livingsystemscoaching.be

## About the (systemic) editor: James Campbell

Language is a wonder. Even when we speak the same mother tongue, we do so in our unique way. Face to face we have many tools that aid understanding. But reading challenges us to grasp an author's intentions rather than giving their words our own meaning. This is where I believe an editor (but not all editors) can be a friend [1] to the writer. I try to do the minimum necessary to a text while ensuring that the author's meaning is clear. I'm constantly checking with myself and the author that my opinions, beliefs and ideas are not slipping into the book unnoticed. At the same time I try to remove ambiguities and add fluency. English versions of books tend to be the ones upon which further translations are based and this, too, informs how I edit. Finally, there comes a point in the process when a gestalt emerges: the letters, spaces, words and ideas have become a book. One I hope the author can be proud of. And then I know we are almost home.

I was born in London in 1950 of Scottish parents and now live in an intentional community, in Eindhoven, the Netherlands, with my wife and 10-year-old daughter. I grew up playing football, mountain-biking and reading poetry. Football is now limited to watching Manchester United, and the Netherlands has no mountains; but the joy, inspiration and support of poetry increases with each passing year. I first experienced systemic work around 1997 and, in the 20+ years since, I have followed many training courses and workshops, from weekends to year-longs, with Judith Hemming, Jan Jacob Stam and others. I've been general editing for about 11 years and systemic editing for about 6 . My earlier activities include studying for a BSc in Chinese Medicine and many years of global sales-management roles. My life always feels lighter and more real in those moments when I feel here and true contact becomes possible.

I can be contacted via `www.thelastword.eu`

James Campbell

---

[1] look online for William Stafford's thoughts on the writing process

## Some words from the illustrator: Hans Hoegaerts

I'm a Belgian based illustrator and tool designer. I'm offering visual support to authors, coaches and organisations who seek to move beyond the written word.

I'm getting really excited with all things related to visual language, transformation processes, cultural (re)design, team dynamics and organisational design. This interest originated in different HR roles as an employee. When I took the leap to become an independent, I sharpened my purpose in life and my pencils to become a fervent proponent of visual language.

In roaming these broad and interesting professional fields I encountered Philippe, with whom I share a great passion for visual language, designing processes in its broadest form and hybrid thinking. Since the moment we met, a whole caleidoscope of ideas, models and tools have emerged from our brains.

I insist that an image is not necessarily the final goal. The image is the mean to expand and deepen the discussion, the presentation, the concept and the understanding. Images are not intended as side dishes, they are complements to the written and spoken language.

Asking about the 'why' of my passion? I humbly refer to brighter minds that formulated my point of view in a few elegant quotes:

- *"If I can't picture it, I can't understand it"*, Albert Einstein

- *"It is impossible to even think without a mental picture"*, Aristotle

- *"Man's mind cannot understand thoughts without images of them"*, Thomas Aquinias

- *"The evolution of images is a kind of intermediate between that of the perceptions and that of the intelligence"*, Jean Piaget

- *"There are images I need to complete my own reality"*, Jim Morrison

I've been, am and will always be on the lookout for new and interesting ways to work visually in combination with the drawing process. Among those are some trainings that made me very happy:

- Lego Serious Play ®
- Voice Dialogue
- Clean Language

But what makes me really happy is your question regarding visual work. You can contact me via hans@hanshoegaerts.be or hans@visualchangeagent.com

# Bibliography

[1]    Aaron Antonovsky. *Health, Stress and Coping*. San Francisco: Jossey-Bass Publishers, 1979.

[2]    Marianne Bentzen. *The Neuroaffective Picture Book*. Trowbridge: Paragon Publishing, 2015.

[3]    Wilfred Bion. *Experiences in Groups*. London: Routledge, 1968.

[4]    Sandra L Bloom and Brian Farragher. *Restoring Sanctuary*. Oxford: Oxford University Press, 2013.

[5]    Danielle Braun and Jitske Kramer. *De Corporate Tribe. Organisatielessen uit de antropologie*. Alphen aan den Rijn: Vakmedianet, 2015.

[6]    Arthur Brock. *Wealth a Living Systems Model*. 2014. URL: http://artbrock.com.

[7]    Doc Childre and Bruce Cryer. *From Chaos to Coherence*. Oxforn: Butterworth & Heinemann, 1995.

[8]    Dan Booth Cohen. *I Carry Your Heart in My Heart: Family Constellations in Prison*. Heidelberg: Carl Auer International, 2009.

[9]    J. Collins. *Good to great*. New York: Harper Collins, 2011.

[10]   Geoff Colvin. *Talent is overrated*. London: Penguin, 2008.

[11]   Charles R. Figley. "Compassion fatigue as secondary traumatic stress disorder: An overview". In: *Figley CR, editor. Compassion fatigue: Coping with secondary traumatic stress disorder in those who treat the traumatized*. New York: Brunner-Routledge, 1995, pp. 1–20.

[12]   Viktor Frankl. *Man's Search for Meaning*. Boston: Beacon Press, 1959.

[13]   Yiannis Gabriel. "Organizations and Their Discontents: Miasma, Toxicity and Violation". In: *Critical Management Studies 4 Conference Cambridge July 4-6, 2005*. The Tanaka Business School. 2005.

[14]   Stephen Gilligan. *The Courage to Love*. New York: W.W. Norton & Company, 1997.

[15]   Daniel Goleman. *Emotional Intelligence*. Michigan: Bantam Books, 1995.

[16]   Ronald A Heifeitz, Marty Linsky, and Alexander Grashow. *The Practice of Adaptive Leadership*. Brighton: Harvard Business Press, 2009.

[17]   Khaled Hosseini. *The Kite Runner*. NewYork: Riverside Books, 2003.

[18]   Frederic Laloux. *Reinventing Organisations*. Paris: Diateino, 2014.

[19]   Peter Levine. *In an unspoken voice*. Berkeley: North Atlantic Books, 2012.

[20]   Chloé Meredith. "Connecting the dots. A social network perspective on social-organizational processes in secondary schools". PhD thesis. Leuven: KU Leuven, 2017.

[21]   Arnold Mindell. *Sitting in the Fire*. Portland: Lao Tse Press, 2014.

[22]   Arnold Mindell. *The Deep Democracy of Open Forums*. Newburyport: Hampton Roads Publishing, 2002.

[23]   Babette Rothschild. *The Body Remembers. The Psychophysiology of Trauma and Trauma Treatment*. New York: W.W. Norton & Company, 2000.

[24]   Franz Rupert. *Splits in the Soul*. Steyning: Green Balloon Publishing, 2011.

[25]   Daniel Siegel. *Mindsight The New Science of Personal Transformation*. New York: Bantam, 2010.

[26]   David J. Snowden and Mary E. Boone. "Decision Making. A Leader's Framework for Decision Making". In: *Harvard Business Review* (Nov. 2007).

[27]    Erik de Soir. *Redders in nood*. Tielt: Lannoo Campus, 2013.

[28]    Anngwyn St. Just. *A question of balance*. South Carolina:
        BookSurge Publishing, 2008.

[29]    Howard Stein. *Listening Deeply*. Boulder: Westview Press, 1994.

[30]    Nassim Taleb. *Antifragility*. Random House Trade Paperbacks: New
        York, 2012.

[31]    Nassim Taleb. *The Black Swan*. Random House Trade Paperbacks:
        New York, 2008.

[32]    William Tate. *The Search for Leadership An Organizational
        Perspective*. Charmouth: Triarchy Press, 2009.

[33]    Friedemann Schultz von Thun. *Störungen und Klärungen:
        Allgemeine Psychologie der Kommunikation*. Reinbek: Rowohlt
        Verlag, 2010.

[34]    Dave Ulrich and Wayne Brockband. *The HR Value Propostion*.
        Brighton: Harvard Business Press, 2005.

[35]    Pat Vivian and Shana Hormann. *Organizational Trauma and
        Healing*. North Charleston: CreateSpace, 2013.

# Index